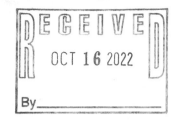

LET'S
MOUNTAIN
BIKE!

LET'S
MOUNTAIN
BIKE!

The Complete Guide to Mountain Biking

PAUL MOLENBERG

gatekeeper press

Columbus, Ohio

Let's Mountain Bike!: The Complete Guide to Mountain Biking

Published by Gatekeeper Press
2167 Stringtown Rd, Suite 109
Columbus, OH 43123-2989
www.GatekeeperPress.com

ISBN (paperback): 9781642374018
eISBN: 9781642374025

Printed in the United States of America

Contents

Part Three: Riding Skills

Part Four: Fitness Training

Part Five: Everything Else

> *"The mountains are calling and I must go."*
>
> -- John Muir

Introduction

HAVE YOU EVER gone mountain biking? Imagine flying through the forest with the wind whistling in your ears and the tires crunching the ground below. Trees are zipping by as the narrow winding trail rapidly unfolds before you. Your senses are fully engaged, and you're feeling a connection with the terrain as it dictates your every move . . . flowing over and around the bumps, through the turns, and over the hills. Your heart is pounding and you're ready for anything. This is when you grin broadly, knowing that there's nothing else you would rather be doing.

The mood will begin to take hold as soon as you leave the motorized clamor of the asphalt jungle and enter the serenity of the natural world. Then, as you set off through some incredible landscape, the thrill of the action will quickly take hold of your attention. You could be whipping down a trail through a thick forest, skillfully navigating your way along a rocky riverbank, or even weaving your way through the wind-worn canyons and rock outcroppings of a desert landscape. These are the types of places that will provide some of the most incredible cycling experiences of your life.

Most people know how to ride a bike; it's an activity that's typically learned in childhood. But if you've never mountain biked on the narrow single-lane trails called "single-tracks," then you're not familiar with the thrill of real mountain biking and how much fun it can be. It's much more than just riding a bike. It's an awesome experience that's difficult to meaningfully describe to those who've never tried it, something that instills a passion that can turn into an outright addiction and a way of life.

All work and no play can be a real drag on the psyche. Busy schedules, work, bills, deadlines, homework, and other obligations can keep one from cutting loose and having fun. Mountain biking provides a sense of mental well-being that can positively affect other aspects of your life. It's a great outlet from the everyday grind and high-pressure expectations. Even if you had a really bad day but are still able to get out on the trails, your troubles will dissipate and feel less important. Biking brings fresh perspective and meaning to life: it's the perfect antidepressant and mood elevator. That's what you call mountain bike therapy! When it comes to exercise, there isn't a more enjoyable way of getting into shape as you gain improvements to the performance of your heart, lungs, muscles, and your sense of balance.

It doesn't take a "natural athlete" to participate in this sport, just the ability to learn basic technique, positioning, and balance. Using the instructions in this book, you'll learn the skills and techniques needed to improve and become more confident in biking. You'll be riding faster on longer and more challenging trails, all while knowing you can handle it. Quite a few mountain bikers crave the thrill of speed and action, but statistics show that the vast majority are not racers. With mountain biking, *you* decide how much you want to push yourself and how much risk you want to take. Many mountain bikers simply enjoy casual recreational rides devoid of motor vehicles, all while taking in the aesthetic beauty of the landscape. You can maintain a comfortable speed and make occasional stops to take in the beautiful and fascinating views. You don't have to be a risk taker to have great mountain biking experiences.

It's true that there are inherent risks with mountain biking, but you don't have to get hurt; it's not a foregone destiny. A big emphasis on safety has been placed throughout the pages of this book. You'll learn how to see the dangers, anticipate them, and take corrective action to prevent accidents. Some riders get into trouble due to a lack of awareness of their limitations. As a beginner, you must know and understand your skill level. You need to be aware that there are some things that you're not good at yet. You'll start with short rides that are not too challenging, and then work your way up. Remaining crash-free involves keeping to trails that are within your abilities, riding at speeds that are below your upper boundary, applying basic skills, foreseeing danger, and knowing what actions may get you into trouble.

There have been many advances in the technology of mountain bikes, which in large part has been driven by professional racers. Their need to gain an advantage and stay ahead of the competition has created an ever-present demand for better technology. In turn, manufacturers have come to rely on this input to create new and exciting design improvements to high-end bikes, improvements that inevitably trickle down to the lower models. As a result, modern bikes now have better functioning components with higher reliability, more comfort, and lower weight. This has given all types of riders the ability to challenge themselves against increasingly difficult trails.

These days, participants of mountain biking come in all ages, from kids to seniors, and include both men and women. In 2016, the sport saw 8.6 million participants in the U.S. alone[1].

- In addition, 4.3 million new bikes were sold, which represents about 25 percent of the bicycle sales market[2].

- Although a good portion of these mountain bikes are ridden in urban settings, off-road riding is gaining ground and growing tremendously.

Access to trails will be your first consideration. Many people don't realize how many trails are nearby and available for use. You don't have to live in the mountains to find them. They can be found in most areas, including major metropolises. Take, for example, New York City. When an outsider envisions New York, they don't imagine parks or places suitable for mountain biking. But in the boroughs of Manhattan, Queens, and Staten Island, city parks containing several miles of challenging single-track are being enjoyed by mountain bikers. (This is a great way for people living in the inner city to connect with nature.) For longer rides, a thirty-minute drive out of New York City will bring you to state parks with even more trails. This scenario holds true for nearly all major metropolitan areas. The trails are there; you just have to know how to find them.

When I first began mountain biking, I had many unanswered questions. I sought information from various sources to find out what I needed to know, and some things I learned the hard way: by trial and error. Eventually it all started coming together, and the knowledge that I have now accumulated has allowed me to feel confident and ride well. This book is a collection of that knowledge, providing comprehensive information, advice, and tips for all riders, whether you're a total beginner or you're more experienced. You'll find extensive content on the types of bikes, equipment, and upgrades; how to make purchases; how to set up the bike; and maintenance. The book also offers tips on how to locate trails, what to bring on a ride, how to ride the trails, skills training, and how to identify and react to potential hazards. It should answer all of your questions as you enter and progress into your mountain biking journey.

To the many curious people who've never experienced mountain biking: You've got to try this. It will become an activity you'll enjoy for many years to come.

Welcome . . . to the Amazing Sport of Mountain Biking

> *"Until mountain biking came along, the bike scene was ruled by a small elite cadre of people who seemed allergic to enthusiasm."*
>
> -- Jacquie Phelan,
> Mountain Bike Hall of Fame inductee

PART ONE

The Bikes

IF YOU'RE NEW to the sport of mountain biking, chances are you need a bike. Choosing the right one for your needs is not always easy, as there are many types, configurations, sizes, and manufacturers. It's fairly common and all too easy for an uninformed beginner to choose a bike that's unsuitable for the type of riding they'll be doing. But when time is taken to learn more about the variety of bikes available and the sport in general, it makes choosing the right one easier and more enjoyable. And the day you get a new bike will be a great day.

For most people, the price tag is a big consideration. They can come in a huge range of prices, but the old saying holds true: You get what you pay for. In the case of mountain bikes, going too cheap means you'll have a heavy bike that starts falling apart after the first couple of rides. They can be dangerous; brakes will break and chains will fall off. At the higher end of the scale, improvements jump up the price in leaps and bounds.

Figuring out the most appropriate category of mountain bike is the first step, and then you'll be ready to look at options such as frame material, suspension design, and components such as rims, tires, forks, shocks, seats, seat posts, handlebars, derailleurs, gears, and brakes. These are all considerations that can greatly change the weight, performance, and price of a bike.

If you have an older bike and are looking to upgrade to something newer, you're probably aware that there have been many changes in bike technology. Today's mountain bikes are lighter and have greatly improved suspension and brakes. They've become better overall performers by providing faster and smoother rides, which directly translates to more fun.

> *"It is by riding a bicycle that you learn the contours of a country best, since you have to sweat up the hills and coast down them."*
>
> -- Ernest Hemingway

CHAPTER ONE
The Categories

WITH A HEAVIER frame, wide knobby tires, and a suspension system, mountain bikes are designed to provide good performance and durability on rough terrain. They are made to go where street bikes never could. The variety of available mountain bike categories provides options for the different types of terrain and riding styles. Since mountain biking is an activity that's heavily dependent on having the right equipment, it's important to figure out which category is best for you. The bike you choose should match up with the type of terrain that you'll spend the most time riding on: the ones closest to home.

Know Your Local Trails

The best way to figure out what type of bike you need is to first investigate and understand your local trails. By checking out the ones you'll be riding the most, you can match the bike to the conditions.

Park maps can be helpful in finding trails that are suitable for mountain biking, but there are also several smartphone apps dedicated to providing this information. Some will even work with GPS to give your location within the park. Although you'll find that the majority of park trails are mapped, sometimes you may have to explore an area with unmapped trails. The positive side of this is the opportunity to discover some great single-track. If you have no trail riding experience or no access to a mountain bike, a nice hike is always a good option for learning the particular features and challenges of local trails. Here are some dynamics that should be considered when judging what type of bike is the most suitable:

- Do the trails have a lot of roots, rocks, and ruts?
- Are they smooth and flowing?
- How long and steep are the uphill sections?
- Are the downhills steep?
- Are there boulders and ledges?
- Will you be riding on snow or sand?
- Will you be riding in bike parks?
- Will you be competing in races?
- Are you only interested in casual riding?

By first learning the trails and parks that are readily available to you, along with a reasonable assessment of your *potential* riding ability, you'll be able to make an informed decision of which type of bike is the most appropriate. If you're a beginner, keep in mind that the trails you'll initially need to ride will be shorter and less technical. If they have too many roots and rocks, or if the inclines and declines are too steep, you shouldn't be attempting it. A mishap or excessive exhaustion could cause you to resent the sport. It's best to start on the easier trails, and as you gain experience and build your stamina, you can then advance.

Choosing a Category

There are several categories of mountain bikes on the market, including the Hardtail Cross Country (XC), the full suspension Cross-Country/Trailbike, the Enduro/All-Mountain/Aggressive Trailbike, and the Downhill/Gravity Driven bike. The biggest differentiators among them are their frame designs and suspension systems. Bikes with plus-size and fat-size tires create even more options for the consumer to choose from.

Hardtail Cross-Country (XC)

Specialized S-Works Epic Hardtail

Originally, mountain bikes had no suspension system at all, but, nowadays, almost all mountain bikes come with suspension forks in the front. "Hardtail" mountain bikes have no suspension in the rear. One of the benefits of a solid rear end is the lack of "pedal bob," which is the tendency of a rear suspension to bob up and down from the surges of each pedal stroke. The solid rear end transfers more of the rider's muscle power to forward motion, giving hardtails a pedaling efficiency advantage. Other advantages include a significantly lower weight and fewer moving parts, which translates to fewer mechanical problems and costs.

Hardtails are great on smoother terrain, but without a rear shock absorber, rough terrain will cause the rear end to bounce. The tire will then have less contact with the ground, which will result in reduced stability, control, and braking. As you try to finesse your way over obstacles, your arms and legs will need to act as shock absorbers. All of this will put your mountain biking skills to the test by training you to choose the best path (called line) for your wheel, which, on the positive side, is an essential skill to develop.

The lower cost of hardtails makes them a good entry level choice, but they should not be regarded as a beginner's bike. Many cross-country racers prefer them due to their pedaling efficiency and lighter weight. If most of your rides are on smooth, flowing trails or even on pavement, then a hardtail is probably the best choice for you. If you anticipate some rough rides, you should consider a full suspension bike. You'll get less beat up, which equates to more enjoyment.

Cross-Country (XC) / Trail Bikes

Specialized Epic Pro

Cross-Country (XC) bikes and Trail bikes have rear suspension systems that absorb bumps on the trail for a smoother ride and greater comfort. Because the tire moves with the terrain and stays better connected to it, these bikes provide better control and more efficient braking than a hardtail. This will enhance your performance when the going gets rough.

Suspension travel is measured by the rear wheels' maximum vertical movement. XC bikes typically have a range of 100 to 140 millimeters. With an exception for extremely technical terrain, this is enough travel to make your ride smoother and easier to manage. Weighing between 20 and 30 pounds, they're lighter than long-travel bikes made of the same frame material. This can be a big advantage on long and steep uphill climbs.

Cross-country/trail bikes are the most popular type on the market. They are versatile enough to handle various trail conditions, making them the top choice for mountain bikers. Overall, this category gives you good versatility and speed. However, you should carefully evaluate the trail conditions that you'll be riding on the most. If they're persistently rough and rocky, you may be better served with a bike in the enduro/all-mountain/aggressive trailbike category.

Enduro/All-Mountain/Aggressive Trailbike

Specialized Enduro

Enduro, All-Mountain, or Aggressive Trailbike, whichever name you choose to call them, are bikes that are capable of handling most trail conditions. They fill a gap between cross-country riding and downhill riding, readily adept at both climbing hills and tackling technical descents. These bikes are intended for riders who can make full use of their extensive terrain handling characteristics. It's a style of riding that requires exceptional bike handling skills.

These bikes have 150 to 160 mm of suspension travel, which can readily handle descents with drops and other radical trail features. The frame is more beefed up than XC bikes, the forks are longer, and the head angle is more sloped back, all of which makes riding downhill a little less scary and more manageable. In short, trails that are too grueling for XC bikes can be handled much better with an aggressive trailbike.

The features of these bikes increase the weight (between 26 and 34 pounds), and the more laid back geometry is not the most ideal for climbing, but they're still light and versatile enough to get you up the hill. If you're a strong, conditioned rider who does well with climbing, this shouldn't be an issue.

These are do-it-all bikes that can be used on a wide variety of terrain. Whether you need this kind of bike or not largely depends on the trails you'll be commonly riding. If it's seriously rough terrain with a lot of technical challenges, this type of bike is probably a good option. This is also a good choice for enduro racing, which is more technically challenging than XC race courses. However, if you're looking for a bike that's capable of high speed downhill runs, the Downhill category bikes are the reigning champions.

Downhill / Freeride / Gravity Driven

Specialized Demo 8

Downhill mountain bikes are designed for gravity-driven downhill riding with extreme terrain conditions. For this, they have beefy frames, oversized suspension, thick and wide tires, and the largest brake discs among all mountain bikes. The suspensions have between 170 to 250 mm of travel, enough to soak up any big impacts, including huge drops. These bikes weigh in at 32 to 40 pounds.

Because they're designed with a laid back or "slack" head tube angle, the front tire is further out in front. This helps prevent the rider from being pitched over the bars on the steepest hills and makes the bike feel rock steady when pointed sharply downhill. Although they're the best for descending, they're terrible at uphill climbing. These bikes are only meant to be taken to the top of the mountain by ski lift or automobile, then ridden down at high velocity on some of the most severe and challenging terrain. The Freeride discipline does not have the same focus on downhill speed. Instead, it involves riding off of anything you can find, such as big ledge drops and platforms.

Downhill bikes are mainly limited to designated trails and closed course tracks, not trails shared by hikers and horses. If you don't live near any designated trails, you won't have much use for this kind of bike. But if high elevation is readily available and you want the thrill of screaming down a mountain, you'll probably find it to be the ultimate in fun. It's a popular sport, but it's also dangerous and takes the utmost skill, experience, and fitness. Full body armor is recommended because crashes with serious injuries are an ever-present possibility.

Fat Tire & Plus-Sized Bikes

Specialized Fatboy SE

For riding on light snow, hard-pack snow, sandy trails, or beaches, the fat tire mountain bike has become a popular option. Due to their superior stability and trail-gripping power, these bikes are even being used for cross-country riding. With four to five inches of tire width, their footprint provides extra grip and a soft ride that hooks many riders. Their cushioning effect absorbs trail vibrations and smaller impacts, thereby reducing the need for suspension systems, although you can find front and rear suspensions incorporated into some models. One of the drawbacks is the tire's squishy feeling during hard cornering, as if it wants to roll off the rim. Another issue is the extra rolling resistance making the bike slower. But for those who want a grippy ride that can float over rough terrain, this is the ticket.

Bikes made for "plus-sized" tires are another option for cross-country riding. While a regular tire may be in the range of two inches wide with a fat tire four to five inches wide, plus-size tires come in at around three inches wide. This in-the-middle size offers some relief to the high rolling resistance of fat tires while still providing upgraded traction benefits. They also have a lower weight and a more solid feel in the turns than their fat cousins.

More Categories

There are a couple variations of the above that are designed for specific applications. The **Hardtail Dirt Jump Bike** is a smaller framed, more maneuverable hardtail designed for jumping on ready-made tracks. These excel with stunts such as the back flip. **Slopestyle** bikes are similar to dirt jump but have dual suspension, which allows riders to

fly higher. These are primarily used in bike parks that have a unique variety of jumps, drops, quarter-pikes, and other wooden obstacles. Both of these variations have a more affordable price tag than their bigger cousins and are an appealing option for the younger, stunt-oriented BMX crowd.

The **Single Speed** bike is just that. Its chain runs directly from a single chainring to a single rear sprocket. This kind of bike poses serious challenges when riding uphill, but has a distinct advantage of being lightweight and simple. There are no gears to change … no derailleurs, no shifters, and no rear suspension. Some riders love these

minimalist bikes because they challenge you and force you to compensate for the lack of gearing using strength and endurance.

We can't get through this list without mentioning **Electric** bikes. The technology has come a long way for power assisted bicycles, and they're now available in a variety of mountain bike types including hardtail, dual suspension, downhill, and fat tire bikes. There's a lot of controversy over these bikes within the cycling world. Although they're not for everyone, they appeal to some people. E-bikes can really bring the mountain biking experience to those who may not be inclined to obtain the fitness required to climb the tougher hills or who have a disability that would otherwise make it impossible. The fact that they can open the world of mountain biking to more people is a wonderful thing.

When you talk about their usefulness with downhill mountain biking, that's a whole other aspect of the electric advantage. No longer will you have to wait or pay for the ski lift to get your heavy ride back to the top; instead, just ride up under power. But if you're interested in cross-country riding and you're a healthy individual, carefully consider your lifetime fitness goals. Do you want to be an ever-improving athlete? If this is the case, an electric bike may not be your best choice.

Making a Selection

It's important to note that some bikes have performance features similar to bikes in other categories, so you should consider your options carefully. For example, a full suspension XC with an advanced suspension system could have the pedaling efficiency of a hardtail. A full suspension bike could also be lighter in weight than a hardtail due to its superior frame and component material. A high-end enduro could be lighter than an XC, and a downhill bike could be lighter than an enduro bike. Quality and price play a big part in performance and weight characteristics, which can give high-end bikes the ability to perform well in the arena of a closely related category.

When selecting a bike, it's important to know what caliber of bike you really need. Of course, the more you spend, the better the bike that you'll have, but determining what's important enough to pay extra for and figuring out where you can save money will require some investigation. Deciding which grade of components and materials to put in your "must have" bucket is an important step in finding the right bike. The idea is to get the most performance possible with the money that you have. The following chapters should help direct you to making the best possible purchase.

CHAPTER TWO

Frames

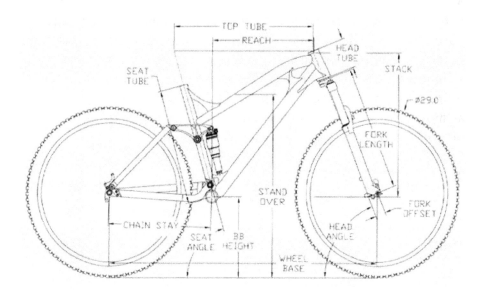

FRAMES ARE THE core of the machine, and their geometry greatly affects the riding experience. Manufacturers design them based on the performance expectations of the type of bike and its intended use. The variations in frame geometry make each bike's ride qualities feel unique; it all depends on what the manufacturer is going for. Pedaling efficiency, cornering stability, and descending/ ascending abilities are some of the things that are affected. Due to all of the possible variations, it's good to know what ride characteristics you're looking for when hunting for the right bike. Some examples:

- A "steep" head tube angle will put your weight further forward for superior climbing performance but will make descending trickier.

- A shorter wheelbase will allow for tighter turns, while a longer wheelbase gives more high speed stability.

- A lower bottom bracket will make the bike feel more "sunk in" and stable on the turns but will increase the chance of the pedals hitting obstacles.

Frame Sizes

It's important to have a frame size that's best suited for your body. If it's too small, you'll feel low and crunched up; if it's too big, you'll feel high and stretched out. Frame size directly affects your comfort and how well you can handle the bike. An ill-fitted bike is also a safety issue and can be a potential contributing factor in accidents.

Seat tube length is a basic measurement for determining frame size, but different manufacturers vary in the ways to take this measurement, which makes numerical bike sizing misleading. It doesn't take into account the top tube length, which is also an important dimension because this determines your arm reach. Since most frames are designed with proportional seat and top tubes, manufacturers typically use the more common designations of small, medium, large, extra-large and XXL. The following chart is for adult sizes and is just an estimate:

BIKE SIZE	RIDER HEIGHT	SEAT TUBE LENGTH
SMALL	5'2" - 5'6"	15" - 16"
MEDIUM	5'6" - 5'10"	17" - 18"
LARGE	5'10" - 6'1"	19" - 20"
EXTRA-LARGE	6'1" - 6'4"	21" - 22"
XXL	6'5" - 6'7"	23" - 24"

Due to variations in the leg and torso lengths of different individuals and the variations in frame geometry between the different manufacturers and models, those at a borderline height will need a little experimentation with each bike that's being considered. One way of determining the right size is by physically checking how you fit. To do this, the saddle height and the saddle setback will need to be adjusted.

(Refer to chapter seven for the set-up procedures.) If one or more of the adjustments have reached the end of their limit, you have the wrong size frame. For example:

If you have the saddle adjusted equal in height to the handlebars, but the seat post is extended past its limit line, you probably need a larger frame.

If you have the saddle setback adjusted all the way forward, but your reach to the handlebar still doesn't provide sufficient bend at the elbows, you probably need a smaller frame.

Women Specific Bikes

Although mountain bikes can be used by either sex, many women require different frame geometry than men to get the optimal fit. The average woman generally has a smaller stature than men with proportionately longer legs, a shorter torso, and narrower shoulders.

To accommodate these differences, many bike manufacturers have models designed specifically for women. The geometry and certain components of these bikes are a better fit for a woman's physique. They're slightly taller (proportionately to the rest of the frame) for longer legs, have slightly shorter top tubes for shorter torsos, and narrower handle bars for narrower shoulders. Taking women's overall shorter height into consideration, manufacturers also design these bikes with a lower stand over height and shorter crank lengths.

To determine if this is the type of bike you need, you should test the fit of both regular and women-specific to see which suits you best. Depending on your body dimensions, you may or may not need a women-specific mountain bike. The following chart is an estimate of their sizes:

BIKE SIZE	RIDER HEIGHT	SEAT TUBE LENGTH
EXTRA-SMALL	4'10" - 5'2"	13" - 14"
SMALL	5'2" - 5'6"	15" - 16"
MEDIUM	5'6" - 5'10"	17" - 18"
LARGE	5'10" - 6'1"	19" - 20"

Frame Material

Frame material is an important factor because it affects the weight, flexibility, durability, and price of the bike. While aluminum and carbon fiber are by far the most popular, steel and titanium are also described here for comparison. Each has their own unique set of properties and price that needs to be considered when making a selection.

Aluminum: Aluminum alloy frames are popular due to their lighter weight and reasonable price. They're widely considered the best buy for entry and mid-level bikes. Since aluminum is not as strong as steel, more material is needed to make up the difference, which is why the tubing is wider. The larger diameter tubes cause them to ride stiffer than bikes with steel alloy frames, a characteristic that gives them livelier handling in tight riding situations. This is a quality that many riders like, but this stiffness will also transfer trail chatter and vibration through the bike, which can result in a harsher ride.

Aluminum also has the ability to resist corrosion, making it more suitable for wet climates. A well-made aluminum frame will provide many years of reliable use. Lightweight and strong, it's the best value for the money.

Carbon Fiber: Carbon fiber has become the standard material for higher-end bikes. It's a non-metallic material that's more expensive than steel and aluminum but is lightweight, tough, and does not corrode. It's actually one of the strongest engineered materials in the world. Many big strides have been made in the advancement of carbon fiber manufacturing technology. Entire fuselages of some of the latest commercial and military aircraft are now being manufactured from this material.

This ultra-lightweight substance is an excellent choice for bike frames and has become very popular with cyclists. It provides an advantage in strength and weight over metal frames. Its stiffness and flexibility strikes a good balance between that of aluminum and steel. If you're the type of rider who wants the lightest frame, you'll find it worth the additional cost. When you're pushing the limits of the sport by riding competitively, it could make the difference between winning and losing.

Although prices have slowly come down due to increased sales volume, they are still on the expensive side and will probably remain so for the foreseeable future. This is due to the cost of the raw carbon fiber material, the cost of the unique molds required for each type and size of frame, and the amount of hand labor that goes into each one. Higher-end frames typically have carbon fiber material that was made with labor intensive layup processes. They're lighter in weight, have increased strength, and allow a small amount of flex in key areas. In comparison, less expensive carbon fiber frames can be harsh-riding and run the risk of cracking under extreme impacts. Always choose a reputable manufacturer to ensure that you're getting a good quality carbon fiber frame.

Steel: Steel alloy frames are the heaviest but also the least expensive of the frame materials. Steel has high strength, which gives it more durability and makes it less likely to crack or dent in an accident. However, this heavy weight will increase the effort that's required for climbing hills and can also make these bikes feel less nimble. Manufacturers will often make the tubes with a smaller diameter to offset the heavier weight, but this tends to make them more flexible, resulting in a spongier ride. The positive side of this flexing is reduced fatigue that results from trail vibrations.

One more thing to consider with steel frames is their tendency to rust over time in wet climates. If you anticipate a lot of exposure to water, it may not be the best choice. If you are going with a steel frame, make sure that it's the more common chromoly blend of steel, which is stronger and more durable.

Titanium: Titanium alloy is a less common frame material, even though it's the fourth most common metallic element on earth. This lower usage is due to its high price, which is in part due to the tremendous amount of energy that's required to extract it from the earth. Another reason lies in the fabrication process, which tends to be problematic due to the difficulties involved with manipulating the tubing and welding the joints.

Titanium does offer some big advantages over other metals, including the highest strength to weight ratio. This gives manufacturers the ability to make the tubing thinner in places to increase flexibility for absorbing trail vibrations, while shaping the tubing wider in other places where greater stiffness is required. Titanium's fatigue life, which is a measure of how many times a material can be stressed without damage, is nearly infinite, and its ability to resist corrosion means it won't rust, another highly desirable quality. These factors will surely allow titanium frames to outlast all others. It will always be a high-cost frame material, but if you can afford the premium price tag, it will provide excellent strength, flexibility, and durability in a lightweight frame that will last a lifetime.

Rear Suspension Systems

The rear suspension plays a big role in the performance and handling of the bike. This system is made up of the frame's pivoting rear triangle and the rear shock absorber that it actuates. There are many variations of this, each with unique features designed to match with frames and forks so that all parts work together to give the bike its ride characteristics.

Since about 2003, bike manufacturers have made big improvements to rear suspensions by reducing pedal bob, which is the tendency of the rear shock to compress with each pedal stroke, resulting in a loss of pedaling efficiency. Working closely with the shock absorber manufacturers, they have overcome this inherent efficiency problem with a force called anti-squat. Through years of improvements in both rear linkage arrangements and rear shock technology, most can now handle it fairly well. In fact, the pedaling platforms of some XC models are so good that they closely match the performance of a hardtail while still providing good shock absorption.

The degree of complexity of the suspension system can affect the price of a mountain bike. Different bike manufacturers use one of several different suspension designs, with new variations always in the works. All the different jargon that's used in the industry for these systems can make understanding the designs very complicated. Although it's not important to be intimately familiar with all the variations, you should at least be familiar with two basic designs that all the variations are based on: the Single-Pivot and the Four Bar Linkage. Which system is best really comes down to what feels right for you; there is no one best choice. Test riding bikes at local shops is the easiest way to find one that suits your personal preferences.

Single Pivot: This is the simplest but least popular suspension design. It consists of a swing-arm that pivots at the frame just forward of the bottom bracket. The advantages of this system are its light weight, ease of maintenance, and lower cost. A disadvantage of this design is that it creates some degree of brake interference, which is a compression of the shock while braking. Examples of manufacturers that have used this system on some of their bikes are Cannondale, Devinci, Diamondback, Orange, Santa Cruz, and Trek.

Orange Five AM

Four Bar Linkage: This design uses four pivot points to complete the suspension. These pivots join the linkages at varying locations depending on the configuration. Multiple patented designs have been derived from this basic concept, each with different appearances and performance. Some may have the shock connected to the bottom tube and others connected to the top tube, but they're all part of the same four bar family. These include the DW Link (Ibis, Turner, Pivot, Independent

Fabrications, Iron Horse); the Horst Link (Specialized, Scott, Norco, Cube); the Active Braking Pivot (Trek, Kona) and the Virtual Pivot Point (Santa Cruz, Intense).

Ibis Mojo (DW Link)

Specialized Epic (Horst Link)

Trek EX 9 (ABP Link)

Intense Spider2 (VPP Link)

> *"The most expensive component is the one that breaks."*
>
> -- Farrell's Law of New-Fangled Gadgetry

CHAPTER THREE
Components

BIKE MANUFACTURERS COMMONLY use the same frame design across their entire range of price offerings of individual models. What typically differentiates these bikes is the quality of the attached components. This is something that makes a huge difference in their performance and, of course, their price. Knowing what components to look for in a mountain bike and making a wise purchase could be the difference between having a good time and experiencing frustration. This is the kind of sport where equipment matters...a lot. Key components that need to be considered are the wheels, the suspension, the brakes, and the drivetrain.

Wheels

Wheels can be considered the most vital components of a bike because they transfer your pedaling power to the ground and affect the bike's control and performance. Because it's desirable to do these things with the highest efficiency, it's important to make well-informed choices in wheel size, material, and tire design.

One big consideration is weight. Since the centrifugal force created by a tire's rotation is magnified outward, it causes the tire's weight to become greater than its actual (static) weight. This is known as rotational kinetic energy. It's mainly a factor during acceleration because the influence of this energy dissipates as the bike's momentum takes over. Manufacturers have designed lighter wheels in order to lessen this effect and create faster accelerating bikes. Most modern rims are now made of aluminum, and a smaller percentage are made of carbon fiber. This type of weight advantage will have a bigger impact on a bike's performance than cutting down a bike's weight in other ways.

Wheel Diameters

Wheel size is one of the main considerations when selecting a new bike. With adult=sized mountain bikes, there are three different rim diameter sizes available: the 26 inch, the 27½ inch, and the 29 inch. Frames and some of the components are designed for specific wheel sizes, a pairing that ensures that the bike has optimal handling and operation. In most cases, mixing a frame with a different wheel size than what it was designed for will cause problems and is not recommended.

Having a choice in wheel size has widened the purchasing options for consumers, so it's important to have some knowledge of the pros and cons of each. Which one you go with is largely dependent on personal preference, body size, riding style, and what discipline of the sport you're involved in. The following is a brief description of the performance that each size provides.

26": The 26er is the original mountain bike wheel size and had long been the industry standard. But nowadays the demand for bikes with wheels in this size is dramatically reduced, so many dealers no longer carry them. It has also become increasingly harder to find replacement tires. However, this size does remain on the market to some degree, especially with Slopestyle, Dirt Jump, and Downhill bikes. You can also find cross-country 26ers being ridden all across the land, and used ones are always available for sale.

This is the smallest of the wheel sizes and as such, has more torque and requires slightly less leg strength per wheel revolution. This makes them very capable climbers on steep hills with good traction and gives them great acceleration in situations such as popping out of a turn or getting up a sudden incline. The shorter wheelbase and smaller tire size also allow for sharper carving around the corners and the ability to quickly flick around objects, giving aggressive riders the advantage on trails with tight turns, switchbacks, rock gardens, etc. This extra agility will train one's eyes and mind to pick out the best path for the tire (called line), which in turn will result in more skilled and proficient riders.

Having smaller wheels means that the rims, tires, forks, and frame all weigh less than larger-wheeled bikes made from the same materials, which is a distinct advantage. The disadvantage comes from the fact that they don't travel as far per wheel revolution, making them slower on the flats and on the type of hills where torque is less of a factor.

29": This popular size has mostly taken over the hardtail market and is a top seller in the full suspension market. Several aspects of 29ers differentiate them from the 26ers; the most significant is the ease with which the large diameter allows them to roll over objects. This has the effect of smoothing out the ride and bringing more comfort, something that is especially beneficial for hardtails or bikes with short travel suspension. And when the trail is a balancing act over wet and slippery roots and rocks, the increased traction and roll-over ability of the bigger tires provide a distinct advantage. A downside of this roll-over capability is that it can put riders in the habit of simply plowing over rough terrain without concern, thereby removing the need and desire to sharpen line selection skills.

While the 29ers can be less nimble in tight turns, wide, sweeping turns will feel more stable because the bottom bracket of 29ers sits lower in relation to the wheel axles. This puts your weight at a lower center of gravity and gives you a sense of being more sunk-in and stable, a feature that allows you to rail those types of turns. The lower torque of the 29ers makes them less likely to break traction, which is especially helpful on climbs with loose terrain. This reduced torque does require more strength to accelerate from a stop, which is most noticeable when starting out on an incline. But once you get these tires up to speed, they carry their momentum well, making them faster on the majority of rides.

For beginners, a 29er is easier to ride. Its roll-over capability empowers riders to charge over the rough terrain with less fear. And when competing in cross-country races, the advantage is definitely with the 29ers. In most cases, these races do not have highly technical courses that require a lot of sharp agility. This allows the 29ers to glide through the course quicker and with better time results. As a consequence, XC races these days are dominated by the 29ers. For shorter riders, bikes fitted with tires of this diameter can feel large and unwieldy. If you're 5'5" or less, smaller diameter wheels will probably suit you better.

27.5": This brings us to the third size on the market, the 27.5 inch, otherwise known as a "27-five" or a 650b (based on an older road bike standard). Due to the big differences in the advantages and disadvantages of both the 26ers and the 29ers, an intermediary size was seen by numerous manufacturers as an important addition to the line-up.

The 27.5 inch wheels are somewhat of a hybrid that has good performance in most situations, taking some of the advantages of both the 29ers and the 26ers while reducing some of the disadvantages. Its responsiveness and compactness is similar to the 26ers while possessing speed, stability, and roll-over capability that's closer to the 29ers. Its weight falls in between the other sizes, which is a reasonable compromise. This intermediate size also has more options for suspension system designs, which means they can be combined with even the longest forks and shocks.

While the 27-five doesn't completely eliminate all of the disadvantages of the other sizes, it could very well be a happy medium that works best for most people. In fact, if you're interested in an Enduro/All Mountain/Aggressive Trailbike category, this could be the optimal size.

Conclusion: Depending on who you talk to, you'll get different opinions on which wheel size is better. But much depends on what kind of rider you are and what type of trail conditions you'll be riding on most of the time. In all likelihood, your selection will be a good one, and it's hard to go wrong. Here are a few more points that may help with the decision:

- If you're a downhiller and need long stroke suspension on a nimble bike, a 29er may not be the best choice.

- If you're an experienced rider who frequently rides highly technical trails and likes to use a lot of body language to whip around and pop out of tight corners, a 26er may suit you well.

- If you're a relatively new rider with little or no experience, a 29er could be a good choice because its superior roll-over ability will make riding easier.

- If you're a cross-country racer who wants to make the best times, a 29er is probably the best choice.

- If you're going for a fat tire or a plus-sized bike, it's important to understand that the outer diameter of the tire is going to be bigger than a regular tire. For example, a 27.5 plus will have an outside diameter that is close to a 29er.

- If you want overall versatility, which is a common situation, the 27.5" wheel is the way to go. They're a great compromise between the 26ers and the 29ers.

Tires

Tires come in a variety of widths and tread patterns that affect the two main factors of a tire's performance: traction and rolling resistance. If you have a tire with great traction, its grip to the terrain will slow you down with its increased rolling resistance. Likewise, if your tire has low rolling resistance, it may spin out on loose terrain due to a lack of traction. There are also differences in sidewall thicknesses and compounds that affect the tire's puncture resistance and its ability to resist wearing out.

New bikes generally come packaged with tires that are suited for the bike's intended purpose. For example, an XC will most likely have a tire that is balanced between good traction and relatively low rolling resistance, while a downhill bike will have a wider and thicker tire with softer rubber to give it great traction. Since Downhill Mountain Biking mainly uses gravity for propulsion, rolling resistance is much less of a concern.

When you're faced with selecting a tire for your bike, traction is the bigger consideration and should be given higher priority. As you shop for tires, you'll discover a large and confusing array of tires that can make selection difficult. While some tires are made for specific terrain conditions, others will try to cover a broad range of conditions. You'll find that every tire manufacturer has its own way of describing the virtues of its tires. But once you understand tire widths, tread patterns, thicknesses, and compounds, you'll be able to identify what you need. After that, it's just a matter of choosing one manufacturer over the others based on reputation, reviews, etc.

Width: The width of a tire's tread determines how much surface area is contacting the ground. Increased contact provides higher traction but also increases the rolling resistance. A narrow tread will have less rolling resistance but will also have less traction. In general, most XC bikes will use tires in the width range of 1.9" to 2.2", enduro bikes with 2.1" to 2.4", downhill bikes with 2.3" to 2.5", plus-size tires at 2.8" to 3.0", and fat tires around 4.0". The different tread widths of standard tires can all mount to modern rims due to the use of a similar "casing" width, which is the tire's measurement from bead to bead. Plus-size tires and fat tires each have specifically designed rims.

Thickness: Generally, this is determined by the thickness of the thread of the cloth material that's embedded within the rubber. A thick thread means that the tire will have more rubber, which all combined provides better protection against punctures, but it will have increased weight and less compliance during an impact. A thinner thread means that the tire will have a thinner wall, which reduces its weight and provides more compliance but has a higher puncture risk. Thread thickness is measured by threads per inch (TPI), which is a standard measurement used in tire descriptions. Most XC bikes will have tires with 120 TPI, enduros with 60 or 120 TPI, and downhill bikes with a 2-ply 60 TPI in order to withstand rough trails with lots of sharp-edged rocks.

Compounds: Tire manufacturers add different ingredients to the rubber in order to achieve specific traction and wear characteristics. These rubber compounds are made to be anywhere from soft to medium to hard. A soft rubber tire will have great traction on loose terrain and during cornering but will have a high rolling resistance on hard pack. A hard rubber tire will have better longevity and will provide the best energy transfer to the ground due to its low rolling resistance but will have a tendency to slip on loose terrain. There are no designations that show a tire's hardness. The best way to tell is by pinching the knobs and wiggling them back and forth. Keep in mind that bigger knobs will be harder to wiggle, which is also a characteristic that actually lowers rolling resistance. All in all, a tire that's slightly on the softer side will be best for most conditions.

Tread patterns: Small, closely spaced knobs translate to less rolling resistance and greater speeds on hard terrain but will not provide sufficient traction on loose terrain. On the flip side, large and widely spaced knobs will have great traction and speed on loose terrain but will have a high rolling resistance on hard terrain. Unless you're racing on hard pack or riding through mud, medium-sized and widely spaced knobs will work best on a variety of terrain conditions. Some tires will have flatter profile knobs across the middle with more aggressive square knobs on the sides. This improves rolling resistance while providing good cornering traction.

Some bike manufacturers will use different tires front and rear. Since front wheel slipping will often lead to a crash, a more aggressive tread in the front is an advantage; and since most of the bike weight is carried by the rear tire, a smoother tread in the rear provides the advantage of less rolling resistance. Using two front tires to provide good cornering performance is also a possibility.

There is no easy answer on what the best tire is. The most important thing is to have tires that match the terrain that you'll be riding on the most. The following are examples of different tread patterns and manufacturers, along with the terrain conditions that they're best suited for.

Hard pack/ Dry terrain

Kenda Small Block Eight

- Closely spaced knobs
- Low rolling resistance
- Fast accelerating on hardpack
- Numerous knobs provide multiple contact points for hard pack traction

Dry to moist hard pack / Some loose terrain

Specialized S-Works The Captain

- Closely spaced center knobs for lower rolling resistance
- Wide spaced edge knobs for cornering traction
- Versatile use

Dry to wet terrain / Loose terrain

Michelin Wild Grip'r

- Wider spaced knobs for good traction on a variety of terrain
- Edge knobs designed for cornering
- Rolls decently

Mud

Continental Mud King

- Spiked knobs for traction
- Knobs widely spaced to shed mud
- Slow rolling on other terrain

Tire Valves: There are two types of tire valves: the Presta and the Schrader. The Presta valve has a smaller diameter than the Schrader valve, which means a smaller stem hole. This makes the rim stronger because the hole is the weak point and the most likely location for the rim to bend or crack. It also allows manufacturers to make rims narrower and lighter.

The Schrader is the same valve that's used on a car tire, which means that it can be accessed by any service station pump. Presta valves are found only on bicycle tires, so first-time riders will probably need to purchase a pump that can accept this type. Alternatively, an adapter can be used that fits onto the Presta to allow a connection with a Schrader pump.

Presta   Schrader

Forks

Because fork length and features can vary, some consideration is necessary when choosing a bike. Typically, the length is matched to the frame's geometry to provide the optimal handling characteristics for the intended application. There are two basic types of suspension forks: air and coil.

Air: Air forks provide shock absorption from the compression of air in a chamber. Some models have secondary chambers that bleed air from the primary chamber when a higher compression is reached, giving it a more steady resistance throughout the stroke. Air forks provide the ability to custom tune the settings to personal preferences of ride quality based on rider weight, style of riding, and terrain conditions. Simpler models will only have an air pressure adjustment and basic rebound adjustment. More expensive models use dials or internal valves for additional forms of adjustment. Disadvantages of air forks include the periodic maintenance that's required due to their multiple seals and a heat buildup that worsens during big downhill runs, which can result in an inconsistent feel. For average trail riding, these disadvantages are not serious and are acceptable tradeoffs for the savings in weight.

Coil: Coil sprung forks are heavier than air shocks because they use a spring inside the fork to provide shock absorption. Springs can be made from either a steel alloy or the lighter but more expensive titanium alloy. The advantages of coil forks are a sturdier and tougher construction that requires less maintenance, a slightly better absorption of small bumps, and smooth, even resistance throughout the entire compression stroke. Preload is added to these forks by adjusting a knob . . . the more preload it has, the firmer it feels. Although coil forks are less expensive, they are typically used only with downhill bikes due to their heavy weight.

Beware of forks and shocks that are of cheap quality from unknown manufacturers. They will only disappoint you if you're at all serious about the sport. Unless you're buying a bike that's strictly for downhill gravity assisted riding, only consider a bike with air forks due to their lighter weight.

You can save money by getting a lower model that has simpler adjustments, but some basic features are still necessary. One of those is rebound damping, which sets the fork's speed rate of re-extension after being compressed. Another feature commonly found is a lock-out switch that can partially and fully stop all movement of the fork. Locking the forks can allow more pedaling energy to transfer to forward motion, which can be helpful during climbs.

Shocks

Rear shocks use the same basic concept as forks, except on a smaller scale. Their length is typically matched to the rear suspension system for optimal performance. Because of their lighter weight, air shocks are the best option on XC bikes. You may have seen spring type shocks on low-end bikes, but their only useful purpose is for looks because they're heavy and have too much pedaling bounce, making them impracticable for trail riding. When it comes to enduro, freeride, and downhill bikes, spring shocks do have advantages because of their ability to absorb big hits. But even on these bikes, modern air shocks can be found that rival the performance of springs.

Shocks can have many adjustments, including rebound damping, which functions the same as the fork's rebound adjustment, and compression damping, which is the shock's resistance to being compressed. Higher compression damping will reduce pedaling bob but will result in a less comfortable ride. Some models will have this pre-set and not adjustable, which is OK if the bike has a good pedaling platform. Usually, there is some degree of inherent pedal-bob that robs energy from forward momentum. One option for coping with this is a system that locks and partially locks out the shock, either automatically with a sensor, or manually with a switch that has descending mode for full travel, trail mode for limited travel, and climbing mode to almost completely lock it out.

Disc Brakes

With awesome braking power at your disposal, you can take on steep downhills with much less fear. Just knowing that your brakes will quickly scrub off the speed will give you the confidence to go faster. Modern disc brakes fill this role very nicely, and for this reason, they are now installed on all but the lowest quality mountain bikes. When it comes to the old-style rim brakes, there are a number of drawbacks including:

- Inferior performance requiring extra distance to stop.

- Poor operation when they're wet or muddy.

- The rims are beefier and heavier because the pads can wear into them.

- If the rims get hit and develop a wobble, the braking performance will be affected.

Once you've used disc brakes, it will be hard to imagine riding without them. Starting with a light squeeze of the levers, you'll be able to feel the brakes begin working. They'll give you complete control of your braking power and speed, even in wet or muddy conditions. Disc brakes are the new standard and are a definite advantage over rim brakes.

Basically, there are two types of disc brake systems: mechanical, which is cable operated; and hydraulic, which uses fluid. The advantages of mechanical brakes are their lower cost, easier maintenance, and lighter weight. A disadvantage is cable stretch. This can cause a spongy feel, reduced braking power, and will require more frequent manual adjustments. Cables are also susceptible to mud and debris buildup that can cause binding, but with a little care and maintenance, mechanical disc brakes will work just fine and can be a good lower cost option.

Hydraulic disc brakes will give you smoother performance, more control, and better reliability. The hoses and reservoirs create a closed system that water, dirt, and debris cannot penetrate. However, a small leak can cause a loss of power, making frequent inspections absolutely essential. Many systems have a self-adjusting mechanism that keeps the reach of the brake lever in the same position when the brake pads wear down. Hydraulic disc brakes are the hot ticket item and have truly played a role in defining the modern mountain bike.

Disc brake rotors come in a variety of sizes including 140mm, 160mm, 180mm, and 200mm. The larger rotors will have greatest stopping power but will also add weight to the bike. This is why the largest sizes are commonly found on downhill bikes.

Higher quality brakes will allow more modulation, which is the brake's ability to apply partial pressure so that you can ease your braking power on and off, as opposed to sudden on/off braking. Cheap brakes that lock up easily are dangerous and should be avoided.

Gears

The front chainring(s) and the rear cassette are the gears of a bicycle's drivetrain, which also includes the derailleurs, the chain, and the pedal cranks. Front chainrings can either have one, two, or three "rings"; and the rear cassette can have 11, 12, or even 13 "cogs." The most common combinations are 1x11, 1x12, 1x13, 2x10, 2x11, 3x10, and 3x11. The lowest gear is a combination of the smallest chainring to the largest cog. This is sometimes referred to as the "granny gear." It's an ultra-low gear that can be especially helpful on the steepest climbs. The highest gear is a combination of the largest chainring to the smallest cog. This end of the scale is good for smooth downhill runs that generally take you to speeds of twenty-five mph and above.

The triple chainring will give you the most gearing options, which can have some advantage in situations such as rolling hills. The dual chainring will typically have enough gearing range for any situation. The single ring is a good and viable option. No front shifter equates to simpler gear selection, fast and precise shifting, lighter weight, and less maintenance. The small size of the ring also gives it greater ground clearance, which is an advantage on rocky terrain. A disadvantage is its narrower range of gear choices, which means it may not have either an ultra-low gear or an ultra-high gear.

With a single chainring, you do have the option of swapping it out with one that has more teeth for a higher range or one with fewer teeth for a lower range. If you're doing a lot of climbing, a 30- or 32-tooth ring may be acceptable. If your climbs are extreme, you may want a 28- or even a 26-tooth ring. If you're on mostly flat trails, a 36-tooth ring will prevent over-spinning at higher speeds. Upgrading to an oval ring can also provide a performance advantage by smoothing the power surges created by the pedal strokes, thereby reducing the chances of rear tire slippage during climbing.

Groupsets

A groupset is a component manufacturer's product series collection that consists of the drivetrain components, the shifters, the wheel hubs, and the brakes. It does not apply to the bike's frame, rims, tires, forks, handlebar, seat and pedals. The level of quality of the groupset can greatly affect the price of the bike. Typically, the biggest advantage of higher end sets is the weight savings from the premium materials that are used, such as titanium, magnesium, and carbon fiber.

Performance differences also become more noticeable as you go further up the product line. As an example: with the chain on the large chainring while crossed over to the large cog, it maximizes tension and puts a strain on the components. This could lead to shifting problems on low end components, but higher end components can handle it smoothly.

New bikes are sold with either a single groupset of components or a combination of parts from different sets to provide both value and performance. They may put higher end components where there is much heavier use and performance is a bigger issue, such as the rear derailleur. Doing this helps to keep the overall cost of the bike down. Another mix you may find is a different component manufacturer between the brakes and the drive train. This is simply the bike manufacturers' choice and does not create a compatibility issue. However, it's better if the rear derailleur, shifters, and cassette are of the same manufacturer because mixing these could cause operational problems.

The biggest manufacturers of mountain bike groupsets are SRAM and Shimano. They maintain a full range of product offerings that vary in quality and price. Check their websites to see the latest offerings and get an idea of what you want. Top end products add a lot of cost to the bike, so unless you're trying to shed every possible ounce and can afford it, something from the middle of the product line can be a good choice. After the parts wear out, you can always upgrade to something from the higher end.

Manufacturers continue to advance the technology of their components and regularly come out with new product series. One of the more notable ones is electronic shifting, which has been slowly gaining traction on road bikes since its introduction in 2009 and is now available on some high-end mountain bike models. This system uses handlebar-mounted switches that send an electronic signal by wire to a battery=powered motor. This motor then turns a worm gear that moves the derailleurs to shift the gears. This system increases the bike's cost, but those who can afford it will enjoy the virtues of nearly-instant gear shifting.

> *"The market is never saturated with a good product, but it is very quickly saturated with a bad one."*
>
> --Henry Ford

CHAPTER FOUR

The Purchase

AT THIS POINT you've probably figured out which bike category and wheel size is best suited for you. It's also probably clear that you'll need to spend a bit of money to get something decent. Of course, you'll need to keep it within your budget, so the big question to ask yourself is: How much bike do I need?

Clearly, the more you spend, the better the bike you'll have, but determining what's important enough to pay extra for and figuring out where you can save money will require some investigation. Factors that should be considered are quality, performance, weight, and price. Deciding which grade of components and materials to put in your "must have" bucket is an important first step in finding the right bike. The idea is to get the most performance possible with the money that you have. Keep in mind that you'll probably love the sport of mountain biking more than you think. If you get a lower-end entry level bike, you'll end up wanting to upgrade your components or switch to a higher level bike. In either case, it would have been less expensive to get a bike with the features that you wanted to have in the first place.

The Considerations

Quality can be found with bikes that are made by reputable manufacturers. In your search for the right bike, you'll probably run into some manufacturers that you've never heard of. Do some research to find out more about the company. Read online and magazine reviews. Find out how long they've been in business, where the frames are manufactured, and where the bikes are assembled. Also find out about the manufacturer's warranty policy. A limited lifetime warranty on the frame and a limited one-year warranty on the complete bicycle are very common. Component manufacturers may offer additional warranties.

Performance is important to consider because the level of componentry will determine the smoothness and reliability of the drivetrain, the stopping power and reliability of the brakes, and the performance of the suspension system. Although you don't want to overspend, there are some minimum standards that you should strive for.

Weight is a factor that needs consideration, but it is not as critical as quality and performance. With higher end bikes, the price you have to pay to save weight goes up in leaps and bounds. A lower weight will give you an edge if you're a racer going against competition that's closely matched in fitness and skill. But for most people, getting up the steep inclines will be your biggest challenge. A lighter bike would certainly help, but it comes at a higher price. If you're physically overweight, it would be more economical to shed some body weight instead.

Price is a key concern for many people. A new mountain bike may cost as much as one month's rent or a mortgage payment . . . or it could cost more than a decent used car. Either way, this is a major purchase. Some people close to you may try to discourage you from spending so much money on a bike, but don't let them. This bike could end up being your prized possession and is an investment in yourself for something that you'll be spending a lot of time with. Remember, you're worth it.

The following features will make a decent entry level bike:

- Aluminum frame
- Tubeless ready rims
- Air forks and shocks with rebound adjustment
- Mechanical disc brakes
- Mid-level components

Here are some of the major premium upgrades that you may want to consider:

- Carbon fiber frame
- Carbon fiber rims
- Air forks and shocks with multiple adjustment options
- Hydraulic disc brakes
- Top-level components

It's by no means necessary to get high-end premium components unless you can afford them or you're a competitive racer looking to get an edge on the competition. There are many combinations of options that will put you in the upper end of mountain bikes, with every upgrade dramatically driving the price higher. More of these parts are now being manufactured out of carbon fiber and titanium, adding to the myriad of available options for consumers.

When a product earns good reviews, it tends to drive up its sales. As the product's sales and production level increases, it becomes mainstream. This lowers the manufacturing cost per unit. These savings are typically passed on to the consumer, which further drives up the demand for the product. We can find solace with this process, as it brings us affordability, quality, and innovation.

The Price Points

When looking at mountain bikes and comparing specs, you'll find that there's a variety of component combinations and price levels. You'll obviously want to get the most you can for your money, so you'll need to do some careful shopping. The following is a list of price points (in U.S. dollars) where you can start to see various improvements. This will give you an idea of what you can generally expect for new model bikes:

1. **$200:** These bikes are so cheap that they are unusable for trail riding in any meaningful way. You will not find bikes at this price level in any reputable bike shop.

2. **$500:** Decent aluminum and chromoly frame hardtails can be found at this price level, but the components will be low-end. This could be a good value for someone who's just riding fire roads with no steep inclines and declines. Full suspension models at this price will be unusable for trail riding; the lack of quality and heavy weight makes them impracticable and are best suited for "urban" riders.

3. **$1000:** Hardtail 29ers and 27.5's with mid-level components. This could be a good choice for limited budgets. Full suspension bikes at this price are not a good idea because they will likely have low-level components and a rear suspension platform with excessive pedal bob. At this price, it would be best to stick with hardtails.

4. **$1500:** Hardtails with quality components. Full suspension bikes begin to improve in both suspension design and components. This is a good entry-level price-point.

5. **$2000:** Full suspension bikes with all of the aforementioned entry level features. A higher quality starts to show at this mid-range. This could be a good price level for those who have a serious interest in the sport but are looking for an entry-level bike.

6. **$3500:** For serious riders. At this level you'll begin to find carbon fiber frames and upgraded components. For those who don't want just an entry-level bike.

7. **$5000 and up:** For professional riders and those with high discretionary income. You'll find exotic materials on all components along with the latest in technology. Is it worth it? Yes. You do get what you pay for, but each improvement increases the price in big leaps, which by ratio doesn't match the performance improvements that you get with equivalent price increases in the lower models.

The Best Deal

The big questions are where and when to buy. Great bikes can certainly be found at the following sources:

Sporting Good Stores: It's possible to find some bikes to consider in large sporting good chains; some of these stores will actually have a good selection of mid-range bikes to choose from. They may even be able to order a higher model for you, but this won't give you the opportunity to physically compare the bikes. You may also see some low-end models that are catered to urban riders. That's not what you're after.

Internet Shopping: When shopping on the internet, you can find a lot of bikes at various prices. Without a doubt, it's the easiest and fastest way to compare specs and prices. A lot of information can be obtained this way. You can then just order the bike and have it delivered directly to your door. What could be more convenient? There's a lot to be said about internet shopping. If you find a great buy and are willing to take a chance on whether the bike you have chosen will be a match for you or not, by all means go for it.

There are, however, a few issues with purchasing a bike this way. Unless you can go to the actual store of the website you're visiting, you won't have any hands-on experience with the bikes; you won't be able to give them a test ride to compare the feel of the different variations in frame geometry, the smoothness of the shifting, the power of the brakes, the general feel of the bike, and if it fits your body comfortably. Proper fitting can be estimated by taking body measurements, but you won't have the opportunity to see if the fit of one bike feels better than another. Internet shopping also means that you won't have face-to-face conversations with a sales person, which can often be helpful in getting a deeper understanding of the differences between the models. Last but not least, you will not get any type of service agreement to go along with your bike purchase.

Local Bike Shops: Local bike shops are a great place to buy quality bikes. If you live in a populated area, there should be several shops within an hour drive of your home. Although having a regular shop close by to help with all of your cycling needs is optimal, visit as many as you can to find the one with the best knowledge, selection, and price. You should be able to find a helpful and courteous staff of bike enthusiasts who can answer your questions, adjust the bikes for you, and set you up with test rides. Although a ride in the parking lot will not tell you how they will perform on the trails, you'll at least be able to compare the basic differences. Some shops have loaner bikes that you can test out on the local trails for a fee.

Many shops will include service agreements, including some that offer free tune-ups for as long as you own the bike. Routinely having your bike adjusted will make a huge difference in ride quality. And if you ever have the need for an urgent repair, you'll probably get priority attention. These kinds of services are a huge consideration because if you plan on keeping your investment in tip-top shape, a local bike shop will make it much easier and simpler.

Sometimes, bike shops have deeply discounted prices. If you're looking to buy the current year's model, you'll pay a higher price for the latest and greatest. But if having the latest model is not such a big concern for you, buying the previous year's model could be a way to save some money. The new models hit the floor around late August and the older models will then be marked down. As time goes by, the price drops even further, and by December you'll find some really deep discounts. It's not uncommon to see 40 percent off the regular retail price. Some stores may even have surplus from the previous two or three years and sell them at low clearance prices. By getting an older model, you could very well price yourself into a bike that has the features you need and want.

Buying a Used Bike

If you're unable to find a new bike that's within your budget while meeting your expectations, buying a used bike can be a great alternative. It's a way to get into the sport with less money without compromising on features. It's possible to get an awesome deal on a great used bike. The trick is being able to recognize the ones that are in good condition while knowing their fair market value. This requires a thorough knowledge of bikes before you begin your search. It's also important to have reasonable caution when dealing with unknown sellers.

Use the following guide to assist you in successfully purchasing a used bike:

1. Explore the world of new bikes by test riding several models. Feel how smooth the new bikes can shift gears and how well they can brake. This will be your performance comparison baseline. You can then more easily recognize any deficiencies or defects when you test ride used bikes. You should also learn the market value of new bikes so that you know how much you're going to save with a used bike.

2. Put together a list of bikes from current ads that meet your search criteria and are close to your budget. Examples of good places to shop are eBay and Pinkbike. You can even try generic sales outlets such as Craigslist. If possible, stick with well-known brands that are not more than a few years old. Look for bikes that, at the least, have everything on the aforementioned list of features for entry-level bikes. If it doesn't, you'll need to budget in the cost of upgrading the bike.

3. Form a list of questions that you'll be asking each seller, such as: How often was the bike ridden? How many miles/kilometers are on it? Has it been crashed? How often? How bad? (Crashes are not uncommon and does not necessarily mean it's a no-go.) Is there any damage? What parts have

been replaced? (Be wary of a bike that has a lot of alternate replacement parts. It may not conform to the manufacturer's specifications and thus has bad ride qualities.) Has it been ridden in the mud? (This tends to wear down chains and gears quicker.) How frequently has it been maintained? Why are you selling it?

4. Check out the bike in person. All second-hand bikes are going to have wear and tear, so you'll need to do a thorough inspection to determine its fair value or whether the bike should even be purchased. After all, there are no warranties on used bikes. When you go, bring somebody with you who also knows bikes. A second person can help identify problems, assist with price negotiation, and be influential in preventing you from making a hasty, emotion-based decision. Here's a list of some important things to check for when looking at a used bike:

   a. Frame: Check the frame for cracks, giving extra attention to the stress areas. This includes where the tubes join at the head and bottom brackets. Cracks can be small, so look closely. Bring a flashlight so you can see it better. Signs of a crack include bulges in the metal and telltale cracks in the paint. If any cracks are spotted on the frame, don't buy the bike.

   b. Handlebar: Check that the handlebar is not bent or cracked.

   c. Drivetrain: Check for a dirty drivetrain, a sure sign of neglect. Check the condition of the gear teeth. They should be rounded. If they look narrow or curved in the opposite direction of the chain travel, it means they're worn out and are due for replacement. Test ride the bike and try all the gears, especially the more frequently used center sprockets. The gears should shift smoothly without getting hung up. Try standing pedaling using a lot of pressure on the down stroke to check for skipping, which indicates an excessively worn chain. Check shifter cables for fraying.

   d. Shocks: Check for leaks around the dust seals. This could mean that the shocks are due for a rebuild. Also, find out when they were last serviced and if the seller has receipts to back it up.

   e. Rims: Check the rims for cracks and dents. Spin the wheel with your finger along the edge of the rim to see if it's straight. If not, small wobbles can be straightened by adjusting the spokes, but large wobbles may require a rim replacement.

f. Tires: Used tires will be worn to some degree. Check how much wear is showing on the edges of the knobs. If they look rough and rounded, they may need to be replaced, which should be factored into the price.

g. Brakes: Check how much wear the brake pads have; they should have some meat left to them. Spin the tire to see if the disc wobbles excessively (more than 1mm). If it does, it will need to be replaced. For hydraulic brakes, check for leaks by looking for any trace of oil on the line connections. It may show up as a clump of dirt. For mechanical brakes, check for cable fray. Finally, check for proper operation of the brakes and how quickly and smoothly the bike stops.

h. Bottom bracket bearing: Give the cranks a firm spin backwards; the bottom bracket bearing should allow it to spin freely two to three revolutions without any strange noises. Any roughness could mean a bad bearing.

i. Headset bearing: Squeeze the brakes and rock the bike back and forth. There should be no play or noises coming from the headset. If there is, it could mean a worn headset bearing.

If the bike has too many problems, consider walking away from it. The cost of repairs could be expensive and not worth the hassle. That's not the best way to get into the sport. Wear and tear also devalues the bike. If the price does not account for the condition and you can't get an agreement on a reasonable offer, you'll need to look elsewhere. Finding a good bike at a good price is going to take some time and will require patience. And patience will reward you in the end.

CHAPTER FIVE

Upgrades

UPON PURCHASING A new or used bike, you may want to immediately upgrade certain things. For performance, some of the best upgrades are tubeless tires, adjustable height seat posts, saddles, clip-in pedals, wide handlebars, and short stems. For comfort, the saddle, pedals, and handlebar are points of contact with your body, making them important considerations. When it comes to wheel sets, suspension, drivetrain, and brake components, it's often more cost effective to buy a bike with the product level you want rather than upgrading it afterward.

Tubeless Tires

For the money, tubeless tires are one of the best performance upgrades you can make. Inner tubes are highly susceptible to pinch flats, which happen when your tire hits a sharp-edged object with an impact big enough to compress it against the rim. This tends to pinch the inner tube, causing two small "snake bite" holes. To prevent this, the tires would have to be filled fairly solid to resist compression, but this higher pressure will cause a loss of traction, which will impair performance.

Enter tubeless. Tubeless wheels have tires that are sealed against the rim to eliminate the need of an inner tube. With no tube, there's no pinch flat problem, which means that lower tire pressures can be used. Lower tire pressure will allow the tire to grip the terrain much better, thereby increasing the responsiveness and control of your ride. Having "grippy" tires will make it feel like you're glued to the ground and will also make the sharp bumps feel softer by allowing the tires to easily deform to the rocks and roots instead of bouncing off of them. Additionally, vibrations created by the terrain will be reduced, which provides a smoother ride with less fatigue. Note: When switching to tubeless, the weight difference as well as the rolling resistance are negligible and won't be noticed.

Tubeless specific rims have no holes for the spokes, but they are expensive. Tubeless ready rims are less expensive and are common on newer bikes. These have spoke holes that need to be covered with a rubber rim strip or with specially designed rim tape to prevent leakage. Their inner wall is ridged to facilitate a seal between the rim and a specifically designed tubeless ready tire, which has a soft and thick rubber bead. Sealant is also used, which has the added benefit of automatically sealing smaller punctures. Always closely follow the manufacturer's installation instructions.

Modern mountain bikes usually come with tubeless ready rims and tires so that you can easily make the transition. If you go tubeless using a kit, make sure you check the kit manufacturer's web site for compatibility between your rims and tires. If you have the wrong combination, you may end up blowing your tires off the rim during installation or worse yet, while you're out on the trail. Here are a few possible disadvantages of tubeless tires:

- The conversion takes some work and money, but the reality is that it's not difficult when the proper steps are followed.

- There's a possibility of "burping" out air during hard riding. This is caused when a sideways tire compression allows air to escape past the rim. If this happens, you'll have to stop to pump up your tire.

- If you use a tire pressure that's too low, you run the risk of damaging your rim.

- If you have larger puncture or cut while out on a ride, you can still have a flat. Installing an inner tube will get you on your way, but the sealant will make it a messy affair.

- The sealant dries up and will need to be replaced at least every three months.

Adjustable Height Seat Post

An adjustable height seat post (dropper post) is another great upgrade. Lowering your seat will make the riding experience much more lively and pleasurable. The reason for this is pretty basic: When riding with your seat post in its normal position, your center of gravity is relatively high (the height that's needed for maximum power generation when pedaling). When traveling downhill, your pedaling power is no longer an issue. In fact, having your center of gravity up high when you're pointed downhill can feel downright scary and increases the risk of tipping over the side or flipping over the handlebar.

The solution is to lower your seat post on the downhills. With the seat out of your way, you can lower your body so that your center of gravity is at a lower and more manageable level. In this crouched down position, you'll be able to absorb bumps with your knees and elbows while easily shifting your weight to a more rearward location to hit your balance point. You'll also have the clearance to move your hips left and right as you deftly maneuver through technical situations. All of this makes for good, controlled descents.

Descents are not the only time you would use a dropper post. Having your seat lowered on turns and through rough terrain keeps the seat from hitting the inside of your legs when you're trying to move the bike from side to side. Your range of motion will not be restricted, and you'll have the versatility to move the bike around any which way that's needed. Simply put: It'll make you a better rider.

Because of the constantly varying terrain during trail riding, lowering your seat manually is a cumbersome task that requires frequent dismounts to make height adjustments. The solution is a dropper seat post. By pushing a lever on your handlebar, the seat will drop down to the low position. With another push of the lever, it pops up to the normal position. This allows you to make changes on the fly. Having this ability encourages you to change the height position much more frequently, resulting in a more engaging ride that better promotes your skills. Although these seat posts are a little heavier and more expensive, the tradeoff for the performance advantages are well worth it and should be a must-have upgrade for any serious trail rider.

Saddles

If you're new to biking or haven't spent a significant amount of time on the saddle lately, you're most likely going to end up with a sore behind. Saddle soreness is the result of continuous unnatural pressure on the soft tissue between your sit bones and the saddle. These pressure points (a.k.a. hot spots) can sometimes lead to unbearable pain, an effect that's often exacerbated from bouncing on rough terrain. Shifting around on the saddle or standing on the pedals from time to time can help but can only go so far. This comfort issue makes the saddle one of the more important components to consider.

Before you run off and buy a new saddle, there are a number of things that should be tried first. Most importantly, make sure that you're wearing padded biking shorts. This is a good way to cushion your behind and is highly recommended apparel for all bikers.

A poor riding position can also cause soreness, so the first step in trying to end saddle soreness is to make sure that your bike is properly set up. (See chapter seven for saddle set-up procedures.) The following are some examples of improper adjustments and the effects that they can have on your body:

- A saddle that's set too high will cause your hips to rock as your legs try to reach the bottom of the pedal strokes. This increases grinding at the pressure points.

- A saddle that's tilted too high can create extra pressure on the crotch.

- A saddle with a low tilt can cause you to constantly slide forward to the wrong part of the seat.

- Incorrect forward and aft positioning can also put your bones on the wrong part of the saddle, something that can negatively change how you're rubbing against it as you pedal.

Don't just tolerate pain and discomfort; make sure your adjustments are optimal. When you're a beginner, keep your rides short. After a few weeks of taking short, high intensity rides at regular intervals, your soft tissue will begin to adjust and toughen up. When this adjustment period is over, a little soreness from a long ride is normal, but it should not be significantly painful. If the pain doesn't subside, it may be time to change your saddle.

Different people have different pelvic bone structures. With your bike set up properly, how your pelvic bones rest on the saddle comes down to the match-up between bones and seat. Ideally, these bones should come into contact with the most padded portion of the seat and should stay there without excessive rubbing. There's a big variety of saddle designs to choose from, with differences in padding, side to side curvature, width, and designs such as split seats. Which saddle is best is a matter of the individual's match-up, but when you find the right one, it can make a big difference in comfort.

You might get lucky and find a good replacement right away, but sometimes it's a trial and error process until you find the right one. If you bought a bike from a good shop, they should let you make a swap, or they may have loaners that you could try out before making an expensive purchase. Another possibility is to borrow saddles from friends to see which one works best for you.

You may have the temptation to immediately go out and get a big, soft, thickly padded saddle. These types of saddles may feel a little better but come with a big weight penalty. Another problem is that they can also create more skin friction, which can lead to another type of irritation, called chafing. Not only is this uncomfortable, but it can result in poor pedaling technique by causing you to kick your knees outward. Their softness will also create a bouncing effect, which is yet another energy wasting motion. If you only go for the occasional short recreational ride, a softer saddle may work for you, but many riders prefer a firmer, narrower seat for better pedaling efficiency.

Women can also suffer from saddle soreness. The problem is that most bikes have saddles designed for males by default. Since women typically have a wider pelvic structure than men, a women specific saddle may be necessary. These are available as both an aftermarket product and as a standard feature on women specific bikes.

Pedals

You've probably noticed that most new bikes either do not have pedals or they're simply the inexpensive plastic type. Pedal choice is an individual preference and is normally left to the consumers as an aftermarket selection. Mountain bike pedals come in two basic categories to choose from: clipless (clip-ins) and platform transfer pedals (flats). There are positives with both kinds, but which one you choose will make a difference in the performance of your riding.

Clipless (Clip-in Pedals): Clipless pedals actually require clipping in. A cleat that's mounted to a special stiff-soled shoe clips into a spring-loaded mechanism on the pedal. It sounds silly to call them clipless when you're actually clipping them in, but this has a history: Before the mechanized pedal was invented, flat pedals came with a cage that had leather or nylon straps that you cinched down across your toes. This cage was called a toe clip, or clip for short, and helped to increase the rider's pedaling efficiency by preventing their shoes from sliding off the pedals. The problem with these cages was their inherent danger due to the degree of difficulty in removing your foot during a crash.

When manufacturers developed mechanized retention pedals that allowed shoes to easily disengage, they became a popular replacement for toe clips. Because these new retention pedals secured your foot without a clip, they were named "clipless" pedals. The thing is, toe clips are now obsolete because they're no longer used for mountain biking, so the name "clipless" has no relevance. You're actually clipping in to these retention pedals, so it's become increasingly popular to refer to them as "clip-in pedals". This is a much more logical term, and will also be referred to as such in this book. Sometimes you may even hear riders use the slang version "clips," which is also a good and relevant name.

Some say clip-in pedals give you an advantage in pedaling efficiency by allowing your muscle power to be more evenly distributed throughout the pedaling circle. (See Chapter Nine on pedaling) Although it hasn't been scientifically proven to have a significant advantage over flats, there may at least be a psychological advantage. Pedaling power is especially important during a strenuous uphill ride when every possible advantage should be used . . . even those that are mental. Clip-ins pedals will provide a stable connection to the pedals by keeping your feet from bouncing off, even on the roughest terrain. And by keeping your feet in a consistent and predictable position, it will make it far less likely that a positioning mistake will be made unless you become unclipped.

New riders are typically apprehensive about clipping-in because there may come an occasion when a rider can't get both feet unclipped in time as they're crashing. This could cause additional injuries from being tangled up with the bike. But depending on the individual, and with a little getting used to, clipping in and out can be done without fear. Releasing from the pedal only takes a small twist of your foot to disengage the cleat from the mechanism. Once unclipping becomes second nature, you'll be instinctively unclipping whenever needed. You may like the increased control so much that you never want to go back to flats.

There are different types of clip-in pedals to choose from. Pictured below are two of the most common, the Shimano SPD system and the Crankbrothers "eggbeater-style" system. The Shimanos have been around for a while and are proven performers that have the advantage of adjustable tension to control how easy they can clip out. The Crankbrothers are also efficient at clipping in and out but are known for their reliable performance in the muddiest conditions. Other brands include Look, Time, and Speedplay. Which one you go with is a matter of personal preference.

Shimano SPD system   *Crankbrothers system*

Platform Transfer Pedals (Flats): Flats have no attachment to hold your feet to the pedals. The preferred type is an aluminum alloy with replaceable metal pins to provide an enhanced grip. Using them in combination with special mountain bike shoes that have flat, sticky-soft soles will optimize the grip and control. With a good shoe/pedal combination, the grip can rival that of clip-in pedals. Flats are commonly used with Slopestyle, Dirt Jump, and Downhill bikes, but are also great for trail and enduro riding.

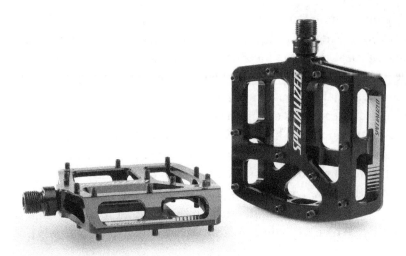

Flat pedals do have some riding advantages. They allow you to take your feet off at any time without hesitation, making it easier to push away from the bike during a crash. They also make it easy to quickly put a foot down if you get off balance; once stabilized, you can instantly resume your pedaling. Just knowing that you have this option can provide enough confidence to aggressively push through tough sections of the trail with less fear. The only potential drawback of removing your feet from these pedals is the risk of tearing up your shins on the sharp metal pins if you're not careful.

There are other ways that flats can make you a better rider. Without being solidly clipped in, you can get the feel for the most natural and stable foot position on the pedals to best transfer the forces through your feet, ankles, and knees. This optimal alignment will provide the basis for proper riding, braking, and pedaling techniques. You'll move more actively with the trail to stay balanced on your pedals, you'll be forced to shift more smoothly so that your feet don't fly off the pedals, and you'll learn to pedal as fluidly as possible for the best efficiency.

It's recommended that new riders take some time on flat pedals to develop proper technical riding skills before moving on to clip-in pedals. Not for just a few rides, but for at least a good couple months. After you gain some finesse with your technical skills and learn to become intimate with the ground you're riding on, you can then consider investing in some clip-in pedals and shoes. But even if you switch to clip-ins, you should occasionally switch back to flats for a few rides to sharpen your skills.

Flats are a good investment, even if you end up switching to clip-ins. The end result is that they'll make you a better rider. When selecting a pair for your bike, it's not necessary to buy high-end flats; mid-level pedals will work just fine.

Handlebars

The handlebars' width and shape determine your comfort and how efficiently you can control the steering, which directly impacts how well you can handle the bike. This makes having the right bar a high priority. If the bike you purchased doesn't have a handlebar that's best suited for your dimensions, you may need to replace it.

Handlebar width: Rough, technical terrain has a tendency to push your wheel around. If your bar is too narrow, you'll have less leverage to resist these pushes. As you're negotiating your way over and around roots and rocks, narrow bars will compromise your control and cause your wheel to move where you don't want it to. Narrow bars can also make the steering feel twitchy because small movement of the bars translates to bigger movement of the wheel. Wide bars (generally in the range of 27 to 32 inches in width) will make it easier to stay in control by giving you the leverage you need to hold the wheel steady while limiting how much your wheel moves with every push and pull of the bars.

Imagine you're climbing a technical trail, and suddenly a rock pushes your wheel to one side, causing you to overcompensate with an excessively sharp turn in the other direction. This could result in sudden loss of momentum or could even cause a crash. A wide bar will allow you to more easily resist that sideways push and keep your wheel on track.

The drawbacks of a wider bar is a slightly less aerodynamic stance, and you may have to occasionally swerve a little further to keep the end of your bar from hitting trees. But the valuable control that you gain from having a wide bar will more than offset these minor compromises. It's important to note that if the bar is too wide, it will limit your range of motion and increase the distance that the bar has to move to make a turn, making tight turns more difficult.

Manufacturers normally match bar width to frame size, but just as people are different, so too are the handlebar requirements of individuals. Arm length, torso length, and shoulder width are the variables that determine an individual's ideal width. As a general rule of thumb, a good compromise between comfort, leverage, and control is in the size range of four to six inches wider than your shoulders. Another method is to get on the ground into a natural push-up position and measure the distance from the outside of your palms. This dimension is likely to be your ideal handlebar width.

Rise and sweep: Another important factor is a handlebar's shape, which is determined by its "rise" and "sweep." Rise is the upward bend of the bar just outside of the center mounting area. The amount of rise needed depends on what height feels right to you. Sweep is a backward bend in the bar, measured in degrees. The purpose of sweep is to make the bar feel more comfortable, but the degree of the bend varies between models because not everyone's wrists and arms are the same. Too much back sweep will cause your elbows to move inward excessively which could affect control of the bike and possibly compromise safety.

It's important to have a handlebar that feels right for you. The fix may be as easy as rotating the bar to a position that feels more natural, or you may need to replace the bar. If you need to buy a new handlebar, you'll find that the majority of them are aluminum. Carbon fiber bars are also available. Although they're lighter, they may transmit the trail vibrations a little more, and they usually come at a higher price. Check the reviews to ensure that you're getting a good quality bar that's known for its strength and durability.

Stems

If you go with wide bars, you should also use a shorter stem. This is the piece that connects the handlebars to the forks' steering tube. Its length is measured from the center of the steering post clamp to the center of the handlebar clamp.

Stock stems can often be too long for use with wide bars. The best choice is a stem in the range of 30 to 70 mm. A stem in this length will shift your weight back, which will lighten the front tire and give the bike a livelier feel. Some may say that this will negatively affect hill climbs and turns, but shifting your weight a little forward on the seat will make up the difference. A short stem configuration will also restore a bend at your elbows that was lost with a wide bar setup, thereby putting your body into a better riding stance.

Changing the stem length is for the purpose of changing your weight distribution over the front tire for a different handling characteristic. It is not intended to act as a fit device for adjusting your posture. If your seat position is correct but your cockpit is too far forward and it's causing you to lie too flat, your frame size may be too big. Conversely, if it's too close and is causing you to sit too upright, you probably have a frame size that's too small.

In the end, finding out which size bar and stem combination is right for you may require some experimenting. If you're purchasing a new stem, stem angle needs to be considered and is one of the factors that determines handlebar height. There are a variety of stems on the market with varying angles. Finding the right angle depends on what height you want to set your handlebars.

> *"Before anything else, preparation is the key to success"*
>
> --Alexander Graham Bell

PART TWO

Preparing to Ride

WHAT WE DO to prepare ourselves, our bikes, and our gear will largely determine the enjoyment and success of our rides. Distractions from being ill prepared could potentially turn your ride into a negative experience. When you're properly equipped, set up, and dialed in, your focus can then be turned to your performance on the bike. This important section of the book covers the accessories and equipment that you should have, how to properly set up the bike, and the recommended gear to pack for the different kinds of rides.

CHAPTER SIX

Accessorizing

ALTHOUGH THE ONGOING costs of this sport are relatively modest, the initial investment of the bike and the necessary accessories are by far the biggest expenditure. If your budget is tight, the best advice is to invest in the best bike that you can afford, and then work on getting accessories in order of priority. If you're buying the bike from a bike shop, there's a good possibility that they'll give you a discount on accessories and a window of time to make the purchases. The following is a list of items that you'll need to support your new-found sport. From these accessories, some are more urgent than others, but most will have to be purchased at some point in time.

Vehicle Bike Racks

Except for those lucky enough to have trails close to their front door, most people will need to transport their bike to their riding locations. Unless you own a truck or a good sized SUV, you'll need a vehicle bike rack to do this. Basically, there are three types: roof mounted, hitch mounted, and trunk mounted. Each has its own unique characteristics to consider. The biggest selections will be online, but your bike shop should have some in stock. Choose carefully, as a quality rack will provide many years of use.

Roof Mounted: The biggest advantage of the roof-mounted system is that it can also be configured for use with other gear, such as cargo containers, skis, canoes, and surfboards, making it an obvious choice for multi-sport enthusiasts. This versatility tends to make it the most expensive type of bike rack, but it will provide the most stable and protective way to carry your bike(s). Disadvantages of this system are the increased wind resistance when driving, the inability to drive into parking garages, and the height the bikes need to be lifted to get them onto the rack.

Hitch Mounted: This type of rack requires your vehicle to have a hitch receiver. If it does not, one can be installed for about $200 U.S. Once you have a receiver, this is the easiest rack to use. Simply slide the hitch into the receiver and lock it in place. This is a very stable attachment that keeps the rack from shifting or moving during travel. With your rack hitched-in, it's completely ready to be loaded with bikes. Two styles of racks are available: A top tube rack that holds the bike by the frame and a tray rack that cradles the bikes' tires. The tray rack is best if you don't want anything contacting your bike frame and possibly scuffing it.

Trunk Mounted: These racks are secured to your vehicle by a set of adjustable nylon straps that attach to the edges of your trunk lid and possibly your bumper. They tend to have the lowest price and are smaller and easier to store than the other types. One of the drawbacks is that they run the risk of scuffing your vehicle or your bike, but with a little care, they can still be a good choice. It's important to note that the bikes tend to shift and the straps tend to loosen during transport, which may require occasional re-checks on longer trips. Also, if you're carrying multiple bikes, they'll be positioned close together, so extra care will need to be taken to keep them from rubbing against each other.

Helmets

This accessory is a must-have right from the get-go and should be worn on every ride. Your brain is without question the most vital part of your body that needs to be protected. A blow to the head could cause a traumatic brain injury and a cognitive disability[3]. Obviously, that's not worth risking.

Most cross-country riders will use open-face helmets. These typically come with a visor, which is a primary difference from road bike helmets. Downhill riders typically use full-face type helmets for added protection. There's a big range of prices between the different makes and models. This is for a variety of reasons including better adjustability, more popular styling, better padding, or better ventilation. A helmet in the mid-price range can be a good option if it's a reputable brand and is well fitting and comfortable.

Since everyone's head shape is a little different, you'll need to try on different helmets at the bike shop to see which ones fit you the best. Because you'll normally wear sunglasses while riding, put them on before trying on helmets to make sure that they don't interfere with the straps. After the helmet is adjusted and tightened per the manufacturer's instructions, it should feel snug yet comfortable, and there shouldn't be any excessive movement when you pull it back and forth. Check that the side straps form a "Y" in front and behind your ears without crossing over them. You should also be able to open and close your jaw without discomfort.

Eyewear

You'll look much cooler with a sharp pair of sunglasses as you're ripping the single-track, but the most important benefit is the protection that they provide. Every cyclist should be wearing a pair to prevent the risk of eye injury. As you ride down the trails, your eyes are exposed to a lot of dangers, such as mud and rocks kicked up from riders ahead of you, various flying insects, and low hanging branches. As you move through the environment, any of these things can fly into your face, so you need to be protected.

If you're considering cheap sunglasses, you're not going to get the features that you want and need. They should have good impact resistance, UV protection, and enough comfort for a whole day of trail riding. These are not cheap, but for your eyes, it's worth it. Look for sport sunglasses that have rubberized nose and ear pieces to provide good comfort and a grip that prevents slippage. If the nose piece is adjustable for a customized fit, that's even better.

The correct lens tint is another consideration. Basically, there are three types of lenses you should have for different conditions: tinted for UV protection on bright, sunny days while on wide open trails; yellow to brighten things up on cloudy days and in shaded forests; and clear for nighttime riding. Instead of having three different glasses, another option is to invest in glasses that have interchangeable lenses.

Quite often, rides are in places where the lighting conditions vary dramatically. One minute you're in an open field bathed in bright sunlight, and the next you're under a dark forested canopy. With dark glasses on, this could impede your ability to see obstacles coming up and could easily become the cause of a crash. One possible solution is to use glasses with photochromic lenses. These will automatically darken when exposed to sunlight and lighten when they're in the shade. Although this shift is a bit slow and the contrast from light tint to dark tint is limited, this type of sunglass will provide a degree of versatility when conditions change.

Downhill mountain bikers with full-face helmets should use goggles for maximum eye protection. For muddy conditions, you can apply layered tear-off film to the goggles. When one film gets soiled, you just grab the tab and tear it off to expose the next clean layer.

Body Armor

Although nobody wants crashes, the danger is ever-present. This is especially true with downhill mountain biking, where riders often take big risks. This is when full body armor, including suits that protect everything from shoulders to ankles, is essential. The downside of being fully armored is the restricted movement, possible discomfort, and increased heat buildup, making this degree of protection impractical for cross-country riding.

For riding cross-country, you can find adequate protection using kneepads, elbow pads, and shin guards, all of which offer protection in the bodily areas that are most likely to suffer injury in the event of a crash. Generally, if you're riding on technically challenging terrain that poses a higher risk of making mistakes, the benefits of wearing armor is greatest. Whether you choose to wear protective gear or not is a matter of personal preference, but if you do decide to wear it, be aware of the false sense of security it may provide . . . something that may cause you to ride beyond the limit of your abilities and ultimately put you at a higher risk of crashing.

Gloves are essential in that they will save your skin in a crash. For mountain biking, the full-fingered type offers the best protection. Make sure the gloves fit snugly so that they don't impede braking and shifting. Some gloves have extra padding in the palms to help with vibration, but gloves without padding allow you to better sense the terrain. It's a personal choice, but a better option for the vibration issue is to switch to a quality set of handgrips.

Padded Shorts

Shorts designed specifically for mountain biking have built-in padding, called a chamois, that will increase your comfort and your ability to ride for long periods of time. At least for men, this is the fashion in the mountain biking world. Women and road bikers typically use padded Lycra shorts. An exception to this is in cross-country racing where aerodynamic tights are still used by many racers. Overall, mountain bike shorts are more comfortable and have a more casual look and feel.

It's not necessary to wear underwear when using padded shorts; the chamois is made to go right against your skin. But if you do, make sure it's a pair made from moisture-wicking fabric designed for athletic use. Whether you're wearing underwear or not, skin chafing can sometimes be a problem. To remedy this, a skin lubricant, sometimes called chamois cream or chamois butter, is available at any bike shop and should be used before every ride to keep you comfortable.

Shoes

Clip-in Shoes: If you choose clip-in pedals, you'll need shoes that are designed to clip into them. The cleats that mount to these shoes need to match the retention system of the pedals. Since shoes can accommodate different types of cleats, the cleats are supplied with the pedals, not the shoes. You'll need a pair that's designed specifically for mountain biking. These will have knobby soles and recessed cleat mounts for walking on the trail when necessary, as opposed to road bike shoes which typically have cleats that protrude beyond the soles.

Clip-in shoes have rigid soles with relatively rigid uppers for better transfer of energy and increased pedaling efficiency. This stiffness will evenly distribute the forces along the full length of the foot for increased comfort. Clip-in shoes for downhill mountain biking have softer and more flexible soles and are used with large-platform clip-in pedals. The extra flexibility gives better contact with the platform, and if there's a need to walk the bike through a particularly tough section of trail, the extra grip of a rubber sole makes the task easier.

Flat Pedal Shoes: If you're going with flat pedals, the shoes should be the mountain bike specific type. These will have soft, grippy soles to stay better connected to the pedals while being stiffer for pedaling efficiency. Consider investing in a pair that has good quality and superior comfort to prevent annoying distractions from foot chafing, cramping, and fatigue. Running, basketball, and tennis shoes with knobby or hard rubber soles are not recommended because they have a greater tendency to slip off the pedals. Skate shoes are the closest thing but still fall short of the stiffness, grip performance, lightness, and durability of bike specific flat pedal shoes.

You don't need top of the line shoes . . . find a pair that is lightweight, comfortable and has a good closure system, such as buckle straps. The fit should be a little snugger than your everyday shoes; your toes should still be able to wiggle, but your heel should stay in place. If you need better arch support than the shoe provides, you can always add an insert. Just make sure that it feels comfortable in every way. This will ensure that your feet remain sore-free on long rides.

Hydration Backpacks

When exercising, proper hydration will help you achieve better performance. If you allow yourself to become dehydrated, you'll be more fatigued, you'll suffer from poor performance and reduced coordination, and you'll be more susceptible to muscle cramping. Preventing these maladies entails bringing enough water with you so that you don't run out.

For shorter rides in cooler weather, your water requirements will be lower. In those situations, a water bottle may be all you need. If you have a hardtail, you may be able to fit two bottle cages to the frame. For average to long rides, high intensity rides, and hot weather rides, you'll need more than just a bottle or two of water. In these circumstances, a hydration pack is the way to go. They have the added benefit of a convenient sip tube that's easy to drink from while you're on the move, which means that you'll drink more often and perform better.

Hydration packs come in a variety of sizes and features. For mountain biking, the most common sizes have either a two-liter or a three-liter water bladder. Any bigger would be too heavy and unnecessary. The two-liter is a good compact size with just enough storage space for all the necessary items you need to bring on shorter rides. The three-liter is a common size because you can simply fill the bladder with less water for shorter rides, and they have ample storage space for longer rides. Hydration fanny packs are also a good option, as they keep the weight at the hips and off of the shoulders.

Tire Pumps

A pump is a must-have item when you own a mountain bike because properly inflated tires will give you better riding performance. All tires tend to bleed out air, so you should check the pressure and fill them as necessary before every ride. This is best accomplished with a quality floor pump that has a built-in pressure gauge. There are many makes and models to choose from, but a moderately priced pump will work just fine. For the most versatility, make sure that the one you choose can accommodate both Presta and Schrader valves.

Because mountain bike tires use far less pressure than road bikes, you should avoid pumps with very high-pressure capability, such as 220 psi. These are mainly designed for road bike tires, which average 120 psi and need only a small volume of air. These high-pressure pumps put out a low volume of air per pump stroke, which means that they require excessive pumping to fill your large mountain bike tires. A floor pump that is rated as low as 90 psi will have a high-volume output per stroke and will fill your tires fairly rapidly. This high volume is also beneficial for seating a tubeless tire to the rim, which can be frustratingly difficult with a low-volume pump.

Flat tires can occur somewhat regularly. If you use inner tubes, you'll get pinch flats and punctures, and if you're tubeless, you could burp out air or tear a sidewall. For this reason, you should always carry along a mini-pump and one or two spare inner tubes. Mini-pumps are lightweight and will easily fit into your hydration pack. Because they require a lot of pumping to fill a new tube, a pump with a CO_2 cartridge fitting will greatly reduce the amount of pumping. Just be aware that CO_2 cartridges can get wasted if a mistake is made during inflation, and they can also be an ongoing expense.

Another option in an emergency situation is to use a puncture repair kit. This is especially useful when you have used up your spare tubes and have no other option. They are lightweight and easy to take along but require some know-how to use them properly. A repaired inner tube should still be replaced after you're done with your ride.

Suspension Pumps

New bikes with an air shock and/or forks often come with a suspension pump, otherwise known as a shock pump. These are pumps that can create much higher pressures than what high-volume tire pumps are capable of. If you don't have one, it would be a good idea to pick one up to accomplish suspension adjustments. A bike shop can help you get your suspension set up, but there's a good chance that you'll still want to fine tune it to match your riding preferences and conditions. Even if you like your current setup, in time it will probably need readjustment.

The better shock pumps come with extra features such as a bleed button that allows you to let out some air without unhooking the nozzle. Overall, these pumps are not very expensive and should be something you have in your possession.

Smartphones / GPS Units

Smartphones' GPS capability has greatly enhanced the mountain biking experience by providing exact coordinates of your location at any given time. Apps that use this capability will also allow you to record your statistics while you ride. When compared to stand alone GPS cycle computers, smartphones offer the advantages of having a built-in compass, additional locater capabilities using cell phone towers, and the ability to instantly upload data.

Smartphone apps can track your ride while measuring your progress and then save the map for future reference for comparing your ride times, your fastest speeds, average speeds, distances traveled, total ascent (based on the known geography of the land), and many other parameters. Knowing your previous statistics allows you to compete against yourself and provides inspiration to keep up the pace. You can also compare what you did differently on your better days. Maybe you had more sleep the night before, your nutritional intake was better, or your pre-ride routine was different that day. Whatever the case may be, you'll be able to figure out what adjustments need to be made for future rides.

One of the more popular apps used by many mountain bikers is **Strava**. It's a type of social networking platform for biking and other activities. It tracks elapsed time, distance, elevation gains, and average speed, and it will work with separately purchased heart rate, cadence, and speed sensors. What's unique about this app is its ability to compare your ride time against your previous rides and that of other riders, both friends and strangers. Before you embark on your ride, you can view a list of existing segmented challenges on the map. When you complete your ride, you'll be placed on a leaderboard on each of the segments with your ranked position, based on time.

If you're the competitive type (as many cyclists are), you'll try to get a higher placing on the leaderboards. This is a great motivator and will keep you from becoming complacent. Always pushing to do better, you'll improve your speed and fitness as well as your ranking on the list. Velo News said it best: "*Besting personal milestones are one thing; crushing your buddy's best time up a local climb with data to prove it, is something else entirely.*" The only drawback to these challenges is a possible recklessness that can go with these types of all-out efforts. Going downhill on multi-use single-track, you could be a danger to other trail users. You must remain cautious and alert while using this app, because it's easy to disregard safety when you're obsessed with getting the fastest time.

Another advantage of using a smartphone while you ride is the option of listening to music. Some find this an enjoyable addition to the ride, while others prefer to hear only the natural sounds of the environment. For those who want it, music can be inspirational and will break the silence that makes you susceptible to unnecessary stray thoughts or overthinking your bike handling. It also has the psychological benefit of diluting the sound of your breathing when it's heavy, strained, and constantly reminding you of your efforts. If you do choose to listen to music, use just one of the earbuds and keep the volume low so that you can hear the sounds around you, including those from other trail users or from your riding partners.

Smartphone holders are available on the market that are designed to attach to your handlebar. The problem is that if you crash, your expensive piece of electronics could become trail litter. And if you're using an ear bud cord, you'll be tethered to your bike. This is a bad setup because you need the ability to move freely over the bike for proper handling. A handlebar mount should only be used under these circumstances:

- It's mounted in an impact-resistant case.
- It's used with a wireless Bluetooth earbud that doesn't easily fall out of your ear.
- It's used in dry, non-dusty conditions.
- Your ride is on the short side. A screen that's lit full time will rapidly drain the battery.
- You understand that you'll often be too preoccupied to pay attention to the screen.

If you're planning on using an armband holder, consider the possibility that your phone could bear the full impact in a crash situation. The best solution is to have a hydration pack that has a conveniently placed pocket designed to hold a smartphone or to put the phone in the back pocket of your jersey.

CHAPTER SEVEN

Bike Setup

CHAPTER TWO GAVE instructions for setting up the bike to determine your ideal frame size. This was helpful while shopping in the store, but when it comes to riding the trails, your setup needs to be scrutinized a little more closely. Getting your machine dialed in to your bodily dimensions while taking your level of flexibility into account will ensure maximum maneuverability, control, pedaling efficiency, and comfort. It's all about accommodating the setup to your personal requirements, which will ultimately contribute to the development of good riding skills.

Not everyone's mechanical abilities are the same; some will be able to do all of these adjustments on their own like a pro, and others will need to bring the bike to a shop to have them done. If you're comfortable doing it yourself but are not completely sure about your finished work, you can always have the shop double check it. Remember to always properly torque all fasteners and make sure all clamps and adjusting mechanisms are tight and properly seated.

If you're strictly interested in gravity driven (downhill) mountain biking or freestyle riding, these instructions generally won't apply. For cross-country and enduro riding with multi-faceted conditions, including flats, downhills, and uphills, these instructions are for you. For the best results, follow these steps in the listed order.

Crank Arm Length

The crank arms connect the pedals to the bottom bracket axle. The standard arm length on mountain bikes is typically 175mm. Lengths of 165mm, 170mm, and 180mm can also be found. Basically, taller riders on extra-large frames might do better with 180mm, and shorter riders on small frames with 165mm or 170mm. There may be other reasons why one might be interested in changing the crank arm length. For hill climbing, a longer crank length will give you better leverage for pushing the pedal. A shorter crank length will give more distance per pedal revolution in any given gear, which can have some advantages in cross-country racing. Another advantage of a shorter length is the increased ground clearance for rocks, lessening the possibility of a pedal strike. It's important to note that if there's too big of a mismatch between crank length and body size, it will negatively affect pedaling performance. Their length can also affect your leg reach to the pedal, so any changes will require repositioning of the seat height.

Seat Height

The seat height will affect power generation, pedaling efficiency, endurance, comfort, and joint health. If it's set too high, your legs will straighten out too much at the bottom of the pedal stroke, causing your hips to move downward to make up for lost leverage. Not only does this create inefficiency, but it'll cause your hips to rock up and down and make your sit bones grind excessively against the saddle. If your seat height is set too low, your knees will bend too much at the top of the pedal stroke. Since this is where your power production begins, you won't have the best leverage as you begin pushing down. This will give you a less efficient range of motion, resulting in less available power, and will also put more pressure on the knees, raising the possibility of developing future knee problems.

Setting the seat height so that it feels right is actually quite simple. It's a matter of determining the degree of leg bend, which can be accomplished with an inexpensive device called a goniometer. This is simply a protractor with long arms and is easily found online. Leg length will be the primary driver of seat height, but for every individual leg length, there's a range of possible seat heights. Where you lie in this range is dependent on your personal flexibility and whether you need less emphasis on either your quads or your hamstrings. That being said, if your body will allow it, a seat on the slightly high side can have power generation benefits.

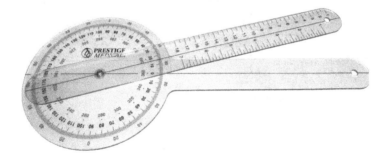

With your riding shoes on, sit on the bike next to a wall, supporting yourself with one hand. It's helpful to have an additional person for this measurement while you're trying to stay balanced. Clip-in if you're using clip-in pedals, and then rotate them backward until one of them is at bottom dead center. Holding your foot level, your lower leg should have a slight bend in the range of 25 to 30 degrees, as measured along the leg bones with the goniometer. If you want to take some stress off of your hamstrings, move the seat until your leg angle is at 30 degrees. If you want to take some stress off of your quads and your knees, move the seat until the angle is at 25 degrees. Check your other leg; if you have one leg that's longer than the other, go with the measurement of the shorter one. Once you've found the correct leg bend, lock down the seat post. If you ever switch from flat pedals to clip-ins or vice versa, you'll need to recheck the seat height and adjust if necessary.

Go for a ten-minute ride to check that your hips don't swivel and that the rotation feels right. The seat height may seem high because both feet won't touch the ground when you're at a stop, but this is normal and you'll quickly get used to it. With your joints warmed up, recheck your measurement. If it still checks out, then your seat height is properly set. If you're not using an adjustable height seat post, you'll need to make a mark on the post so that you can easily get back to the correct seat post height after manually dropping the seat on descents. Once set, there should be no reason to adjust it again.

Saddle Setback

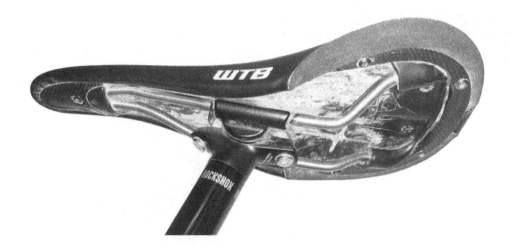

Saddle setback is the forward and aft positioning of the seat. Like height positioning, setback makes a significant difference in your pedaling efficiency by affecting where stress is placed on the knees: too far forward puts more stress on the front of the knees, and too far back puts more stress on the back of the knees. When the setback is adjusted correctly, your knees will be in the right place for providing maximum pedaling leverage while alleviating painful side effects. Follow these directions to obtain the optimal setting:

1. Supporting yourself against a wall, put your pedals in a horizontal position, one foot in front of the other and parallel to the floor. Sit with your pelvic bones placed on the part of the saddle that you normally sit on when riding on level ground. This is usually the widest and softest part

of the saddle. Sometimes it may take riding around a little to settle in to your normal spot.

2. Have someone hold a weighted string against the bottom of the kneecap of your forward leg. The string should lie at the center of the pedal axle. If the string is too far forward or aft, loosen the seat post bolts and slide the saddle forward or aft on its rails.

3. Keep adjusting and rechecking until you get it right, then switch legs and try again. It should be the same as the other side unless there is a difference in leg length, in which case you'll need to split the difference. After checking and rechecking, you'll nail down the correct saddle setback.

4. At this point you should have a comfortable reach to the handlebar with some bend at the elbows, assuming you have the correct frame size.

5. If you made an adjustment to your setback, your leg reach could have been affected. Re-check your saddle height to make sure your knee flexion is still optimal.

Saddle Tilt

An improperly tilted saddle can lead to serious discomfort and could even be the direct cause of your soreness and numbness. If it's tilted up too high, it could be putting excessive pressure on your crotch area. If it's tilted too far downward, you'll slide forward and sit on the wrong part of the seat, causing your sit bones to grow uncomfortable. This could also put too much pressure on your hands as you try to keep yourself pushed back, leading to hand numbness and, subsequently, bike control issues.

To find the tilt that's best for you, start with a level seat and ride with it for a short time to see how it feels. If it's not right, adjust it by a degree or two and try riding again for a while. To determine the level, you can use a bubble level or a smartphone level app. You shouldn't have to move it more than a degree or two in either direction to get comfortable.

Handlebar Position

Now that your saddle is perfectly adjusted, it's time to adjust the handlebar. Handlebars are designed to rotate through a set range of motion, with normal positioning set for an upward rise and a backward sweep. How far upward and how far backward it needs to be is a matter of comfort and personal preference. This setting will impact your hands, wrists, and forearms. If it's set wrong and left uncorrected, it could cause fatigue, numbness, or even pain. Ideally, you should have a natural wrist position with maximum hand-to-grip contact. Follow these steps to find your optimal position:

1. Loosen the stem to handlebar bolts just enough to allow for rotation.

2. Sit on your bike while mounted in a trainer unit or by having someone hold you upright from behind.

3. Hold your arms out in front of you at handgrip width, with your palms down and wrists level. Relax your hands and wrists as much as possible and slowly let your arms down until your hands rest lightly on the grips. This is your natural hand and wrist position.

4. Rotate the bar to match this natural position. Recheck and readjust as necessary until it feels right. If it doesn't feel natural in any position, you'll need to find a bar that has a more comfortable sweep angle. Rotating or changing the bar could affect the handlebar height, which should be checked next.

Handlebar Height

Typically, handlebars should be set to one inch above the top of the seat to three inches below the seat. A height that puts you into an aggressive stance while in the seated position is best, but comfort is also an issue, so you don't want to have a stance that's too low. Flexible and athletic riders, or those on the taller side, usually prefer the handlebar lower; and recreational riders, or those on the shorter side, usually prefer the handlebar higher. If you're a new rider, you may prefer a more upright position, even though you should try to get used to a lower stance. There are a few possible ways of changing the handlebar height, each requiring some degree of technical know-how:

*   Move the height adjustment spacers to either above or below the stem as needed. This feature is only available on modern bikes equipped with a threadless stem that clamps to the outside of the steering tube.

*   Replace the stem with one that has either more or less degree in rise. Just remember, a steeper angle will slightly reduce your reach to the bars because the stem will have a shorter effective length due to its reduced parallelism to the ground.

*   If you need to go significantly lower, it's possible to turn your stem upside down to point downward.

*   Change to bars with a different rise.

Brake Levers and Gear Shifters

Now that your handlebar and seat are in the correct position, your brake levers and gear shifters are most assuredly in the wrong position. Whether you bought your bike new or used, they will probably not be set up in the optimal positions for your personal requirements. Having these controls positioned for your body dimensions and movements will give you the strongest braking power and the most natural shifting. This will  help you to function at your best and remain solidly in control of your bike.

Your brakes' potential power is directly related to how much force you can apply to the levers. If you use all of your fingers, you'll be able to squeeze extra hard. But this will severely reduce your hold on the handgrips, which means less bike control at a time when you need it the most . . . during braking. This will also cause your hands and wrists to become more fatigued, compounding the problem of staying in control. By pulling near the end of the levers, good leverage can still be obtained with a couple of fingers. In fact, just one finger at the far end of each lever will usually provide all the braking power you'll need with any modern disc-brake system.

To get the lever in a position that allows a one-finger pull, it will need to be moved inward until your forefinger lines up with the end of the blade. Some bikes have a combined brake lever and shifter mount, which usually makes setting up their positioning easy. Bikes with separate mounts typically come set up with the brake levers on the outward side of the shifters, which doesn't always allow your finger to be positioned at the end of the lever. One remedy is to switch your brake levers to the inward side of the gear shifters, and then reposition both to the optimal distances.

The shifters should be put into a position that allows you to easily reach them without the possibility of your thumbs accidentally bumping or rubbing against them when you're grabbing the handgrips. It's not a big concern if your thumbs don't completely cover the shifter paddle when changing gears, as long as you can push the paddles with your thumbs all the way through their motion without removing any part of your hand from the grips.

The rotational position of the brake levers (the tilt) is also important for comfort, safety, and control. Optimally, they should be positioned so that your wrists are straight and in line with your hands. This will help to reduce forearm fatigue. The position of your body will determine arm angle . . . so exactly what body position do you use for reference? The answer depends on how often you're off of the saddle and the steepness of the hills that you typically ride.

When riding down steep hills, you'll be doing a lot of braking. You'll be off the saddle, but your body will be in a low, stretched out, and leaned-back position, which means that your brake levers will need to be rotated fairly high to keep your wrist aligned. This high-lever position may seem too high when you're in a normal seated position, but having a comfortable hand/wrist position when the brakes get their highest use should get priority.

When riding down not-so-steep hills, your chest will be somewhat over the handlebars. To keep your wrist more in line with your hands, your levers will need to be rotated downward but should not exceed a 45-degree tilt. This compromise will give you the freedom to move your body up or down as required.

To move the levers, loosen the mounting screws just enough to allow the clamp to rotate. When tightening down your levers, make sure that the clamps are tight enough to keep them from moving by themselves, but not so tight that they don't move if there is a crash. This allows them to rotate instead of just breaking off. To make it easy to return them to the same position, measure the angle and make a note of it for future reference.

Lastly, if the reach of your brake levers feels like it's too far out from the handlebar, you can adjust the point at which your brakes engage as you pull the lever inward. This is called the "reach adjustment" and is something that all brakes have at the levers. This adjustment is dependent on the length of your fingers and should be set at a distance that's comfortable and allows some finger bend when you're pulling the lever but not yet applying braking power.

Cleats

Bike shoe cleats need to be adjusted for optimal foot positioning. This will help with power production, reducing injuries from repetitive motion, and making it easier to engage and disengage from the pedals. No matter which type of clip-ins you're using, where you tighten down your cleats will have a significant impact. As an example, when the cleats are too far forward, even by a few millimeters, the tendons and muscles toward the front of the feet must compensate for the reduced leverage, which could lead to ankle pain or knee problems.

There are two cleat positions that need to be addressed: the fore/aft positioning and the lateral positioning (rotated for toe in or toe out). Before you begin these adjustments, loosen or tighten the cleat mounting screws until they can move against the soles with some resistance. This will help to hold them in position until you're ready to fully tighten down the screws.

For most people, the ideal location of the forward/rearward positioning puts the ball of the foot (the joint that's behind the big toe) just slightly forward of the pedals' axle. To find this location, put your shoes on and use your finger to locate the center of the ball of your feet. Write a line on a piece of masking tape and use it to mark this location on the edge of your shoes. Remove your shoes and move the cleats until they are positioned 10-12 mm behind this mark. While this is generally a good position, it may not work for everyone. If you have extra-long feet, you may need the cleat a few millimeters further rearward, and if you have short feet, you may need the cleat a few millimeters further forward to obtain your optimal positioning.

The cleats' lateral adjustment will determine which way your toes points in relation to the centerline of the bike. This setting should emulate the natural positioning of your feet. To determine this, walk a few strides forward and come to a stop with your feet at a normal distance apart. It's likely that your toes will not be pointing directly forward, and one foot may be different than the other. These are the angles that you'll need to set your cleats to. Simply point one arm of a goniometer straight forward and the other arm along the centerline of your foot, then transfer this angle to your cleats. Another possible way to measure this angle is with a smartphone compass to check the number of degrees that your feet are from the centerline.

Once you have the cleats positioned just right, fully tighten down the mounting screws. When you go for a ride, you'll notice that your shoes can move around a bit. There's three to six degrees of free lateral rotation intentionally designed into most pedal/cleat combinations, called "pedal float." This helps to cut down repetitive motion injuries that would likely occur if you were solidly locked in. Some pedals, such as the SPDs, have a tension adjustment that varies the amount of float. This adjustment should be set to give the proper degrees of float, not too much and not too little.

With your cleats correctly positioned, your feet will stay more or less at the center of the float. Just be sure that your heels do not contact the chain stay or the swing arm. If they do, you'll need to slightly change your adjustments until no contact is made.

Suspension Adjustments

It would be nice if you could just get on your recently purchased mountain bike and go trail riding without having to mess with anything, but it's just not that easy. The effectiveness of your suspension's operation depends on how well it's dialed in. When properly set up, it protects your body from vibrations and shocks while keeping your tires better connected to the trail. With all the possible adjustments that a suspension system can come with, it can seem like a complicated task. But once you understand a few basic concepts and are familiar with the methods of adjustment, you'll have no problem with it.

When you first get a new or used bike, the suspension system will have to be set up to match your body weight, the riding conditions of your trails, your riding style, and your abilities. Preload, rebound damping, and compression damping are the primary types of adjustments for both forks and shocks. They need to be set up in a way that can absorb the small impacts and vibrations while at the same time able to absorb big impacts without bottoming out. It's usually a compromise between the two, and it may take some experimentation until you have it dialed in the way you like it. Fortunately, once you have your suspension set, you'll only need to check it periodically.

Fork Preload

Preload is the forks' built in resistance to compression, and it is measured by the distance that the preloaded fork compresses when a rider in full gear sits on the bike. The distance of this seated compression is called the sag. Its setting determines how much travel is remaining to absorb shocks and how easily it can reach the end of its travel and bottom out. Having the proper sag will also allow the wheels to better hug the contours of the terrain for the best possible ride quality.

A stiff setup means less sag. With stiffer settings, bigger impacts can be absorbed without bottoming out. If your rides are full of big impacts, you'll need to adjust the forks for a stiff setup. Just be careful not to make them too stiff, or you'll have excessive chatter and your tire will be less connected to the ground. A soft setup means more sag, which will soak up more chatter from the trail and your tire will feel more connected to the ground.

The best setup will put your sag as soft as possible to utilize the entire stroke of the fork during the biggest impacts, which typically occurs a couple of times during a normal cross country ride. If it's set too soft, you'll bottom out too easily on medium-sized impacts and you won't get protection from the bigger impacts. The normal sag setting for a cross-country bike is about 25 percent of the total travel; and for downhill bikes, it's about 40 percent.

The degree of adjustability you actually have depends on the length of the forks. Some forks have a scale for sag printed directly on the upper tube. Since the sag distance on the fork is calculated as a percentage of the total available for travel, long travel forks will have longer sag distance. This gives them the ability to soak up small and medium bumps while easily providing big impact protection. There are far less options on very short travel forks. In fact, for bikes with only three inches of travel, it may come down to a choice of either soft or firm. The following is a general guide for adjusting your fork sag:

1. If your forks don't have an O-ring around the upper tube, put a zip tie just above the forks' dust seal.

2. If your fork is equipped with a travel adjust dial, set it to maximum travel.

3. If you have a climbing/descending mode switch, set it to descending.

4. Make sure the lock-out is unlocked.

5. Compress the fork a couple of times to break it in.

6. Being careful not to compress the fork or slide the O-ring or the zip tie against the dust seal.

7. Put all of your riding gear on, including a full water bladder.

8. With your bike supported by someone else who's holding the seat post, slowly mount the bike and get into a slightly leaned forward "ready" position to compress the fork.

9. Slowly dismount the bike, being careful not to further compress the shock.

10. Measure the distance of the O-ring or zip-tie from the seal. Compare this distance to the total fork travel and calculate the difference into a percentage (travel distance ÷ total fork distance x 100).

11. Adjust the forks to the desired sag. This is accomplished by adding or removing air with a shock pump connected to the Schrader valve(s) located at the end(s) of the fork. If your fork has both upper and lower valves, you should add or remove air evenly between the two.

12. For coil shocks, turn the preload knob located at the top of the fork in a clockwise direction to increase the preload and a counterclockwise direction to decrease the preload.

Fork & Shock Preload Chart

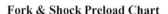

SOFT   40%   35%   30%   25%   20%   FIRM

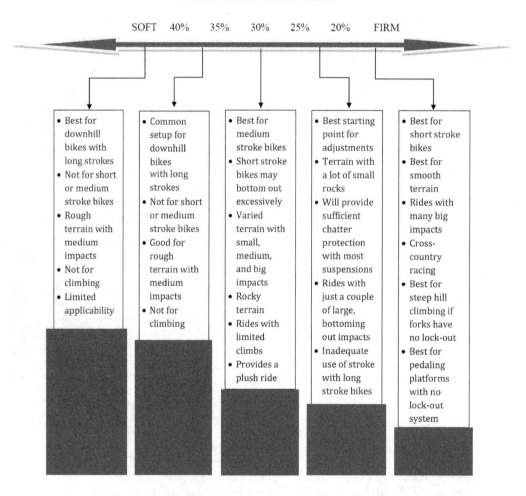

• Best for downhill bikes with long strokes • Not for short or medium stroke bikes • Rough terrain with medium impacts • Not for climbing • Limited applicability	• Common setup for downhill bikes with long strokes • Not for short or medium stroke bikes • Good for rough terrain with medium impacts • Not for climbing	• Best for medium stroke bikes • Short stroke bikes may bottom out excessively • Varied terrain with small, medium, and big impacts • Rocky terrain • Rides with limited climbs • Provides a plush ride	• Best starting point for adjustments • Terrain with a lot of small rocks • Will provide sufficient chatter protection with most suspensions • Rides with just a couple of large, bottoming out impacts • Inadequate use of stroke with long stroke bikes	• Best for short stroke bikes • Best for smooth terrain • Rides with many big impacts • Cross-country racing • Best for steep hill climbing if forks have no lock-out • Best for pedaling platforms with no lock-out system

This chart is only a rough guide. The setting you use should reflect the range given in the owner's manual or the manufacturer's web site, while giving consideration to the riding conditions of the trails you normally use. It may take some experimentation to find the setting that works best for you.

Rear Shock Preload

The rear shock preload (sag) adjustment is even more critical than the forks because it affects the suspension's pedaling platform. Set it too soft, and you'll find yourself bobbing up and down with every pedal stroke, which severely affects your efficiency. Set it too firm, and it'll feel like a hardtail, defeating the reason you own a full-suspension bike. The concept is to keep the rider and the bike level while the wheels move up and down with the terrain. All decent, modern full-suspension bikes have a pedaling platform system that provides a somewhere-in-between setting that feels just right. It's simply a matter of adjusting your preload until you hit that sweet spot.

The difference between the rear shock and the forks is that the shock's total travel distance is not a straightforward number. A rear suspension with five inches of travel refers to its wheel travel, not the shock travel, as it is with forks. To find the total shock travel, you can refer to the spec sheet on the shock manufacturer's web site. Perform the following steps to check your current sag and adjust the preload for the proper sag:

1. If your shock does not have an O-ring around the shaft, put a zip tie just above the dust seal.

2. If you have rebound adjustment, turn it all the way counterclockwise to its minimum position.

3. If you have a climbing/descending mode switch, set it to descending.

4. Put all of your riding gear on, including a full water bladder.

5. Supporting yourself with a wall or a table, slowly mount your bike and get into a seated position to compress the shock. Wait about 30 seconds to allow it to fully settle in.

6. Being careful not to compress the shock any further, carefully dismount the bike.

7. Measure the distance of the O-ring or zip-tie from the seal. Compare this distance to the total shock travel and calculate the difference into a percentage (travel distance ÷ total shock travel x 100).

8. Add or remove air to the shock in five psi increments until the desired sag is achieved, re-checking as you go. Make sure that it's the same percentage as the fork sag for a well-balanced bike.

9. Test ride the bike to check that the setting best matches your terrain and riding conditions. This will also ensure that the shock has completely settled during actual use. Readjust as necessary.

10. For coil sprung shocks, the measurement is taken from the center of the shocks mounting bolts to determine both total travel and the sag percentage.

Rebound Damping

"Rebound" is the shock's or forks' re-extension after being compressed. "Damping" is a resistance setting that serves to slow down the speed rate of the rebound. With no damping or not enough (low resistance), your shock would abruptly snap back to full extension after every compression. This would cause the bike to jump back into the rider and the wheel to separate from the ground like a bucking horse. It would then oscillate by re-compressing and re-extending over and over like a spring.

If there is too much damping (high resistance), the shock will not extend fast enough before the next compression. It will then compress even further on the next impact, and so on. This will cause the shock to pack down with no opportunity to extend. Neither of these extremes is favorable, so a good middle ground setting must be obtained.

Rebound damping adjustments can be made to adjustable forks and shocks by turning a dial, which is usually located at the bottom of the unit. To make full use of your shock and forks, it's important to have full extension between impacts, no matter how frequently they occur. For that, you'll need to obtain a setting that's as low as possible without being abrupt and springy. Try experimenting with the settings in your normal riding area with typical riding conditions. Go to both extremes of the dial and then put it in the middle. From there, turn the dial in increments, testing it until it feels right. Once it's set to where it seems best, leave it there and get used to riding that way because you don't want  to be a never-satisfied tweaker. Just make sure that your forks and rear shock have approximately the same rebound rate.

Compression Damping

Compression damping is the shock's or forks' resistance to being compressed. Its adjustment changes the speed rate of their compression, slowing it down to prevent bottoming out. It also serves to reduce rear shock pedal bob. Your suspension components may or may not have a compression damping adjustment. If they don't, you'll be using the factory's predetermined setting. If they do, you'll want to make adjustments to suit your personal preference and typical riding conditions.

Check the manual for the manufacturer's recommended setting as a starting point for adjustments. If necessary, you can move it from there until it feels optimal. Not enough damping (low resistance) will make it feel soft and supple, but it will bottom out easily while creating excessive pedal bob. Too much damping (high resistance) will make your ride feel excessively stiff and won't allow your tires to stay connected with the terrain. Since neither of these extremes is favorable, an ideal balance must be found that makes the ride as soft as possible without excessively bottoming out.

Damping is controlled by a dial or a knob, usually located at the top of the fork and by a marked adjuster somewhere on the shock. Just like your rebound, you want to be out on a ride when making these adjustments. Check out how often you bottom out at each setting and how much pedaling bob your rear shock seems to allow. Move the adjuster in increments until you are satisfied with the setting. For the most part, set it and forget it.

Tire Pressure

The tires' air pressure determines how much they flatten down when pushed against and how much contact area there is with the ground. This directly affects traction through most aspects of riding, including riding on loose terrain, riding over roots and rocks, and during cornering, braking, climbing, and descending. The tires also complement the suspension system, as their pressure dictates how well they absorb vibrations and small bumps.

Pressure that's too low can be a problem because there's a possibility of damaging the rim. The tire could actually roll off during hard cornering. Underinflated tires will also cause pinch flats on inner tubes, air to burp out with tubeless tires, and an overall mushy feel. Higher pressure means less flattening of the tire and a smaller contact area with the ground. Although this will result in a lowered rolling resistance, too much pressure will cause you to slide in the turns, your tires to bounce and slide off rocks, and your rear tire to more easily slip during hill climbs. You will not have good control of the bike. Over-inflation will also make the ride seem harsh, with no give for absorbing vibrations.

The best set up is to run the tire pressure as low as possible without creating problems from under-inflation. So, what is this pressure? There is no one answer because there are many variables that affect what works best for you. Consider the following:

- Heavy tires with thick sidewalls need less air pressure to support a load. Lightweight tires with thin sidewalls will need more pressure to support the same load. If you're not sure what kind of tire you have, let out all of the air and remove one of the beads from the rim. See how thin the sidewall feels and how easily it wrinkles.

- The wider the tire, the less air pressure is required to support the load.

- The taller the tire, the less air pressure is required to support the load. (e.g., 29" vs. 26")

- A tire with an inner tube will need higher air pressure than a tubeless tire in order to prevent pinch flats.

- The front tire should be anywhere from two to seven psi lower than the rear tire. This will help it hook up better in the turns while the rear tire rolls with less resistance.

Consider the terrain conditions:

- If the terrain has a fairly smooth surface and isn't technically challenging, you'll want to use a higher tire pressure to reduce your rolling resistance, especially if you want to go fast over a long period of time. In this scenario, your tire choice will likely be a lightweight tire with low profile knobs.

- If you'll be riding on rough terrain with lots of rocks, roots, ruts, etc., rolling resistance is not a concern. You'll need a wide tire, and you'll want to use an air pressure that's as low as possible to help the tires conform to the contours of the terrain and absorb the bumps.

- If the rough terrain includes sharp and jagged rocks, you'll need a tire with thick sidewalls and bigger knobs, which will also require less air pressure.

- Loose and sandy terrain will require tires with a little less air pressure for better traction.

- Riding on hard-pack should be with higher pressures for a reduced rolling resistance.

- Riding on pavement will require the tires to have a much higher pressure.

Consider these riding style variables:

- Many experienced riders know how to pick good lines to avoid objects. This helps smooth out the ride and will allow the use of lower air pressure without the worry of rim damage. Conversely, smooth riding will lower traction and bump-compliance concerns, thereby allowing a higher pressure for reduced rolling resistance . . . a setup that some cross-country racers prefer.

- Speed affects how hard you'll hit obstacles. If you typically ride fast over rock gardens, the chances of damaging your rim increases while running low pressure. Alternatively, a higher pressure means that you'll be bouncing off of everything. A happy medium that limits the amount of bouncing while still protecting the rims from damage is usually best.

Your tire's sidewall will show a pressure range in raised lettering. This range can be as wide as 30 psi and is meant for use with inner tubes. In some circumstances, the low limit can be exceeded, but which psi you use depends on the many variables. For average-sized riders (150 to 180 pounds), you can start by setting the pressure anywhere within the tires' given range. Heavier riders should adjust the pressure toward the higher end of the range, and lighter riders toward the lower end of the range.

Ride with this pressure on the trails, and see how well your tires hook up in the turns and how much traction you have on loose terrain. If your ride is rough, you're sliding out, your tire is slipping on the climbs, or you're excessively bouncing off of rocks, your pressure is probably too high. Over-inflation is the most common tire pressure mistake. If you start getting pinch flats, your pressure is probably too low. Always raise or lower your pressure in increments of three to five pounds until it feels right and/or you stop getting flats. Another way to nail down the best pressure is by bracketing. To do this, set your pressure to the middle of the tires' range and test it by going for a ride at your preferred location. If you need more or less pressure, go up or down 1/4 of the range. If you need to adjust it again, go 1/8 of the range up or down. Just remember, it's easier to run the pressure a little on the high side and let out some air if the trail conditions change.

If you're tubeless, you'll be running a lower pressure than you would with tubes. This will probably bring you below the marked minimum pressure on the tire. This is O.K., but if you feel your tire rolling under your rim during hard cornering, or if your tire pressure consistently drops due to burping, the air pressure is probably too low. The following chart is provided as a general air pressure guide for tubeless tires. Fat tires are not included on this chart but will use considerably less pressure than what's listed here. This chart is simply for getting you started and is not intended to be the official pressure for your tires. Remember to take all the variables into consideration when experimenting with different pressures.

Rider and Gear Weight (LBS):		80	90	100	110	120	130	140	150	160	170	180	190	200	210	220	230	240	250
29"	2.8 - 3.0	12	13	14	15	16	17	18	19	20	21	22	23	24	25	26	27	28	29
	2.5 - 2.7	15	16	17	18	19	20	21	22	23	24	25	26	27	28	29	30	31	32
	2.2 - 2.4	18	19	20	21	22	23	24	25	26	27	28	29	30	31	32	33	34	35
	1.9 - 2.1	21	22	23	24	25	26	27	28	29	30	31	32	33	34	35	36	37	38
27.5"	2.8 - 3.0	14	15	16	17	18	19	20	21	22	23	24	25	26	27	28	29	30	31
	2.5 - 2.7	17	18	19	20	21	22	23	24	25	26	27	28	29	30	31	32	33	34
	2.2 - 2.4	20	21	22	23	24	25	26	27	28	29	30	31	32	33	34	35	36	37
	1.9 - 2.1	23	24	25	26	27	28	29	30	31	32	33	34	35	36	37	38	39	40
26"	2.8 - 3.0	16	17	18	19	20	21	22	23	24	25	26	27	28	29	30	31	32	33
	2.5 - 2.7	19	20	21	22	23	24	25	26	27	28	29	30	31	32	33	34	35	36
	2.2 - 2.4	22	23	24	25	26	27	28	29	30	31	32	33	34	35	36	37	38	39
	1.9 - 2.1	25	26	27	28	29	30	31	32	33	34	35	36	37	38	39	40	41	42

It's a good idea to check your tire pressure before every ride in case there's been some leakage. Pressure can vary between gauges by a couple of psi, so to stay consistent, use the same gauge every time, whether it's the one on your pump or a stand-alone pressure gauge. You should learn the feel of your tires' optimal pressure by squeezing them when they're inflated. You won't be able to tell the exact psi, but you'll know when it's way off. This is a handy skill to have when there's no gauge available.

CHAPTER EIGHT

The Rides

THERE MAY BE a temptation to just up and go on a spur of the moment ride. Spontaneity and adventure are truly what makes this sport fun, but there's also an ethic of self-reliance. Riders learn to fix flat tires and repair broken parts to avoid being stranded. They bring enough tools to take care of the most common problems that can occur, as well as emergency first-aid supplies and the know-how to use them. You could potentially end up a great distance from civilization, so making certain pre-ride preparations for possible mishaps and emergencies will help prevent a bad situation from ruining the ride.

Deciding which gear to bring will require careful consideration. Everything you bring will add weight, some items more than others. Being prepared for problems is absolutely vital for having a good experience, which makes certain items worth their penalty in weight. What you don't want to bring are things that you'll never have a need for. Gear requirements are determined by ride time and, to a lesser degree, riding conditions. Ride times are generalized here by one hour, two to four hours, all day, and multi-day.

No matter what ride you're planning, it's always best to prepare your gear and bike the night before. We're all human, and sometimes good intentions of going for a ride the next day get squashed because you slept in too long and it became too late to get everything ready. Don't give yourself any excuses. On the night before your ride, set your tire pressure and make all your bike adjustments, get all your gear together in one spot, and then get to bed at a decent time. With good habits like this, you'll have no reason to opt out in the morning and you'll be far less likely to forget something.

One-Hour Rides

One-hour rides are good for squeezing some fun and physical activity into a busy schedule. They're also good for beginners with limited endurance. It could just be a quickie at a local trail that you're hitting up after work or school: you know the paths and have no chance of getting lost. You won't need a hydration pack; a full water bottle in the cage will do. For storage, a seat bag can hold everything on this list of items:

- Spare tube – even if you have tubeless tires, it's good to have a backup.
- CO_2 cartridge – even though it may not fill your tire to the proper pressure, it's OK for a short ride.
- CO_2 inflator
- (2) Tire levers
- A small size multi-tool
- Zip lock bag with these first aid items: (2) 1" bandages, (2) 2" bandages, (2) 3" bandages, .5 fl. oz. first-aid spray, (2-3) individually wrapped moist towelettes or alcohol wipes
- Identification
- Petty cash ($5 - $10 to get you fed or fixed. You never know.)

Two- to Four-Hour Rides

This is an average mountain bike ride time. You may know the trails really well or you may spend some time exploring uncharted land. Either way, you should be fully prepared in case you're out longer than planned. A two-liter or a three-liter hydration pack is usually necessary. Which size is dependent on a variety of factors such as ambient temperature, your body weight, your personal sweat rate, anticipated distance, total ascension, your chances of getting lost, and the availability of water for refills. If several of these factors are high and no water refills are available, you may want to consider the bigger size. Suntan lotion and bug spray can be applied beforehand and may not be needed while out on a ride of this length in time.

Even though the following list seems large, the items are small and should fit into the hydration pack. You'll never need all of these items on any one ride, but you'll likely use most of them at some point in time. They will help you in what could otherwise be some very unpleasant situations.

- (2) Spare tubes – even if you have tubeless tires, it's good to have one as a backup.

- Patch kit – in case you run out of tubes

- (2) CO_2 cartridges

- CO_2 inflator

- A high quality mini-pump

- (2) Tire levers

- A high-quality multi-tool

- A chain tool and an extra chain link

- An extra derailleur hanger if your frame has a replaceable one

- A first-aid kit or a zip lock bag with these first aid items: (2) 1" bandages, (2) 2" bandages, (2) 3" bandages, .5 fl. oz. first-aid spray, pain relief medicine such as ibuprofen

- Travel size package of baby wipes – this is not only good for cleaning wounds but is also for cleaning yourself, if the need arises.

- Gauze wrap – useful for many types of injuries

- Identification

- Petty cash ($20 in small bills)

- Cell phone – preferably a GPS-equipped smartphone

- One or two energy bars

- A couple of energy gel packages

All-Day Rides

If you're the adventurous type and you're in superior physical condition, an all-day ride may be something you'd like to try. It involves going deep into the backcountry to places you've never been, using trails you've never ridden. Depending on its grandeur, it can be considered an epic ride. This can take you far from civilization, so you need to be prepared and self-sustained with extra supplies that can get you through the entire day, and emergency supplies in case you get stuck for the night.

You need to have the ability to get yourself out of any situation because you may be unable to contact Search and Rescue for help. This is not the kind of ride you take by yourself, nor is it a grab-stuff -and-go kind of ride. The various extra supplies should be well thought out and carefully considered. The load can be reduced by distributing some of these items between the riders in your group. Sharing is the way to go and will ultimately provide better support for all.

Bring items from the previous list along with the following additional supplies:

- Hydration pack with at least three liters of capacity

- Water bottle filled with an energy drink

- Extra energy gel packages

- Extra food (energy bars, apples, bananas, dried fruit, nuts, light sandwiches, etc.) Make sure you have enough to keep you energized for the entire ride.

- Lightweight waterproof jacket (for higher elevations, uncertain weather conditions, or if you're out later than anticipated)

- Leg warmers, arm warmers

- Emergency Mylar blanket

- Water purification tablets

- Bear pepper spray (if bears are known to be in the area)

- Compact bug spray

- Poison oak/ivy block lotion

- Compact suntan lotion

- Lighter

- Compact flashlight or headlamp

- Swiss Army knife

- Whistle

- Roll of Gorilla tape (useful for emergency repairs)

- A few zip ties

- Compact camera (if your phone camera isn't suitable)

- Quality topographical map (A digital version in your smartphone is ideal, but it would be a good idea to have a backup paper version.)

- Compass (if you don't have GPS)

- Cell phone backup battery or a solar-powered phone charger (preferably one that can attach to your hydration pack for on-the-go charging)

Multi-Day Rides

This is an entirely different arena of mountain biking that could consist of an overnight stay with two days of travel, or it could be as long as several nights and many days of travel. Regardless of how many nights you're out, you'll venture deeper into nature than any day trip could ever hope to accomplish. For this kind of activity, you'll need to be skilled with advanced camping techniques. These multi-day rides can be compared to backpacking, in that you need to bring everything with you to be self-sustaining in the wilderness. The difference is that on wheels, you can cover much greater distances. This is a fantastic way of exploring the wilderness far from civilization and is known as "bike packing."

One such ride is the Great Divide Mountain Bike Route, which is the world's longest unpaved cycling route. It runs from Canada to Mexico, following the spine of the Rocky Mountains over a distance of 2,774 miles (4,464 KM). It cuts through five U.S. states: New Mexico, Colorado, Wyoming, Idaho, and Montana; and two Canadian Provinces: Alberta and British Columbia. There's enough trail distance for several smaller epic rides, or for the hardcore adventurists, one very long ride. This is not a trip for the weak-willed or the faint of heart.

To carry all the extra gear that you'll need to bring on these kinds of rides, specialized bags designed for lightweight touring are available that can be attached to your bike.

Saddle Packs provide extended behind-the-seat storage without the use of a heavy rear rack.

Handlebar Bags provide storage in an easy-to-reach location. They also counter the weight of a saddle pack, which is important on the climbs.

Custom Frame Packs use the open area of your frame structure to maximize available storage while providing weight at the center of gravity.

Using a combination of bags will provide maximum storage capacity while keeping the load balanced and lightweight. This is especially important if you're riding single-track and/or technical surfaces. Online search results will show a few different manufacturers that make this type of customized bag system.

For bike packing, there are a lot of different options on which gear to bring. You may not have exactly the right gear on your first bike packing trip, but you'll learn which adjustments need to be made for the next time out. The trick is to keep everything light enough to successfully make your way up the hills and down the trails. Your gear and pack weight should be fifteen pounds or less, not including food, water, and the clothes you're wearing. Accomplishing this requires balancing your needs versus keeping it light. You'll need to minimize your items and make them as light as possible. You should also avoid redundancy and plan multiple uses for your gear, whenever possible.

In addition to the items on the previous lists, the following should also be considered:

- Ultralight backpacking tent. These tents are ideal due to their compact size and light weight. Look for a tent that's in the range of about two pounds (per person). They can be a bit pricey but are well worth the investment. For a lower cost option, a lightweight camping tarp can be used.

- Ultralight down sleeping bag. Look for one that's less than two pounds and is rated for temperatures appropriate for the conditions you're expecting. Typically for late spring, summer, and early fall, a rating of 30-40 degrees F will work in most cases. These bags can also be pricey but are a necessary item for a good night's sleep. A lower cost option would be to just lie on a sleeping pad with enough clothes to keep you warm at night.

- Sleeping pad. Because you'll feel the ground through your sleeping bag, a pad is necessary for your comfort. These are relatively inexpensive and weigh less than a pound.

- Air pillow. Inexpensive and weighing in at just a few ounces, this is an essential item to have.

- Ultralight stove kit. This comes with the stove and cookware that you'll need to prepare food. The kit packs together nicely and weighs as little as 1 ½ pounds for a basic set. The fuel will be additional weight that you'll need to account for. There are different types of fuel-burning stoves, but the simplest and most reliable is the alcohol stove. Propane canister stoves are also a good option, but the simplicity and lighter weight of the alcohol stove makes it the winning choice.

- Food. You'll need more than the sandwiches and snacks aforementioned on the all-day list. Freeze dried camping food is the easiest solution for providing enough to eat without a big weight penalty. Everything from huevos rancheros to ice cream sandwiches are available in lightweight packages. However, your best bet for breakfast is instant oatmeal. This will provide the complex carbohydrates that you need for sustained energy. You can even add freeze dried berries for extra flavor and/or crushed nuts for extra calories and protein.

- Water purification tablets. The water you bring with you will not last long, so at some point you'll have to get water from a natural source. The problem is that it will likely be contaminated with some forms of microscopic organisms. There are a number of purification tablets on the market that can make the water completely safe to drink.

- Recovery drink. At the end of the day's ride you should consume a powdered recovery type athletic drink, mixed with water. This will help prepare your body for the next day's ride.

- Lighting system. There's a good chance you may be caught riding in the dark while trying to find an optimal campsite. A high-power LED handlebar light should be used in combination with a helmet-mounted light.

- Fire starting kit. Several miniature fire-starting kits are available on the market.

- Toiletries. You need to remain civilized but keep your items minimal and light.

- Extra clothes and a change of clothes. It's especially important to regulate your body temperature as you're riding to prevent excessive sweating or chills. The wide swing in temperatures that you'll experience outdoors will require careful planning of which clothes to bring. You don't want to bring too much or too little. Here are some strategies that should help:

    a. Have a versatile use of clothing so that your wardrobe can perform under a variety of circumstances. For example, combining a short-sleeved jersey with arm warmers is better than a long-sleeved jersey because the warmers can come off as the day heats up. The same thing goes for leg warmers.

    b. Dress in layers. The last thing you put on will be the first thing you'll take off. For example, the base layer could be a sleeveless shirt, followed by a short sleeve jersey and arm warmers, and the top layer could be a thermal jacket or vest.

    c. Use breathable fabrics. You don't want clothing that traps moisture. It needs to be able to wick the sweat and moisture from your skin. For example, polyester shirts and wool socks are good choices.

    d. For the campground, a down jacket, a hat or a beanie, and gloves would be good to have.

    e If there's any chance of rain or fog, you should also have waterproof outerwear, such as a hooded rain jacket.

Tips for All-Day and Multi-Day Rides

1. Map your route carefully and give other people the detailed plans of where you're going. For all-day rides, plan a route that will get you back before sundown.

2. If possible, plan all-day trips with most of the climbing in the first part of the ride. That way, you'll be doing more descending on the return. This is more satisfying and is a better strategy for managing your energy reserves.

3. Only attempt this type of ride during favorable seasons. Traveling long distances can be severely hampered by rainy, muddy, and snowy conditions. Lightning and summertime wildfires are hazards that also need to be considered. Use good judgment and consider postponing if necessary.

4. Ideally, a minimum of three riders should be in your group. That way if someone gets seriously hurt, one person can stay behind to provide assistance while the other goes for help. (Hopefully, this situation never happens.)

5. Your fitness level needs to be above average because, if it isn't, the consequences could be dire. On all-day rides you could find yourself completely wiped out at the bottom of a valley, unable to climb your way out before nightfall. On multi-day rides, you could be completely spent after a long and difficult day of riding, only to get up the next morning and do it again . . . not something for the weak. For an all-around positive experience, everyone in the group should have similar physical and mental endurance, along with similar riding skills.

6. Conserve your energy on the climbs. This is where you can prematurely burn yourself out. Keep a slow and steady pace in low gear. You have a lot of distance to cover, so showing off could get you in trouble further into the ride.

7. If you're feeling less than 100 percent due to issues such as respiratory infections, gastrointestinal infections, or even a serious lack of sleep, you should opt out of the ride until you feel better. Not only can these things severely hinder your performance, they could prevent you from completing the ride.

8. Make sure your bike is well tuned and operating flawlessly. Inspect it carefully, and fix anything that's acting up, including any rattles, which may be a sign of something coming loose or may become a source of irritation. Your bike should be in tip-top condition.

9. This is not the type of ride to learn how to do maintenance tasks while out on the trail. You should already have hands-on experience with changing and patching inner tubes, using a chain tool to replace a chain link, changing a derailleur hanger, etc. If you don't have experience with simple maintenance tasks, practice at home before you go.

10. Buy the best quality tools you can afford, including a hand pump and a mountain bike multi-tool. You don't want cheap tools that break easily when you're in the middle of nowhere.

11. Take turns at being the lead rider. This keeps everyone at a pace that covers the most ground possible while remaining in your comfort zones.

12. Don't attempt risky technical drops at high speed. It's best to play it safe when you're far from civilization. Hiking through tough sections is recommended. Wear shoes that have some degree of flex at the toes to make walking easier.

13. You need to keep your carbohydrate level consistent throughout the day. Instead of waiting to get hungry and then eating a big meal, try eating smaller quantities of food throughout the day, including energy gels and trail mixes containing dried fruit and nuts. Take regular breaks at least once an hour to eat a little food. This will help keep you energized and moving. Also, get some protein every two or three hours to prevent protein deficiency.

14. Remain hydrated by drinking water regularly, even if you don't feel thirsty. As a general guide, drink about eight ounces of water every twenty minutes. This amount could vary, but it's a good starting point. Water is your most critical fuel, and remaining hydrated will keep you energized throughout the ride.

15. On single-day trips, know when it's time to turn around and go back. Your group needs to evaluate the remaining daylight hours versus your present location. You will also need to be aware of how much water you have remaining. If your supplies are more than half gone, consider making your way back.

16. Know the wildlife in the area. You need to be knowledgeable on how to avoid predators and how to react if you do encounter one.

Hot Weather Riding

Some of the best rides can be had on long, gorgeous summer days, but when it's during hot weather, especially with high humidity, special precautions must be taken to stay cooler. Although this is most critical on long rides, it's still important on shorter ones. Mountain bikers must adjust for riding in the heat and humidity; otherwise, serious heat related problems can occur.

Your body has a temperature reducing mechanism via the evaporation of sweat. But when cycling in hot weather, it can become overwhelmed. This can even happen during longer rides in moderate temperatures (65 to 80 degrees Fahrenheit). At a certain point, the mechanisms become ineffective, your body's core temperature rises excessively, and you develop what is known as heat exhaustion. Signs of heat exhaustion include feeling weak and fatigued, heavy sweating, nausea, vomiting, dizziness, or a headache.

If this happens to you, the best course of action is to stop cycling, get into the shade, remove some clothing, lie down with your legs raised six to twelve inches, splash water onto your face and torso, and drink cool fluids, preferably a sport drink containing carbohydrates and electrolytes. Do not restart your activity until the symptoms disappear.

If you ignore the signs of heat exhaustion and fail to deal with it, you could quickly develop what is called a heat stroke. This is a complete shutdown of your body's ability to shed heat. This is a life-threatening medical emergency! Even if you survive, it could cause permanent damage to sensitive organs, including the brain and spinal cord.

In addition to the signs of heat exhaustion, a person with heat stroke will be in an altered mental state, could lose consciousness, and could even have a seizure. Their skin will be dry, red, and very warm. If this happens, the victim will need help. Begin aggressive cooling with all available resources, but never give an unresponsive person anything by mouth. Instead, place the victim on their side to protect the airway. Emergency Medical Services will need to be contacted immediately. If heat stroke is recognized early and immediate cooling is administered, the survival rate approaches 90 percent[4].

So, how can all of this be prevented? Dressing lightly with vented apparel provides enough convection of heat while at rest in temperate climates, but while cycling at higher temperatures, the most efficient method of cooling down is by the evaporation of sweat. Body water lost from sweating must be replaced, so enough water must be brought along to last your entire ride. You must not allow yourself to become dehydrated. If you go for a 20-mile ride on a hot summer day, you could sweat out as much as four to eight pounds of water, depending on the individual, the temperature, and the amount of exertion. Some of this will have to be replaced. If you bring along a full 24-ounce bottle, you will only have 1 1/2 pounds of water . . . clearly not enough. To meet your hydration requirements, you'll need a two- or three-liter hydration pack full of ice water along with one or two water bottles filled with a drink containing five to ten percent carbohydrates and some electrolytes.

It's possible to increase your body's ability to dissipate heat by training in hot weather[5]. Try seven to fourteen consecutive days of short rides in the heat before taking a long ride. This will allow your body to acclimate by increasing your sweat production, which in turn keeps your internal temperature lower. Just remember that in all circumstances you'll need to replace the lost fluids.

The following heat index chart was developed by the U.S. National Weather Service[6]. Depending on the color band of the heat index value, the risk for heat-related illness can range from cautionary to extremely dangerous. As the heat index value goes up, more preventive measures are needed to stay protected.

NOAA's National Weather Service

Heat Index

Temperature (°F)

RH (%)	80	82	84	86	88	90	92	94	96	98	100	102	104	106	108	110
40	80	81	83	85	88	91	94	97	101	105	109	114	119	124	130	136
45	80	82	84	87	89	93	96	100	104	109	114	119	124	130	137	
50	81	83	85	88	91	95	99	103	108	113	118	124	131	137		
55	81	84	86	89	93	97	101	106	112	117	124	130	137			
60	82	84	88	91	95	100	105	110	116	123	129	137				
65	82	85	89	93	98	103	108	114	121	128	136					
70	83	86	90	95	100	105	112	119	126	134						
75	84	88	92	97	103	109	116	124	132							
80	84	89	94	100	106	113	121	129								
85	85	90	96	102	110	117	126	135								
90	86	91	98	105	113	122	131									
95	86	93	100	108	117	127										
100	87	95	103	112	121	132										

Relative Humidity (%)

Likelihood of Heat Disorders with Prolonged Exposure or Strenuous Activity

☐ Caution   ☐ Extreme Caution   ▨ Danger   ▧ Extreme Danger

Tips for riding in hot weather:

- Drink plenty of fluids before and after your ride. If you're riding consecutive days, weigh yourself before and after each ride to ensure that you're maintaining your weight. Don't allow yourself to enter a continuous state of dehydration.

- Ride during the coolest part of the day, either very early or very late.

- Ride slower.

- Ride for a shorter duration.

- Take breaks in the shade to drink and cool down. Splash yourself with water, if you have some to spare.

- If possible, pick a riding location that has more shade from tree coverage.

- If possible, pick a riding location that has fewer hill climbs.

- Wear breathable fabric for better sweat evaporation.

- Wear light-colored clothing for better sunlight reflection.

- If riding in extreme conditions, don't do it alone.

Cold Weather Riding

Mountain biking is generally considered a year-round sport, although during the winter some people hang up their bikes in the garage until the weather warms up. Cold weather can sometimes be discouraging and can make getting out the front door the most difficult part. But the winter offers some unique scenery along with peaceful, serene rides that should definitely be experienced. Riding in the off-season will also keep you in shape and will prevent your riding skills from becoming rusty. Even with light snow on the ground (one to five inches), good riding is still possible, especially if you have a fat tire bike.

Unless it's raining, the snow is too deep, or there's some other kind of extreme weather, there's no reason you can't ride in the winter. How cold it gets before you decide it's too much is an individual preference, but some will ride in temperatures as low as ten to twenty degrees below freezing, while others prefer winter temperatures that are a bit warmer.

Even though riding in the winter is physically more difficult, the biggest challenge is regulating body temperature. Wind delivered naturally and by cycling speed creates the perception that the temperature is lower than it actually is and further increases the rate at which heat is lost. This is known as the wind chill factor. Adjusted wind chill temperature has been measured by heat loss experimentation and is shown on indexes such as the one on the chart below, developed by the U.S. National Weather Service[7]. This chart is based on exposure to bare skin and can give you an idea of the maximum ride duration that should be attempted. Clothing that covers up bare skin along with heat generated by exercise will change the rate of heat loss.

Wind Chill Chart

	Temperature (°F)																	
Calm	40	35	30	25	20	15	10	5	0	-5	-10	-15	-20	-25	-30	-35	-40	-45
5	36	31	25	19	13	7	1	-5	-11	-16	-22	-28	-34	-40	-46	-52	-57	-63
10	34	27	21	15	9	3	-4	-10	-16	-22	-28	-35	-41	-47	-53	-59	-66	-72
15	32	25	19	13	6	0	-7	-13	-19	-26	-32	-39	-45	-51	-58	-64	-71	-77
20	30	24	17	11	4	-2	-9	-15	-22	-29	-35	-42	-48	-55	-61	-68	-74	-81
25	29	23	16	9	3	-4	-11	-17	-24	-31	-37	-44	-51	-58	-64	-71	-78	-84
30	28	22	15	8	1	-5	-12	-19	-26	-33	-39	-46	-53	-60	-67	-73	-80	-87
35	28	21	14	7	0	-7	-14	-21	-27	-34	-41	-48	-55	-62	-69	-76	-82	-89
40	27	20	13	6	-1	-8	-15	-22	-29	-36	-43	-50	-57	-64	-71	-78	-84	-91
45	26	19	12	5	-2	-9	-16	-23	-30	-37	-44	-51	-58	-65	-72	-79	-86	-93
50	26	19	12	4	-3	-10	-17	-24	-31	-38	-45	-52	-60	-67	-74	-81	-88	-95
55	25	18	11	4	-3	-11	-18	-25	-32	-39	-46	-54	-61	-68	-75	-82	-89	-97
60	25	17	10	3	-4	-11	-19	-26	-33	-40	-48	-55	-62	-69	-76	-84	-91	-98

Wind (mph)

Frostbite Times ▢ 30 minutes ▢ 10 minutes ▢ 5 minutes

Wind Chill (°F) = 35.74 + 0.6215T - 35.75(V$^{0.16}$) + 0.4275T(V$^{0.16}$)

Where, T = Air Temperatur · (°F) V = Wind Speed (mph)

Effective 11/01/01

Shivering is your body's way of expending energy to warm up and is the first sign that you're losing heat. When the wind chill temperatures become low enough, there's a danger of developing frostbite, which can set in fairly quickly. Areas most affected are hands and feet as well as the areas of exposed skin such as the ears, nose, and lips. An even worse condition, hypothermia, can set in after too much exposure. In severe cases, it can even cause death[8].

If you're underdressed and relying on your activity to warm you up, you'll likely end up losing more heat than your body can produce. This is a losing battle and will lead to a number of cold-related problems, depending on exposure time. At the other end of the spectrum is the danger of heating up too quickly, which will happen when you're overdressed. To check if you're wearing too many clothes, get yourself outdoors for at least ten minutes prior to the start of your ride. At this point you should feel chilled without shivering and your torso should not feel cold. If you feel cozy, warm, and comfortable all over, you probably have too much clothing on. As you heat up during your ride, your body will try to dissipate this excessive heat by sweating, which could then end up freezing in your clothing. And when you stop to rest and have a drink or eat an energy bar, you'll be shivering cold.

Shivering to warm up and sweating to cool down expends precious energy that should instead be used for cycling. Protect yourself from big temperature swings by wearing the correct clothing. The idea is to keep your body at a more or less constant temperature for the optimal performance of your cardiovascular and muscular systems. The best recommendation is to go with thinner, removable layers that can be easily stowed away during the course of the ride. Just make sure that you have enough room in your pack and your pockets to hold all of the clothing that you anticipate removing. Items such as leg warmers, arm warmers, and shoe covers are extremely compact.

How many layers of clothing are needed depends on the outside temperature at your riding location just prior to the start of your ride. No matter what temperature range you're in, the base layer, which is the layer against your skin, as well as the next layer out, should be made from moisture-wicking fabric so that moisture is not retained against your skin. The following are some recommended combinations of cycling clothing for three ranges of temperature - mild, cold and frigid. Each range represents what you may find during a typical day's lows and highs.

Mild Weather (50° - 68°F)

This range can be chilly but also poses the threat of overheating. This is due in part to the changing hourly temperatures as well as exercise-generated heat. You'll need enough clothing to keep yourself from shivering while retaining the flexibility of getting down to shorts and a short-sleeved shirt at the warmest point of the day.

- Base layer: Sleeveless shirt, t-shirt, or short-sleeve cycling jersey
- Intermediate layer: Short-sleeved cycling jersey, long-sleeved cycling jersey
- Outer layer: Arm warmers, light cycling jacket
- Legs: Shorts and leg warmers or knee warmers. Alternatively: Lycra/ spandex pants
- Feet: Wool socks

Cold Weather (32° - 50° F)

This range is above the freezing point but can feel very cold, especially when wind chill is factored in. To protect against heat loss, extra layers that provide the ability to make mid-ride adjustments will be required. Heat loss is greatest from your head, so a skullcap under your helmet can be used to retain heat, but protecting your torso will most affect your overall warmth. Again, make sure you're not overdressed to begin with and are fully prepared to remove layers as the temperature warms.

- Base layer: Sleeveless shirt, t-shirt, or short-sleeved cycling jersey
- Intermediate layer: Short-sleeved cycling jersey (over the sleeveless or t-shirt)
- Intermediate layer: Sleeveless cycling vest, long-sleeved cycling jersey
- Outer layer: Thermal, wind-resistant cycling jacket with a high collar for neck and chin protection
- Legs: Thermal tights
- Hands and feet: Winter weather cycling gloves, thick wool socks, toe warmers, boots or thermal shoe covers
- Head and ears: Skullcap, ear muffs, neck warmer

Frigid Weather (10°- 32° F)

This range is very cold and will require extra forethought and consideration for clothing choice. Riding in temperatures any lower than 10° would be unwise and simply not practicable. Without serious survival preparation, any problem while out on the trail could put you at risk of getting frostbite and hypothermia.

In this temperature range, there's a limit on how much clothing can be removed. But if you do remove clothing, you'll need to have warm base layers made from material such as wool, which provides excellent thermal protection but doesn't hold moisture against your skin. Wool will also continue to insulate when it becomes wet.

When it comes to feet, it's a common mistake to underestimate how cold toes can become when cycling. First of all, there is an inherent lack of circulation in the feet with cycling; and secondly, most regular mountain biking shoes are designed to be ventilated. These issues will cause toes to become numb in no time. If you use clip-in pedals, you may want to switch to flats so that boots can be used. Besides, the snow will clog up your pedals in no time and make clipping in difficult.

- Base layer: T-shirt or short-sleeved jersey
- Intermediate layer: Thick, long-sleeved cycling jersey (two layers in the coldest weather)
- Intermediate layer: Sleeveless cycling vest, wool arm warmers
- Outer layer: Fully insulated cycling jacket that has a wind and waterproof front

- Legs: Thermal tights, thermal knee warmers, wind and waterproof cycling pants
- Hands: Heavily insulated cycling gloves (which lack dexterity) or regular gloves used in combination with bar mitts
- Feet: Two or more layers of thick wool socks (this will require a larger shoe size), thermal shoe covers with cold weather cycling shoes, or fat tire boots
- Head and ears: Balaclava or a skullcap, ear muffs, neck warmer

In these cold weather and frigid weather temperature ranges, additional precautions should be taken to prevent the risk of frostbite and hypothermia. Chemical warming packets can be used in your shoes or gloves if necessary. They're activated by shaking them, which causes a chemical reaction that creates heat. The packets are a low-cost item that can warm up your digits when they're suffering in the cold.

For your hands, bar mitts are pockets that you put your gloved hands into. They mount to the ends of your handlebar to cover your grips and levers. These allow you to use thinner gloves for normal dexterity while keeping your hands warm and dry. Another option, if you're willing to spend the money, is heated handgrips. These wonderful devices are wired to a battery pack that gets strapped to the frame. They will warm your hands nicely while you ride, thereby allowing the use of thinner-palmed gloves. Keeping your hands warm this way can also create an overall feeling of warmth, at least psychologically. This is a big plus in frigid temperatures.

The length of your ride should be considerably shorter than your warm weather rides. How long depends on the wind chill temperature as well as the distance and time it would take you to push your bike back if you have a mechanical breakdown. Being caught out in the cold a long way from where you parked could spell big trouble. At the lowest temperatures, a half-hour ride will probably be about right, and in the not-as-cold weather, your ride should be no more than about an hour to an hour and a half long.

Another thing to be mindful of is the amount of exertion. You should not ride as hard as you would in warmer temperatures because you'll heat up too fast and sweat too much, which could then end up freezing. To prevent this from happening, slow down, keep climbing to a minimum, and remove layers before you sweat too much. With a little forethought and planning, winter weather riding can be an enjoyable way to stay current with your bike handling skills while maintaining your fitness level.

Night Riding

Night riding is a unique experience that gives a completely different dimension to off-road exploration. Even your usual and familiar trails will seem like a whole new place that you're exploring for the first time. With the path eerily illuminated by your shadow-casting lights, the scenery will take on a new and exciting look.

Modern lighting technology provides sophisticated ultra-bright light from compact units that mount to your handlebar and helmet. The handlebar-mounted light will only illuminate the path straight out in front of you, but not the path around the bends. This makes it hard to anticipate what's coming up. A second light mounted to your helmet will illuminate the direction you're looking and intend to travel, and will also take out some of the shadows. You'll know which line to pick, where to turn, which obstacles to avoid, and where the cliffs are. This can make night riding a relatively safe experience, even though your speed perception will be off and it'll feel like you're going faster than normal. If by chance you only have one light, the best location is still on the handlebars, but you'll have to ride much slower.

Always make sure that you know how much remaining battery life you have and how much time you need to return to the trailhead. Batteries usually have a rated run time, but its best to stay conservative and err on the shorter side. You don't want to get caught in the wilderness without light. Running your lights on a setting that's lower than their maximum brightness is one good way to get more time. Battery run time is also an important consideration when purchasing lights, but it would also be wise to find good quality, bright lights. This will allow you to see further and, thus, ride faster.

When planning a night ride, always prepare for the nighttime temperatures, which can be much colder than the daytime. Nocturnal animals will also be out, sometimes in large numbers. You'll sometimes be able to see their eyes reflecting your light as you roll down the trail. For your safety, learn which kinds of creatures you may come across before you begin your ride.

> *"You're moving through a wonderful natural environment and working on balance, timing, depth perception, judgment...it forms a kind of ballet."*
>
> --Charlie Cunningham
>
> Mountain Biking Pioneer

PART THREE

Riding Skills

EVERYBODY WANTS TO do their best and have the ability to keep up with their friends or even compete against them. But how good is your best? How well are you performing? Can you do better? This all depends on how much time you've put into learning proper technique and your fitness level. If you're committed to being your best by consistently working hard to reach your goals, what you put into it will be rewarded.

When it comes to performance, the bike's handling characteristics are a factor, but a rider's skills are the biggest influence. You'll need to discover your weaknesses and focus on improving them through regular practice. How well you prepare your body, your mind, your bike, and your gear all come into play for successful riding. Equally important, remaining crash-free and unhurt should always be a predominant component of your progression. This is best achieved by learning to avoid common mistakes, riding within the limits of your skills, and applying techniques that make you a better rider. There's a fine line between safety and danger that lies at the upper end of your skill limit, and this is where continuous improvement will be made.

Trails with tight turns, rough and rocky sections, and big elevation changes can be unnerving for the inexperienced. Whether you have some experience or you're an absolute beginner, proper techniques need to be learned and practiced to master the trails. This section of the book gives information on basic bike operations, engaging your mind and body, riding tips and techniques, and bike handling skills. Follow closely, and you'll be on track to achieving your best. Good luck.

CHAPTER NINE

Riding Basics

E VERY RIDER NEEDS basic riding skills that are part instinct and part planning. How you position your body for every circumstance, how and when to brake, effective pedaling technique, and proper gear selection are core mountain biking skills. They will be the foundation of everything that you do out on the trails. Follow these lessons closely to develop the skills you need to be a successful and competitive rider.

Body Positioning

One of the most basic things to learn when you first start mountain biking is how to properly position your body. This will determine how well you can maneuver the bike beneath you and how well you can react to the changing terrain. While the seated position undoubtedly provides great stability and pedaling power, it doesn't provide the high degree of maneuverability that's needed to quickly respond to changing terrain. When you're not pedaling, you'll need to be in an off the saddle (standing) position.

Standing on the pedals with bent arms and legs is called the "ready" or "attack" position. By thinking of it as being "ready," you'll be on the lookout and ready to respond to the trail. As your confidence level rises and your riding ability becomes more aggressive, you can think of it as the "attack" position. The ready/attack position allows you to freely maneuver your body to shift your weight over the bike. It also allows you to maneuver the bike without moving your body weight around. This separation creates a unique dynamic. Whether it's sharp turns, rapid braking, descending, sudden elevation changes, or obstacles such as rock gardens and tree roots, you'll be in control. More than that, you'll have the ability to push your skills to aggressively conquer the terrain.

Follow these steps to get into a correct ready/attack position:

1. While on level ground, start riding in a straight line. With the crank arms horizontal, stand on the pedals with your weight centered and balanced squarely upon them. Your feet will be level with each other and your toes will feel level with your heels.

2. Bend your knees and lower your behind, similar to a half squat. This height is limited by the height of your saddle, so if you have a dropper post, you should lower it to give yourself more room. This extra clearance will make it easier to move the bike and your body independently in

response to changing terrain. It also lowers your weight in relation to the ground, making it easier to stay balanced while giving your legs the ability to bend and extend to soak up the bumps.

3. Slightly open your legs at the knees to allow some side-to-side movement of the bike. This differs from the seated position, which requires your legs to be closer together to maximize pedaling efficiency.

4. Lean your torso forward by bending the elbows. You'll be lowering your shoulders toward the handlebars while keeping your back straight. As you do this, move your hips rearward just enough to keep your weight centered and balanced squarely on the pedals. On level ground, this should be slightly back from the normal seated position.

5. Your elbows should be extended slightly more than a 90-degree bend. This will give your arms the ability to flex as needed. They should also be pointed outward and lower than the top of your shoulders, as if you're halfway through a push-up. This is an ideal position for pulling, pushing, providing balance, and flexing to absorb the bumps.

6. Raise your head enough to easily see all the way down the trail. If your helmet has a visor attached, you'll need to raise your head a little further. If this gets uncomfortable over time or causes neck pain, try riding without the visor so that you don't have to tilt your head as far. Because your head is heavy and has the ability to throw off your balance, keep it upright and neutral.

This off-the-saddle, weight-centered, neutral position will be the default. All movements to control the bike will originate from there. Through the course of your ride, your positioning will change often, including where your hips are in relation to the saddle, the degree of bend in your knees and elbows, and the side-to-side lean. Experiment by raising and lowering your torso with your arms and legs, then leaning your bike from side to side while keeping your torso still, and then shifting your weight back by partially straightening out your arms and putting your butt above the open space behind the saddle.

Time spent off the saddle does have a side benefit of minimizing saddle soreness. However, extended amounts of time in the ready/attack position can be tiring as well, so it's good to rest on the saddle when the opportunity arrives. Saddle time should be limited to long sections of flat or lightly rolling ground, soft turns, easy braking, or when maximum pedaling efficiency is required, such as uphill riding. Basically, a combination of on and off the saddle will give the greatest comfort over the duration of a ride.

Weight Distribution

Whether you're seated, standing, climbing, descending, braking, or turning, one aspect of weight distribution needs to remain consistent: keeping the majority of your weight on the pedals and only a little on the handlebars. In the mountain biking world this is known as "light hands, heavy feet."

If you're putting too much weight on your handlebars as you're bouncing on rough terrain, you'll get tossed around a lot more severely, as if the bike is trying to knock you off. As a result, your arms will be more rigid, and your elbows will not be soaking up the bumps the way they should be. This is a rough, uncontrolled way of riding that will cause arm and shoulder fatigue and could lead to costly mistakes being made. Just the opposite, if your weight is too far rearward, you may actually be pulling on the bars; your front end will be too light, and you'll have reduced steering control.

To do it right, keep your weight centered and balanced on the pedals. This puts your center of gravity on the bottom bracket and, hence, evenly balanced between your tires. Your bike will be a lot more responsive and you'll be able to whip it around much better. Your arms will also be more relaxed to soak up the bumps, thereby reducing your chances of getting knocked off the bike.

This all sounds great in concept, but it's not an easy habit to acquire. First of all, your bike must be properly set up for your body; you don't want your machine working against you. Then you must practice, practice, practice. No matter what you're doing, negotiating obstacles, cornering, braking, ascending, descending, think about your hands and your feet. This is an easy thing to forget when you're having fun and you're in the heat of the moment. It's something that must be reminded and re-reminded until balance point awareness becomes a natural part of riding. Once you're consistently and thoughtlessly light on the hands and heavy on the feet, your rides will be much more stable, and you'll be a much better mountain biker.

Braking Basics

Like body positioning, good braking techniques can link together many elements of mountain biking. Doing it correctly will speed up your ride, while improper braking will reduce your performance and can lead to crashes. To get the most speed and control while avoiding mishaps, you need to know when and how to brake. Before we get into these techniques, it's important to understand some braking basics.

- As described in chapter seven, your levers should be set up for a one- or two-finger pull.

- Knowing which lever is the front brake and which is the rear needs to be instinctive. This seems like a no-brainer, but sometimes in the heat of action, a mix up is entirely possible. Getting them mixed up could lead to unwanted costly mistakes. For bikes made in the U.S., the easiest way to remember which is which is by associating the "R" in Right lever with the "R" in Rear brake. Bike manufacturers in some other countries may install the levers in the opposite positions.

- The front brake is the more powerful of the two and can provide as much as 4/5 of your stopping power. The danger of this power is that squeezing too abruptly could lock up the front tire and cause a crash. This is completely avoidable with good brake timing and the proper distribution of your weight; you should have no fear of your front brake.

- Keep both left and right fingers resting on the levers without squeezing them. This is called "covering" the brakes and will help keep you ready to pull at a moment's notice. The exception to this is during situations when your brakes won't be used, such as hill climbing.

Braking Power

Learning to properly harness the power of your brakes, especially the more powerful front brake, will make you a faster and safer rider. With some practice, you'll become intimately familiar with the full stopping power of your machine. If you're new to mountain biking, your initial practice is best accomplished on pavement . . . it's a quick and easy way to better prepare for the trails. You can learn to feel the moment your rear tire begins to rise and how to instinctively prevent it by counteracting with balance and the right braking power. Understanding this power will give you a big boost of confidence and will better prepare you for the trails. The following steps are pretty basic, but they'll teach you how to maximize your brakes.

1. **Brake test:** Preferably on a street with a gentle downhill slope and while in the seated position, get your speed up and then softly and evenly squeeze both brakes until you slowly come to a stop. Do not abruptly pull on the levers. Feel the smoothness of your brakes as you apply even pressure to both front and rear brakes, allowing them to work together. Repeat this a few times with incrementally increasing pressure and notice how quickly you stop. Be careful not to squeeze too hard.

2. **Front brake:** On the same road and at the same speed, practice coming to a stop with only your front brake. At first, gently ease into it with light pressure, then squeeze harder on subsequent tries. You'll soon discover how quickly you can stop with just the front brake. Get to the point where your rear tire almost comes off the ground. Now get into the low attack

position while balancing your weight on the pedals as you try to get the rear end to come up again. There should be a marked difference in your ability to keep it down.

3. **Front brake with heel drop:** Brake again using only the front brake while in a low attack position, keeping your weight centered on the pedals. As you brake, drop your heels so as to drive your inertia forward and down into the pedals. This will transfer the braking force through the tires and into the ground, increasing traction and helping to make your stopping power even stronger. Simultaneously push your palms into the handgrips.

4. **Both brakes:** Now perform the same braking technique except while using both brakes. Try braking even harder, dropping your heels enough to keep the force square into the pedals. After you let off the brakes, level out your heels. Practice timing this while keeping your weight centered on the pedals. Unless you're heading downhill, resist the temptation to lean back to keep the rear end down, which will cause your front tire to un-weight and reduce its stopping power. This could also cause more problems by leaving you unbalanced when you have to maneuver the bike immediately after braking.

Braking with Traction

Braking will always be strongest when it's done without locking up the tires. Once they're locked, the only thing slowing you down are the tires dragging across loose terrain. Braking in this manner will put your safety at risk and is far less efficient than your brake pads squeezing the discs. This will also unnecessarily erode the trail.

Keeping the tires rotating depends on how hard you squeeze the brake levers, how efficiently you distribute your weight, and the available traction, which is determined by the trail surface, tire type, and tire pressure. Stopping distance is another factor to consider and is dependent on the speed that you're travelling and the interaction between the tires and the ground. The lower the degree of traction and the faster your speed, the greater the required stopping distances. This is why it's important to effectively judge your traction and speed to determine how much distance you need to slow down or stop. This comes with practice and experience.

Learning how much braking force is required on all types of surface conditions is the best way to prepare for any given situation. Practice the following basic exercises at your favorite riding location to sharpen your braking skills. Remember to mark or make note of the location of your braking starts and stops so that they can be compared.

1. **Rear wheel braking with traction:** Find a straight trail with a slight decline and a relatively smooth surface. At a moderate to fast speed, pull your rear brake lever with just the right amount of pressure to stop as quickly as possible without breaking traction. The most powerful braking occurs just prior to a skid, so try to bring it to that point by releasing some pressure if you feel/hear your tire begin to skid. Do this in both a seated position and an out-of-the-saddle position with your weight centered.

2. **Feathering the brakes:** This technique can make it easier to stop on loose terrain by preventing your wheels from locking up. Using the same speed and body positions, try stopping as quickly as possible by increasing and decreasing lever pressure to keep it just below the edge of a skid. This is similar to the operation of anti-lock brakes on cars. Most modern mountain bike brakes will allow a wide range of braking pressure, something known as "modulation." Try not to exaggerate your feathering because it doesn't take a lot. Only use this technique when the trail conditions are loose and traction is poor. When you're on firmer terrain, make it a habit to brake with even pressure.

3. **Experimenting with different terrain:** Once you become accustomed to maximizing the brakes, experiment on different types of terrain as they become available. This will provide you with valuable experience that will prove to be useful. Remember to keep your weight centered and your heels lowered when you brake. You should experience excellent stopping power while keeping traction under control.

Final Thoughts on Braking

Brakes can regulate your speed to manageable levels, but you should not make constantly dragging your brakes a standard method of operation. This is a bad habit with potentially negative consequences, especially as you're braking on rough and rocky terrain. It's much better to ride brake free until you hit a smooth spot, and then do the majority of your braking. Getting your braking done quickly and then letting off allows your wheels to spin freely more often, which helps to stabilize your bike. The reason for this is simple: Your wheels are like gyroscopes, helping to keep you upright. You can test this force by taking the front wheel off the bike and giving it a spin as you hold the axle. Tilt it to one side or the other, and you'll feel the gyroscopic forces trying to keep it upright. This force helps to keep the bike stable, but when you're braking, your tires are not rotating freely and the force is negated, resulting in a reduction of the bike's stability and controllability. This is why you should brake sparingly but effectively.

Using the braking exercises, you should have gotten a pretty good feel for stopping distances. Just be aware of the riding conditions while keeping your speed manageable. It's good to gradually push to faster speeds, but you need to know your limits. When riders are traveling faster than their comfort level, they tend to tense up from apprehension. This often leads to braking mistakes and the inevitable crash. Don't let your riding partners push you to go so fast that you can't properly manage the bike.

By braking only when it's necessary and using good techniques, you'll achieve faster speeds, have better control, and get more satisfaction from your rides. Most importantly, knowing when and how to brake for corners and descents will reap the biggest rewards but will require some specialized techniques. These are covered in Chapter Eleven.

Efficient Pedaling

Pedaling can become strenuous and tiring, so techniques that provide the most efficient transfer of muscle power to forward propulsion should be gladly adopted. A beginner may think that there's nothing complicated about it . . . just pedal. But good techniques can be applied to effectively enhance your efficiency, thereby allowing you to pedal longer and harder.

First off, it's important to have your cleats adjusted and your bike properly set up per the instructions in Chapter Seven. This will give your legs the correct amount of extension at the bottom of the pedal stroke while positioning your knees and feet at the correct location over the pedals to provide the optimal leverage.

To aid in maximizing the use of the muscle groups in your legs, keep the outer side of your knees in line with your hips as you rotate the pedals. If you're pedaling with your legs flared outward, you're doing it wrong. This creates a loss in pedaling efficiency while increasing the chances of knee, ankle, or foot problems. This misalignment could be caused by a seat that's too low, improperly positioned cleats, inexperience, or discomfort caused by skin chafing of the inner thighs or the crotch area. If the latter is the case, make sure you apply chamois butter before every ride.

Efficient pedaling requires focused energy, but when other body motions are thrown in, it detracts from your efficiency. If your head is bobbing from side to side, it takes a little away from forward motion. If your shoulders are swaying side to side from the hips, it can disrupt pedaling speed and motion. These things add up and take away. Try tightening your lower abs to stop any sway at the hips. Work on keeping your body still so that your energy is focused and fully utilized.

When it comes to applying power, you don't want to simply press down hard on the down strokes . . . left-right-left-right-left-right. This gives you jerky pulses of power and makes for an inefficient method of pedaling. It also puts too much emphasis on just one group of leg muscles, the quadriceps (the muscles at the front of your thighs). Although these are your strongest pedaling muscles, it is possible to somewhat ease the burden put upon them by making use of supporting muscles.

Rapid quad burn is not the only disadvantage of pedaling with jerky pulses of power. On sand and gravel, this method can cause the rear tire to break traction on the power strokes. And during climbs, a slipping tire will likely result in the need to put your feet down and come to a stop. It's much better to smooth out the power bursts so that they taper off and blend in with each other. To achieve this, power needs to be applied to the pedals before and after each down stroke . . . essentially through as much of the pedaling circle as possible. This is commonly referred to as "pedaling in circles."

During the full revolution of a pedaling circle, the biomechanical forces of pedal resistance and muscle usage are constantly changing. Pedaling in circles will use a wide range of leg muscles to match up with the changing resistance. This sequence of muscle contractions can be complicated, but it really doesn't matter because you don't need to know what every individual muscle is doing. It's simply a matter of training your muscles to naturally and habitually apply power correctly. Once you master pedaling in circles, you'll be spreading the load through more of your leg muscles, thereby giving yourself the ability to pedal more strongly and to travel greater distances.

There are two phases in the pedal stroke: propulsion and recovery. During the upstroke, basically no force can be applied toward rotation. It's a brief moment for muscles to relax and recover. To compensate for these moments with no energy production, it's important to make the propulsive phases of the pedal cycle last as long as possible. By extending the propulsive phase, the pedaling circle will be smooth all the way through.

To understand how the biomechanics work, it's easiest to divide the motion into four sections and reference them to positions on a clock. It's important to note that none of the following clock positions are exact; there may be small variances based on body type and bike setup. All stated foot positions are in relation to the center of gravity. For example: If you're riding uphill and sitting on the nose of your seat, it shifts your pedaling pressure slightly rearward, so heel-toe level in this circumstance is not in relation to the ground.

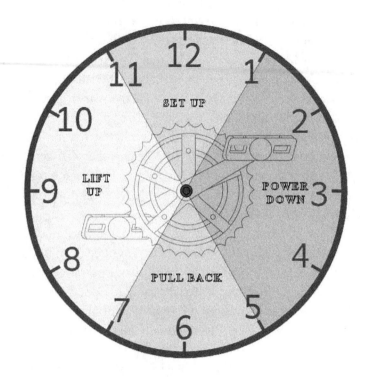

The Down Stroke: 1 o'clock to 5 o'clock. The down stroke is when the greatest amount of power is generated. It begins at about 1 o'clock using a combination of forward and downward forces. Peak power is reached at about three o'clock, at which point the force is purely downward. When your quadriceps muscles are providing the majority of the power, your heels should be moved slightly lower than the rest of your foot in order to activate the hamstrings (the muscles at the back of your thighs) for additional help.

The Bottom Stroke: 5 o'clock to 7 o'clock. As you're nearing the bottom, you'll still be applying a down stroke force, but you'll begin to apply a rearward force by pulling your foot. As you move past bottom center (6 o'clock), your toes will automatically start to tilt downward slightly. At this point, imagine scraping something off the bottom of your shoe onto the edge of a curb . . . your foot will be doing a similar action. Maintain this pulling as far as you can, which usually ends up at about the 7 o'clock range.

The Up Stroke: 7 o'clock to 11 o'clock. No power is generated on the upstroke, but when your cranks are spinning rapidly, your feet can get pushed up by the pedals. In this situation, your feet are creating some resistance, which is a waste of energy.

You'll need to remove all resistance by lifting your knees as quickly as possible to keep weight off the pedals. If you're using clip-ins, it may feel like you're pulling up, but that's not what's happening. Unweighting is the best you could hope for. During this portion of the circle, your toes will be pointed slightly downward, especially during the early part of the stroke.

The Top Stroke: 11 o'clock to 1 o'clock. This is where you can gain additional power prior to the down stroke by pushing forward on the pedals. It's a transitional stroke that switches your ankles from a toe-down position established during the up stroke to a level-foot position for the down stroke. While pushing forward on the pedals, push your butt against the seat for the best leverage. The range for this stroke is relatively short and only continues until your quads take over on the down stroke. When it's combined with the bottom stroke of your opposite foot, it's enough to prevent your down stroke from being a sudden surge.

As far as ankle movement goes, your heels will be pushing down on the down stroke, leveling out at the bottom, moving up on the upstrokes, and then leveling out once again at the top. This may vary slightly based on saddle position and foot/cleat positioning. Ankle movement may initially feel pronounced in a pedaling circle, especially if you're using flat pedals, but the amount of actual movement will be subtle.

All of the above information may be too much to think about as you're spinning the cranks, so what you need is a simpler way to think about it. The idea is to create a single, continuous, smooth operation. Here is a simplified version:

1. Strongly dig in on the down stroke with emphasis on your heels.
2. Scrape when you get near the bottom and keep scraping as long as you can.
3. Lighten your feet on the up stroke.
4. Push forward at the top while leveling your feet for the down stroke.
5. Repeat . . . smoothly and evenly.

Practicing on paved roads or easy fire trails is best. Start at a slow RPM with medium resistance. Once you get the feel of it, up your RPMs a bit and continue practicing. Keep upping your RPMs until just before you feel bouncy on the saddle. Do these in twenty-minute intervals. If you're somewhat comfortable at maintaining smooth pedaling circles at this point, try it out on a single-track, including some small climbs. Just remember to always keep your main focus on bike handling.

You may have one leg that's stronger than the other. This is completely normal, but you'll need to adjust your power to even it out. Overcoming the deficiency between your weaker leg and your stronger leg may take a degree of mental effort, but it's worth it for smoother pedaling. Some say that practicing with a single leg will force you to learn how to apply power more evenly through the circle. This may be true as far as revealing where the dead spots in your pedaling circle are, but it's not a safe activity to do for any extended period of time. One-legged cycling should only be practiced with your bike held steady while mounted in a trainer or while you're on a stationary bike.

Repeatedly practicing circular pedal strokes will make them smooth, natural, and instinctual. By adopting this good habit from the beginning, it'll prevent bad pedal strokes from setting in. And once you master it, you can be a stronger and faster rider while taking on bigger climbs.

Efficient Standing Pedaling

There are times when a sudden burst of power is needed for situations such as getting over the top of a tough climb, getting up a steep mound, or passing another rider. Whatever the need is, when executed properly, standing pedaling will do the trick. Because this sudden burst of power requires extra oxygen for your muscles, your heart rate will increase rapidly to deliver it. To take full advantage of this power and delay over taxing your system, 'pedaling in circles' should be maintained as best as possible. Standing pedaling has a different feel because the top and bottom strokes are shorter, but 'pedaling in circles' is still doable. It may take some practice, but it'll pay off when it's time to deliver sudden power.

1. The down stroke will be enhanced by your body weight and will actually continue until about the 6 o'clock position. Push down hard with your heels while pulling on the bars for maximum power. If needed, it would be acceptable to gently rock the bike from side to side as you push down. If you feel your toes pushing against the front of your shoes, your foot is pointing downward, in which case you'll need to shift your hips back until you feel your heels pushing down.

2. The bottom stroke will still be a scraping action but will extend over a smaller section of the pedaling circle. After reaching the bottom, it may feel as though the pedal wants to spring back up, but don't allow this to throw off your pedal stroke. Instead, work on keeping the movement smooth and continuous.

3. On the up stroke, extra effort will be required to pull your knees up and un-weight the pedals.

4. On the top stroke, you'll still be pushing forward, but it'll be brief as your weight takes over earlier in the down stroke.

Choosing Cadence

Cadence is the speed at which you turn the pedal cranks, measured in RPMs. A high cadence translates to high RPMs, and a low cadence is low RPMs. The speed of your cadence can greatly affect your performance on the trails. Too high, and you'll be bouncing on your saddle; you could lose stability on rough terrain, and your rear tire could break traction and spin. Too low, and you'll be bogging down, wasting energy, and causing your leg muscles to burn out more quickly.

The best cadence for maximizing your pedaling efficiency and obtaining the highest endurance is in the range of 80 to 100 RPM. This range is in the "sweet zone" for power. It's slow enough that you won't feel like you're bouncing on the saddle and fast enough that you're not bogging down and over-expending your leg muscles. This range will provide the best power generation compared to the amount of energy you expend. It also leaves you better prepared for sudden acceleration or sudden hill climbs and gives you a higher level of endurance on long-distance rides.

Since using the optimal cadence is the easiest way to improve your performance, it's important to know how fast your cranks are spinning. There are a few different ways to determine this:

Cadence Sensor. A sensor that mounts to the frame to detect your RPMs at the cranks. It sends a signal to a cycle computer mounted to your handlebar or to a smartphone with an app that detects the signal and audibly reports it through an earbud.

Counting: Done by counting how many times one pedal revolves in a minute. You'll need a stopwatch with easy-to-read numbers attached to your handlebar. Counting to a fraction of a minute can make the task easier. For example, count how many times that one of your pedals revolves for a period of thirty seconds. Double that number, and you have your cadence.

Stationary Bikes: By learning what 80 to 100 RPM feels like on a stationary cycling machine that displays cadence. As you become accustomed to the different RPMs, you'll know what each one feels like. You can then apply that knowledge to outdoor cycling.

The optimal cadence range can only be maintained under ideal trail conditions. Even though this power zone is best for efficiency, this is not road biking. Mountain biking has many variables that can affect your RPMs, such as riding through a rock garden or negotiating tree roots. If the trail starts getting bouncy, slow down your spin so that you remain in full control of your traction and balance. Also, if you're pedaling on a descent with sketchy terrain, a lower cadence will provide smoother pedaling and a more controllable ride.

Gear Selection

In gearing terminology, up-shifting to a "higher" gear means putting it into a harder gear, either by moving the chain to a larger front chainring or to a smaller rear cog. Down-shifting to "lower" gear means putting it into an easier gear, either by moving to a smaller front chainring or a larger rear cog.

The amount of force required to turn the cranks is dependent on the combination of the front ring and the rear cog (gear ratio). Your drivetrain could have a large array of gear choices, depending on the number front chainrings and rear cogs in your drivetrain. For example, if you have a 3x10 gearing, each of the front three chainrings can combine with the ten cogs, giving you a total of thirty gears to choose from. If you have a 2x10 drivetrain, you'll have twenty gears to choose from, and if you have a 1x11 drivetrain, you'll have only eleven gears to choose from. Having a multitude of gears doesn't mean that you need to run through them all to go from a stop to the fastest possible speed. Even if you tried, with multiple rings there's a lot of front-to-rear ratio overlap that would make this impossible.

There is some justification to having all of these extra gears: Let's imagine you have three chainrings and you're on level ground. You start pedaling in a gear that's easy to accelerate from, say the middle chainring and one of the larger cogs. As you build up speed and your cadence increases, you begin using your rear shifter to change the gears one at a time to maintain your preferred cadence. As you're riding along and building speed, the fire road that you're on suddenly slopes downhill, causing your cadence to go up very quickly. But instead of allowing your pedals to spin way too fast while rapidly trying to jam across several cogs in a row, you change to the large chainring to give yourself a big increase in gearing that instantly puts your cadence where you need it. Alternatively, if you run into a sudden and steep uphill climb, you can switch to the small chainring for a bigger increase in cadence and then downshift with your cogs one at a time as it starts to get harder. These are examples of the convenience that overlapping gear ratios can provide.

There's a correct gear for every situation, but with everything that riders must contend with, it will ultimately be good judgment that keeps the crank arms turning effectively. Besides the terrain itself, other variables that affect gear selection include your speed, balance, leg strength, vision for picking the right lines, and level of confidence. Making the right gear choices improves with experience, but there are some basic rules that you should always follow.

Anticipate: You need to anticipate potential shifts beforehand so that you always keep the proper resistance. Don't wait so long to downshift that you start to bog down, especially when climbing. Conversely, waiting too long to upshift will cause your cranks to spin wildly without any resistance, leading to a complete loss of power production. When coasting fast on a downhill, be in a high gear, ready to resume pedaling when the opportunity arrives. With proper anticipation using what you see and feel, you can keep those cranks turning effectively by shifting at the right moments.

Change gears often: Don't be hesitant to change gears as often as necessary. Keep your gear matched to the speed you're going. The gears won't change if you're not pedaling, so to have the option of shifting often, keep the pedals moving. Making full use of all the gears will spread out the wear and tear of your cogs and chainrings, thereby extending their life.

Shift lightly: Drivetrains come in many levels of quality and price, but even the highest-end components can be abused to the point of failure. To promote the longevity of your drivetrain, certain shifting techniques should be used. When you're about to change gears, especially during climbs, first lightly ease off pedaling pressure for the briefest moment. Just easing off a tiny bit during a small portion of a down stroke can take tension off the chain and allow for a smoother shift. The front chainrings are especially susceptible and will require tension relief over a longer portion of the pedal stroke. Shifting under power will also be easier and have better results when it's done with good timing and at higher cadences.

Avoid crossing up your chain: If you have two or three chainrings, stretching the chain over the largest ring to the largest cog puts it at the highest tension with the highest side-to-side force. This extreme position will put an undue strain on the chain and the gear teeth, causing higher friction and faster wear and tear. The small chainring to the small cog will also have a friction-causing side-to-side force, but it leaves the chain with very little tension. This can cause the chain to jump off the gears at the worst moments . . . like when you're negotiating rough, jolting terrain.

Your components will allow these extreme positions to functionally happen, but they're not optimal. In fact, it would be better to stay off the last couple of cogs in a crossover situation. Although you may occasionally find yourself in bad gearing due to riding circumstances, shift to a better arrangement as soon as practicable. Try switching both front and rear gears to middle positions whenever possible. You'll always have the choice of moving one up or one down if the need arises.

> *"Do. Or do not. There is no try."*
>
> -- Yoda
>
> The Empire Strikes Back

CHAPTER TEN

The Zen of Mountain Biking

ALTHOUGH "ZEN" IS a sect of Buddhism, in the west its definition has transformed to something simpler. The most popular definition of Zen is in the Urban Dictionary[9], as follows: *"One way to think of Zen is this: a total state of focus that incorporates a total togetherness of body and mind. Zen is a way of being. It also is a state of mind. Zen involves dropping illusion and seeing things without distortion created by your own thoughts."*

Distraction and lack of concentration is your enemy and can take you down. In applying Zen to mountain biking, a total mind and body togetherness will allow you to flow with your bike and your surroundings without the distraction of thinking everything through. You'll be a master at mountain biking. The following topics can guide you to success, but your personality and drive to commit will ultimately determine how successful you will be.

Visualization

"Good visualization" is an ability to continuously look far enough ahead to foresee the upcoming challenges, anticipate your next moves, and then execute them while simultaneously assessing the next set of challenges, and so on. This is easier said than done because it doesn't come automatically; it's something that must be practiced over and over. But once you get it, your riding prowess will have increased dramatically.

First of all, it's important to understand the two primary types of vision: Central and Peripheral:

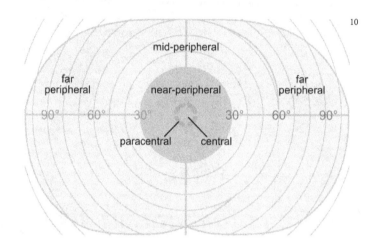

Central Vision: Technically known as Foveal Vision, it uses the central part of your retina. This vision is responsible for providing sharp, detailed information. When you read, you're using your central vision. When you gaze upon an object up the trail, you're using your central vision. It's a focal point that accounts for approximately 50 percent of the information that's provided by your eyes at any given moment.

Peripheral Vision: This is everything that you see outside of your central gaze. It has a wide field of view that doesn't focus on objects and accounts for the other 50 percent of your visual information. Peripheral vision excels at detecting motion, which is a skill that can get better with practice. Juggling is a perfect example. Good jugglers don't stare at their hands or at the objects going round and round. It's all done with peripheral vision. And the more it's practiced, the more accurate it becomes.

Skilled mountain bikers will correctly use central vision to pick out rocks, trees, gaps, drop-offs, etc., on or next to the trail, and peripheral vision to perform the tasks. They'll read what's ahead, evaluate the lines and boundaries, and assess how to set up for them. They'll determine how to go through, over, or around the various objects as well as the best approach to enter into the turns; constantly reading the trail with their central vision and deciding in advance how they're going to deal with it. Their peripheral vision then takes over to follow through with the action that they've planned, without the need to look at or focus on what's already been seen. Their peripheral vision is all that's needed to provide the necessary information to complete the pre-determined action.

A funny thing happens when you stare at an object. Your brain pulls you toward it. This is a known fact[11]. You will actually steer toward the object of your gaze. As you're trying to negotiate everything on the trail, that's the last thing that you need to happen. When you're riding a cliff-side trail and your tire is inches from the edge, there's a temptation to look toward the downslope. But don't do it, this could lead your tire right off the edge!

When it comes to obstacles, the tendency to fixate on what your tire is about to run over will leave insufficient time to determine the best course of action to take, causing the rider to over-react and over-compensate their maneuvers. Fighting the trail in this manner is not only jerky and forced, it can be more exhausting and will put you at a higher risk of crashing.

Get into the habit of continuously scanning the trail far ahead to predetermine your next few moves. You need to look at where you plan on going next, not at what you've already decided to avoid. Try to keep your eyes continuously moving down the trail from one thing to the next, never staring at anything too long. This is not as easy as it sounds; even the best riders have occasions where their central vision drops down to look at the trail directly in front of them. Learning to habitually keep your eyes up will initially take a conscious effort that needs to be practiced every time you ride. But once you get it, you'll be blazing through the trails without hesitation.

As you're moving down the trail, the scenery will be constantly moving. The closer the scenery, the faster it appears to be moving. Your focus should shift up the trail at about the same rate of speed that you're traveling. How far up the trail you need to look is mostly dependent on the speed that you're going. If you're heading downhill at a high rate of speed, you'll need to look quite far down the trail. If you're slowly crawling up a steep hill, you'll probably need to look just a few feet in front of your tire.

Although the bigger struggle is keeping your eyes up and not looking too near, looking too far ahead also comes with a couple of problems:

- You're seeing too much and not assessing the trail properly because the farther into the distance you look, the more real estate your central vision can see and the less detail that can be discerned. Some say you can't look too far ahead, but there is a limit to this. Just keep your eyes on the trail.

- Your peripheral vision's accuracy drops off as it approaches the edges of your field of view. This zone is called your far-peripheral, and it is not very good for detecting what's right in front of you.

- You're probably sitting too upright. Get down lower. Get into the attack position. You'll find that it's harder to stare at the distant horizon while you're in this position.

There's a central vision zone that's just the right distance ahead of you. This "Goldilocks" zone is commensurate with the speed that you're going and the nature of the path that's ahead of you. It should put everything that's closer into your mid-peripheral vision, allowing you to effectively pass over or around almost anything without re-focusing on them. As you go faster, you must look further up the trail to give yourself enough forewarning. And just the reverse, scanning your eyes faster can actually cause you to speed up. It's a self-fulfilling destiny. By the time you've gotten more comfortable with faster speeds, your visual skills will have improved and you'll be better at picking smoother lines without losing your momentum, and vice versa. Continuously practicing good visual techniques will make you a faster, more relaxed, and more confident rider.

Here are a few more vision tips to follow:

- Once you see something, such as a rock, a root, a dip in the trail, or whatever it may be, get your eyes off of it and continue scanning further ahead.

- If you're swerving as you're traveling along a cliff-side trail, you're probably letting the edge get to you. You're not concentrating on the path further ahead and you're tensed up. It can happen to the best riders. To prevent this, you need to make a conscious effort to focus on the trail and let go of your tension.

- Only acknowledge items that are important and will likely require some kind of action on your part. Don't give attention to unimportant details, such as a big rock that's way off to the side, the squirrel that just ran across your trail, or the bugs flying in your face. When you're moving fast, focusing on these kinds of things removes your attention from what you really need to be looking at. Also, if you want to gaze at some beautiful scenery as you're riding, stop the bike and take a look instead of putting yourself at risk.

- There may occasionally be something that you're closing in on and you're not sure how to approach it. Maybe it's something technical and difficult. It would be OK to give it another quick glance, subsequently returning your central vision back to the trail ahead so that the next thing doesn't catch you off guard. If you're still unsure how to handle it, stop and analyze it rather than putting yourself at risk.

- Visualize a path that's as straight as possible to help take out sharp corners and create softer turns. Your line may occasionally take you over some objects instead of around, but this will reduce jerky zig-zagging and will result in a faster ride.

- If a turn is ahead of you, look past it to determine your exit strategy. Sometimes you can see a couple of turns in advance. You should always know what you're going to do after the turn. Then, when you hit the turn, you won't be looking at it. Instead, you may be looking as far as the next turn to get set up for that one.

- Use reference points. For example, if you're going through a turn, one way to force your eyes to keep it in your peripheral vision is to briefly lock onto an object beyond the turn. You'll then smoothly and efficiently complete the turn. Another example is to look at the high points on a trail. By constantly shifting to the next high point, you'll always have complete coverage of the trail. Just remember to always quickly release your vision-lock and continue to scan further up the trail.

- Everything in your field of view will give you an overall sense of the trail and a feel for its flow. It's not just one object after another, but a series of obstacles all strung together, forming a pattern that sets your pace, your techniques, and what lines to take.

Relax!

If you're feeling tense, you'll be riding with stiff, jerky movements. Nothing can make your riding clumsier, more off balance, and more unsafe. This can get you into trouble with some close calls, which will then make you feel even tenser. This becomes self-defeating. Remaining relaxed comes from your state of mind. If you notice that you're tensed up, clear your mind of unwanted emotions and thoughts, think about relaxing your jaw, your neck muscles . . . then your shoulders . . . through your arms and wrists . . . and then your hands and fingers. Your hands should be resting lightly on the grips. Run this relaxation technique in reverse from your fingers and hands on through to your neck and jaw. With the proper state of mind and a loose, relaxed feeling, you'll be poised to make small, rapid adjustments to your balance as it becomes necessary.

Balancing

Balancing is a fundamental mountain biking skill that heavily relies on body positioning, weight shifting . . . and a little Zen. To be a proficient rider, every movement needs to be well-balanced, including reactions to technical trail challenges, braking, cornering, climbing, and descending. If you're frequently imbalanced, controlling your bike will be overly challenging and you'll be more prone to crashes and injuries.

Your sense of balance is maintained by a sensory system that detects acceleration or changes in movement. This system consists of a combination of fluid levels in the labyrinth of your inner ear, your eyesight, your hands and fingers, and the soles of your feet. All of these inputs work together to send signals to the brain. This system can be trained to work better through practice, regardless of current abilities. Training will increase your ability to sense imbalance and to react more quickly to correct it, resulting in a direct improvement to your bike handling performance[12].

Time on the bike provides great balance conditioning if you're proficient with your techniques and flow of movement. But if you don't understand the basics of balancing, excessive shifting around and large, overcompensating adjustments to imbalances will create excessive recovery effort. You'll then become tensed up, thereby compounding the imbalance problem. If you don't take some time to focus on improving your balance, your riding will suffer for it. So how do you improve your balance and stay well centered on your bike without sacrificing your technique? There are many exercises both on and off the bike that you can practice to improve your sense of balance.

Balance Training off the Bike

Off-the-bike balance training will give you an awareness of your center of mass over your feet, which will translate into keeping your weight centered on your pedals. This training entails learning to sense imbalances and quickly recover from them using subtle adjustments. It should be practiced until it becomes an automatic skill, mainly by using weight shifts that pivot from the ankles and the hips. Even athletes in great shape can be challenged by this kind of training until they become proficient at making adjustments.

Imbalances can happen when you involuntarily sway away from your center, so it's important to have an awareness of this natural tendency and to keep it under control. Try standing upright with your feet together, your eyes closed, and your mind clear. Notice how your body subtly and randomly moves side to side and fore and aft. This is your natural sway. Now try lifting one foot up with your eyes still closed. Your sway will increase enough to cause an imbalance that requires a corrective movement at the ankles. Having a good awareness of this ankle activity will make you a much better rider.

Try the following off-the-bike balancing exercises to improve your sense of balance. The best results will usually happen using a few minutes of daily practice, as opposed to longer, less-frequent training sessions. You won't increase your balancing ability overnight; it's going to take some time. The best advice is to start your training early and do it often. Warning: Individuals who suffer from severe balance problems, vertigo, or any orthopedic conditions should seek advice from a physician before starting any type of exercise program.

1. Stand on one foot. This is one of the quickest and easiest ways to improve your balance. Keep your torso upright, hands on the hips, and hold one foot up with a 90-degree bend at the knee. Hold this for about half a minute, and then switch to the other foot for each of these exercises:

   a. Focus your gaze on something stationary nearby to help you detect when you're swaying.

   b. To make it harder to discern movement, focus on something distant. This is where your peripheral vision can be helpful.

   c. Close your eyes. This is much harder because you won't have a visual point of reference.

   d. With eyes open and focused on a nearby object, hop up to switch to the other foot. Upon landing, stabilize your balance for about five seconds. Hop back onto the opposite foot and stabilize again. Repeat this for about a minute. To make it harder, try focusing on a distant object.

2. Stand on a BOSU ball. This half ball/half balance board is available at most gyms, or it can be purchased for use at home. First try standing on the ball with two feet for about a minute. If you can hold this, switch to one foot and hold for at least a minute with each foot. Once you master this, switch the ball around and try standing on the board side, first with two feet and then with one foot at a time.

If you feel that you're advanced enough, you can do bodyweight squats on the board side. Standing with your feet wide apart and your arms outstretched in front of you (holding a stick if you so choose), move your hips back while bending at the knees and hips to lower your torso. Bring yourself down to nearly a level thigh position and then slowly return to the upright position. At first, your legs will be shaky, but that will improve with practice.

3.   Sit on a stability ball. These are also available at most gyms, or they can be purchased for use at home. Sitting on the ball with your hands holding the ball steady, raise one leg until it's straight. Now, slowly raise your arms until they're level with your shoulders. Hold this position for about half a minute and then repeat using the opposite foot. Once you're good at this, hold both legs out with a little bend at the knees, arms raised in the same manner and your torso leaned back a little to counter the weight of your legs. This exercise is excellent for training your body to balance with the hips, which is what you'll use for the majority of adjustments on the bike.

Balance Training on the Bike

Most falls are not even crashes. They're slow-speed losses of balance that put riders on the ground with cuts and scrapes, or worse. When your speed is too slow for the gyroscopic force of the wheels to be of any help, the only thing you have left is your sense of balance. But when the trail gets tricky, your senses and reactions must be exceptional to maintain stability. Slow-speed balance is a skill that must be cultivated. The following are on-the-bike balance exercises that can be done just about anywhere. Give them some practice to really improve your riding.

1.   To stay balanced at a slow speed while remaining precisely on a predetermined line, try following a basketball court border or a painted street line. Go as slow as possible using a low gear while following the line without quivering. If you can hold this over a fairly long distance, practice it again on something a little more risky, such as the edge of a curb.

2.   Still following the line, lean your body to the left and then to the right. Repeat this exercise in the attack/ready position and while shifting your weight forward and then aft. As you get more comfortable doing these exercises, try increasing the amount of lean. Practice this regularly to keep your skills sharp. It can even be part of a pre-ride warm up.

3. Try holding a straight line while riding the bike no-handed. Riding at a moderate pace, work on keeping your body still with your arms down at your sides. Try to increase the amount of time you can hold it. Once you have that mastered, try leaning the bike with your hips to put the bike into a turn. Once you can steer to both the left and the right and then resume a straight line, you'll have developed exceptional balance and a good feel for how your hips can directionally control the bike.

4. Learn to track-stand. While riding normally in the saddle, slowly brake to a complete stop while holding the bike still with the crank arms level and without putting your feet down. Keep your weight pushed into your pedals while making small left-right-left-right steering shifts to help you hold it longer. Stay relaxed and have a soft grip on the handlebars while keeping your corrections minimal. Do this in both the seated position and the attack/ready position. Challenge yourself to hold this as long as possible; if you can do it for half a minute, you're good at it. You can then take it to the next level by occasionally practicing during your trail riding. Just be careful, relaxed, and don't overthink it. This is an extremely useful skill to have out on the trails.

5. Practice slow speed figure eights. This is something that should be done on soft, grassy surfaces just in case you get completely off balance. If you're clipped in to your pedals, be prepared to unclip in a hurry to put your feet down, which in itself is a skill that needs to be practiced. It may be helpful to lay a couple objects on the ground, spaced far enough apart to create a figure-eight pattern around them. Start with a large pattern until it gets easier, and then challenge yourself by tightening it up until you can barely make the turns. Try doing this exercise at various speeds, until you're going so slow that you're almost performing a track stand. This skill is especially useful for situations such as switchbacks.

Final Thoughts on Balance

Balancing requires keeping your weight centered on your pedals and remaining upright. Since riding conditions are often in flux, you'll be constantly moving around to stay centered. No matter which way you need to shift your weight (forward for climbing and accelerating, aft for descending and braking, sideways for turns, etc.), your balance point should always be centered on the pedals.

Sometimes there are personal circumstances that can affect your sense of balance. Because the fluid in your inner ear is the primary sensory input for balance, anything that disrupts its operation can be detrimental, such as an ear infection. Also, if you've been drinking alcohol or if you've taken any kind of drug that alters your state of mind, it's not a good idea to go riding.

Balance is primarily an automatic process of your sensory systems, but intuition sometimes plays a role in reacting to the trails. It comes from your learned experiences of previous imbalances and is a part of becoming a better rider. However, in some situations your intuition will cause you to overreact and inadvertently throw off your balance. For example:

- A steep descent may cause you to unconsciously position your hips way too far back, as if you're trying to get further away from the danger. You'll be at the back end of your weight-shifting range with nowhere else to go but forward. This will leave you unprepared to fully control the bike. Besides not having your weight properly balanced and centered on your pedals, you'll also be unable to pull your handlebars up to lift your front wheel over an object that suddenly appears. You may even flip over backwards when you hit it.

- A rocky, technical section of trail may cause you take a foot off a pedal in an attempt to steady yourself while you struggle to stay in control. Throwing down an anchor in this situation can further throw your balance off. This is a sketchy way to ride and puts you in a situation that you may not be able to recover from. You'll be better off by either coasting through it in the attack position or by pedaling through it while expertly keeping your balance.

- The habit of sticking a foot out in the turns will unweight the tires and possibly throw off your balance, increasing the chance of sliding out. In most cases, you're better off keeping your weight nailed into the pedals so that it transfers firmly into the tires.

Habits like these will take a conscious effort to overcome. Keep practicing the balance exercises of your choice to continuously sharpen your skills and eliminate bad habits. This will pay big dividends out on the trails. With enough practice, you can become a highly skilled rider with a natural ability to stay balanced and centered under most circumstances. Once you're balanced, you'll feel loose and agile, and you'll be able to respond quickly to the changing terrain while staying in control.

On a final note, balance significantly depends on the motor control provided by the brain. During intense physical exercise, the brain's energy consumption increases and has a higher dependency on oxygen for proper functioning. So if you're fatigued from a long, hard, and oxygen-consuming ride, your sense of balance could become impaired because your brain is not getting enough oxygen. Keep this in mind and stay safe!

Aerobic Exercise and Anaerobic Exercise

Aerobic exercise and anaerobic exercise - these two terminologies can cause some confusion, and descriptions can sometimes be complex, but you only need some basic understanding to apply it to the sport. These are two different ways that your muscles burn fuel for energy. With aerobic exercise, the primary fuel is oxygen. For anaerobic exercise, the primary fuel is glucose, which is a type of sugar that's absorbed into the bloodstream and muscle tissues by digestion.

Oxygen is the fuel that muscles use most efficiently and remains the primary source of fuel during low to moderate intensity exercise. This could constitute a good portion of the ride, including level ground, down hills, and over gently rolling landscape. However, you're never fully aerobic or fully anaerobic because you'll always be burning both kinds of fuel. Your metabolism will change the proportions of each to match changes in exercise intensity, but as long as oxygen is still primary, you're still aerobic. As the intensity increases, there will come a point when the maximum amount of oxygen that can be transported and used is reached. This is called VO_2 max. Its timing depends on the individual, and it is a good measure of physical fitness.

When the activity becomes so intense that oxygen delivery can't keep up with the demand (even if VO_2 max is not reached), glucose will become the primary source of fuel and your exercise is considered anaerobic. As glucose is converted to energy in the muscle cells, a by-product called lactic acid (lactate) is formed. Your blood flow will work to remove this acid from your muscles, and your liver will use oxygen to convert it back into glucose. While this is a good recycling arrangement that can help to keep you going, sustained anaerobic exercise will build up lactic acid in muscle tissues because it's not as easily removed from the body as carbon dioxide is. At the point that lactic acid builds up faster than it can be removed, you've hit what's called your "lactate threshold." The timing of this will depend on the individual and is another good measure of physical fitness. As this build-up continues, it will cause a burning sensation in your muscles that comes with a feeling of extreme fatigue. This can progress to nausea and even vomiting and can tense up your muscles so badly that it stops you in your tracks. This is what you call "hitting the wall."

VO_2 max is the best measure for cardiovascular fitness, maximal aerobic power, and long-term endurance, and lactate threshold level is the best measure for climbing ability on long and/or steep hills. Every mountain biker would love to have both a higher VO_2 max and a higher lactate threshold, but this doesn't come easily. Raising them can only be achieved with continued exercise and proper nutrition; there's no shortcut to hard work. But it stands to reason that the better your ability to provide oxygen to your muscles, the longer you can prevent them from going anaerobic. Improving how you breathe is one way to potentially bring some quick results.

Better Breathing

The efficiency of the lungs' ability to oxygenate the blood is an important factor in performance. Proper breathing technique can reduce fatigue and increase stamina, but it's an often overlooked component of athletic training. Breathing is an automatic bodily function that's unique in that it can be regulated voluntarily, which makes it customizable for optimum performance.

Breathing is how air is pulled into the lungs for its oxygen to be absorbed into the blood. The circulatory system then carries the oxygen-rich blood from the lungs to the brain and the muscles' cells for conversion to energy. As a result of this conversion, carbon dioxide is formed as a waste product, which is then carried back to the lungs and exhaled. This cycle repeats over and over very rapidly, but how fast and efficient this happens is a big determination of athletic performance. The more oxygen the muscles can utilize, the better their power generation and endurance will be.

The air we breathe contains 21 percent oxygen, and of this, typically around 40 percent is absorbed into the body. This figure can be improved on and is dependent on a number of factors, including the quantity of blood that your heart is capable of pumping (cardio), your red blood cell count, the condition of your arteries, veins and capillaries (vascular), and the efficiency of your muscle cells.

Improving the performance of your cardiovascular and muscular systems will take some time and work and will be covered in the Conditioning section of the book. Proper hydration is also essential for performance because dehydration causes a reduced blood flow. This has a direct effect on the efficiency of your cardiovascular system and its ability to deliver oxygen[13].

As a mountain biker, you've no doubt experienced the huffing and puffing that comes during intensive efforts, most notably during uphill riding. Maybe there's been a time that you had to get off your bike while gasping for air, nauseated and hunched over. When you're exerting yourself, you're breathing harder to supply more oxygen to your muscles. But if you don't get enough as you push onward, you'll end up reaching your limit and "blowing up." Obviously, we want to prevent this from happening as best as we can. That's why it's important to use the best breathing techniques possible.

Breathing with your Diaphragm

The diaphragm is a large dome-shaped sheet of muscle at the bottom of the rib cage that contracts to pull air into the lungs. This muscle is capable of taking deep breaths that fully inflate the lungs. Diaphragm breathing, otherwise known as belly breathing, is the way everyone breathes when they are born. If you watch a baby breathing, you'll notice their stomach moving up and down. It's a natural way of breathing that can help maximize air intake[14]. The diaphragm truly reigns supreme for moving air. But there are many people who "chest breathe" using their rib intercostal muscles while doing very little breathing with their diaphragm muscle. The rib muscles intended function is primarily to aid in expanding the rib cage, and secondarily to further expand and contract the chest to maximize volume. In any case, about 80 percent of the work should be done by the diaphragm.

Many reasons exist for this chest breathing phenomenon, such as age, chronic stress, a sedentary lifestyle, and slouching. Chest breathing typically results in shallow breaths that do not inflate the lower 1/3 of the lungs. If you're currently a chest breather, it's possible to reverse this, but you'll need to practice diaphragmatic breathing regularly until it becomes second nature. The goal is to activate the diaphragm to the point where you no longer have to think about it. If you're not breathing with your diaphragm 24/7, it will take a conscious effort to correct this.

The diaphragm and the rib intercostal muscles can also become fatigued during prolonged high-intensity exercise. It's what adds to that overall feeling of exhaustion that you get on difficult rides. The more your breathing is strained, the more energy you'll use to breathe and the less energy your legs will receive. Research has shown that making the respiratory muscles stronger will reduce their fatigue during exercise, thereby allowing more blood to flow to the leg muscles. This will have a direct effect on riding performance.

Improving your breathing can increase the dosage of oxygen that your muscles receive while decreasing the work of breathing[15]. Once you're aware of the way you breathe, you can focus on improving your respiratory system and make it work to its fullest potential. It's a quick way to gain significant performance results. If practicing improved breathing techniques helps you make it up a hill or across a finish line a little faster, it's definitely worth trying. The trick is to always breathe diaphragmatically when you're on your bike . . . or during any kind of exercise, for that matter. As a mountain biker and an athlete, diaphragmatic breathing is the best way to utilize as much of your oxygen-absorbing lung tissue as possible and an easy way to enhance performance.

Better Breathing Practices

Any low-cost, safe, and legal performance enhancer should be embraced with open arms. With better breathing, it's possible to avoid, or at least to delay, reaching your VO_2 max. This will allow you to go further and ride harder. Use these breathing techniques for optimal oxygen uptake:

1. Breathing through your nose, mouth, or both - which is best? Because inhaling through the nose allows nostril hairs to filter out particulates, and exhaling through the nose may slow down dehydration, nose

breathing is superior under normal conditions. Maybe you've gotten the advice that it's best to inhale through the nose and exhale through the mouth to regulate breathing. While this may work just fine during casual riding, nose breathing by itself typically doesn't provide enough airflow when you're exercising, and it doesn't come close to supplying the required volume of air during intense cycling. For this reason, a nose/mouth combination will work best.

2.   For sustained efforts that are not at a high level of intensity, relax your jaw and open your mouth enough to allow air to pass through. Breathe in as deeply as you naturally can, filling your lungs from top to bottom.

3.   After every inhalation, pause and hold the lungful for a brief moment. Then as you exhale, slightly purse your lips (close tighter) to provide enough restriction to regulate the pace of your breathing. Pick a pace of exhalation that's comfortable and feels natural for the current degree of exertion. These techniques will give you sustainable energy while preventing you from becoming light-headed or even dizzy from hyperventilation, which is a condition that results from breathing more than is required by your metabolic rate. Hyperventilating will rapidly expel the carbon dioxide (CO_2) in your blood, which will result in a low CO_2 level and a rise in blood pH. This in turn will constrict the blood vessels, thereby reducing blood flow and negatively affecting the function of the muscles. Basically, you need CO_2 in your blood just as much as you need oxygen.

4.   During any kind of effort, exhale to completely but naturally let out all of your air. This important step will provide more room for oxygen on the intake and is an efficient way to breathe. As soon as you've naturally let out all of your air, immediately inhale without a pause.

5.   If your exercise intensity and exertion level has reached the point where the pace of pausing and using pursed lip exhalations doesn't allow enough oxygen, you'll need to drop your jaw further for unrestricted exhales. Remember to keep your face and lips completely relaxed. Use rapid and deep breathing for maximum airflow to provide the oxygen that your body is crying for.

6.   If you're still struggling and your breathing is ragged and out of control, you've probably exceeded your VO_2 max and your lactate threshold. At this point, it's probably best to back off your intensity and recover for a bit.

7.   Always maintain an awareness of your breath while remaining focused on the task at hand.

Mental Focus and State of Mind

The mind is a powerful instrument for achieving goals. It can also be a big roadblock if it provides unnecessary fear or if it wants to quit before the body has reached its physical limitations. Your state of mind is as important, if not more, than any physical skill or ability. It's what determines how well you ride, how safe your ride will be, and how you perceive your exhaustion[16].

If your mind is going over another aspect of your life or debating some kind of problem that you're having, you won't be mentally "in the here and now," and you won't be properly coping with the task at hand. Too much thinking can be a distraction. A cacophony of thoughts in your head will disconnect you from your body, tense you up, and throw you off balance. Try keeping your thoughts simple and basic, such as those dealing with the tasks at hand:

Breathing: Paying attention to your breathing rhythm can clear your mind, relax you, and release your tension. This kind of breathing awareness is the best way to filter out distracting thoughts and help bring focus without fixation.

Looking: Using good vision technique can also give you something to think about that's not distracting. By putting the task of continuously scanning far ahead of you into the forefront of your thoughts, you can alleviate the habit of fixating while blocking out distractions.

Pedaling: If you're not pedaling in circles naturally, you should pay some attention to that as well. It's a rhythmic activity that only needs a low level of thought, so it's a perfect occupier.

Positioning: If you're off the saddle, your thoughts should include moving into the correct body positioning to keep your weight balanced on your pedals. This is something that should be natural, so don't let yourself overthink this.

Conversely, you could be worrying too much about the task at hand, with your focus overly engrossed on certain details of your ride. By fixating on difficult parts of the trail, say a particular rock or boulder that's got you worried, you can tense up and overthink your next course of action. All of this decision making can actually get you into trouble; you're not flowing with the trail and you're probably not using correct vision techniques. Avoid this kind of distraction by continuously scanning ahead, relaxing, and working on your flow. This comes from the mind . . . and it takes some trail experience to master this. You'll know you're flowing when a series of obstacles seem to string together and you're able to glide through it all with very little fear and without any mishaps. You'll be maintaining focus and resisting distractions, whether they come from the environment or from within yourself.

Your emotional state of mind is another factor that affects how you ride. Successful riding and having fun can bring on positive emotions, while a crash can really put you in the negative. Because you'll always have setbacks, it's important to learn how to shrug them off and continue on positively. Try self-talking with positive words. This kind of discipline will give you the ability to bounce back and regain your lost focus. When you're feeling good, you'll do much better. And if you're enjoying yourself, try smiling as you ride. This will all go a long way toward making you a great rider.

Being mentally prepared with strength of mind and clarity of thought applies not only when you're in the moment, but also before you begin your ride. This will determine whether you'll be off to a good start or a bad one and could affect your entire ride. Pre-ride thinking is a good opportunity to strategize how you're going to attack the trails and improve your riding. Take the time to decide how you're going to defeat the challenging parts, no matter what they are: a particularly steep climb, a technical downhill, or a Strava time that you're trying to beat on a particular trail. Go over them in your mind, positively building yourself up with skills that you know you have and with strategies that you know will work.

Going through preparation rituals, whatever they may be, can sometimes provide a sense of readiness for action. Make sure your bike is tuned and ready, your gear is neat and orderly, your electronics are set properly, you've got the right nutrition in you, you're hydrated, you've relieved yourself, and you've done your warm-up exercises. These things can all play a part in feeling mentally prepared. Everybody is different, so do whatever it takes. Just make sure you arrive at the trailhead early enough to get it all done without causing your friends to wait on you.

Mental Imagery

Using mental imagery to visualize what you'll be doing is a basic training tool that's frequently used by athletes. It's an effective technique for acquiring the right motor skills and using good execution. Most elite athletes routinely practice visualization to achieve superior performances. Whether or not this is more effective than actual training is controversial, but the fact remains that it does work[17]. For mountain biking, it's a powerful tool that can have a big impact on riding performance.

There are two different ways of using imagery, internal and external. Internal imagery simulates yourself in the action by looking through your eyes and experiencing the imagined sensations of trail riding with your body. With external imagery, you view yourself from the perspective of an external observer, much like looking at the pictures in your favorite mountain biking magazine and pretending that it's you.

Which version of mental imagery is best is disputed by conflicting studies, so the best advice is to try both to see which one works better for you.

Using imagery takes imagination, especially if you're inventing trails, but if you're mentally going over trails that you're familiar with, it becomes much easier. If there's a particular section or multiple sections that you struggled with or crashed on, close your eyes and visualize yourself doing it better. Try to reproduce a detailed and realistic experience as best as you can by including not only what you see, but also what you typically hear, what you physically feel, the weather, and how you feel mentally. If you can acutely imagine feeling the bike and the trail with your body, you stand the best chance of ingraining improved riding skills. Imagine the feel of the rocks and the bumps under your tires, holding the handlebars, moving your body to keep your balance on the pedals, absorbing shocks, leaning the bike into the turns . . . these are powerful thoughts that can seriously improve your riding.

The beauty of mental imagery is that you can control the speed and the technicality of the trail. On the difficult parts, run it in slow motion to get your technique right. Slowly speed it up until you can do it successfully at full speed. You can do all of this without being afraid and without getting tired. For the best results, keep it real. Choose something that you'll actually be doing, not the monster drop-offs you see in the magazines. Also, imagine success, not failure. Doing the latter will not help you and can actually lead to a failure.

This is an exercise, and like any exercise, it takes practice to get better. You need to be consistent to make a difference. Set aside a certain time of day to do this. It should be in a quiet location where you won't be disturbed. Don't do it so often that you get bored with it. Just ten minutes every other day will be enough.

Mental Toughness

"Mental toughness" is a common term with a wide application in the athletic world. For mountain biking, it's not only applicable, it's an essential quality for successful trail riding. It's a can-do attitude. Riding timid, unsure, scared . . . these things will get you into trouble. So, how do you become mentally tough? How do you change what's going on in your head?

Confidence is the key. By developing the right level of confidence in yourself and your abilities, you'll take your riding skills and physical endurance beyond your perceived limits. Everybody's different and there will always be somebody better than you on any given day. Acknowledge that, but don't let it bother you. Just be aware of your current performance levels and develop specific plans for attaining goals. You know that you have skills and that you have a degree of physical fitness. You just need to leverage what you've got by being mentally tough. This will push you much further than a mind that feels overwhelmed by exhaustion. If you have a competitive nature and a tough attitude, you probably have the mental toughness to win[18].

Personality and individual psychological differences can play a big part in how mentally tough one can be. Those who are driven to win and are willing to push themselves to the edge are usually the ones who succeed in becoming world-class champions. They focus on their goals and don't let go. This high level of internal motivation overrides the pain of competition and brings them to victory.

Don't look for perfection. You'll never be a perfect rider because there's no such thing. Instead, pursue a goal of excellence. Everybody will make some kind of mistake once in a while. It could be a spot you had to put your foot down, a section that you had to get off and walk, or even a crash. Whatever the case, how you recover from it, learn from it, and use it to your advantage is another aspect of mental toughness. Learn not to over-criticize yourself; this will only lead to excessive anger and frustration. It's like saying to yourself: "I can't do it." Once you go down that mental road, you'll end up making more mistakes. Things will just keep getting worse. Instead, give yourself just enough criticism to deal with the situation better the next time, and then put it out of your mind. Continue on with a positive attitude. Coping with mishaps and underperformance by remaining optimistic and keeping it fun is an important component of being confident and tough[19].

Your emotions play a big part, but you'll never be emotionally perfect because having a little fear or a little frustration is natural. But you do need to find a balance because stress, anxiety, and anger are emotions that can become your worst enemy. For example, if you enter a race, you'll definitely have some fear and anxiety on the morning of the race. Having some degree of these emotions can help you perform well, but if you become obsessed with performance and pressure yourself too hard, you'll overemphasize controlling your bike, tense up, and lose your flow. This will hinder your performance and can lead to mishaps. Conversely, if you're carefree, loose, and overly-relaxed, you'll lose focus, which can lead to carelessness and mistakes. To beat the competition, you need to find a balance between your fear and your confidence to obtain your optimal performance level. This is when you'll have the control and focus you need to bring your skills, techniques, and endurance to the edge of their limits . . . and you'll have the mental toughness of a winner.

The Zone

"The Zone" . . . you may have heard of this term. It's associated with the high, error-free performances of elite athletes and is referred to in a variety of sports. Being "in the zone" has been described as: *total concentration and involvement, control, a unity of mind and body and a sense of personal fulfilment at an optimal level of performance[20].*

For mountain biking, this is when your riding will be natural, with no disconnect between your body and your mind; a merge of action and awareness. You'll be relaxed on your bike, but you'll have a high level of focus. On an emotional level, your confidence and self-esteem will be high. Your actions will be accomplished without conscious thought; everything will go well as you ride out the trails. And in spite of the technical difficulties of the terrain, you'll find yourself flowing smoothly. You'll be in the zone.

To achieve this state of being, you need to ride trails that are not too easy or too difficult. If it's too easy, it gives your mind the ability to wander, lose focus, and become disconnected. If the trail is too difficult, you'll be thinking about your difficulties and making decisions like "lift here, lean there, or wiggle around this." In either case, you'll be doing too much thinking and will not attain a total mind-body connection. Of course, you should take rides that push the limits of your abilities to gain experience, but when the level of challenge matches your abilities, this is when you can excel and get into the zone.

Getting into the zone cannot be intentionally achieved; it's something that just happens when everything is working right. The right trail difficulty combined with a clear mind that's confident and focused are the basic requirements. Clear your head of higher level thoughts by concentrating on your breathing. Vision, pedaling, and body position require a somewhat higher level of thought and are tasks that should transpire naturally when you're in the zone. In the book *Foundations of Sport and Exercise Psychology**, ten essential elements of the zone are summarized as follows:

1. ***Balance of challenge and skills:*** *For flow to occur it is imperative that an athlete believes that he or she has the skills to successfully meet the physical, technical, and mental challenges faced*

2. ***Complete absorption in the activity:*** *The participant is so involved in the activity that nothing else seems to matter.*

3. ***Clear goals:*** *Goals are so clearly set that the athlete knows exactly what to do. This clarity of intention facilitates concentration and attention.*

4. ***Merging of action and awareness:*** *The athlete is aware of their actions but not of the awareness itself.*

5. ***Total concentration on the task at hand:*** *Performers report that they feel like a beam of concentrated energy. Crowd noise, opponent reactions, and other distractions simply don't matter. The focus of attention is clearly on the task at hand.*

6. ***Loss of self-consciousness:*** *Performers report that their ego is completely lost in the activity itself.*

7. ***A sense of control:*** *This element of flow refers to the fact that the athlete is not actively aware of control; rather, they are simply not worried by the possibility of lack of control.*

8. ***No goals or rewards external to the activity:*** *The athlete participates purely because of the activity itself, without seeking any other reward.*

9. ***Transformation of time:*** *Athletes in flow typically report that time seems to speed up; although for some it slows down. However, most individuals in flow report transformations in their perceptions of time.*

10. ***Effortless movement:*** *This element refers to the fact that the athlete is performing well but yet is not really thinking about it and doesn't appear to be trying too hard.*

* Reprinted by permission from R.S. Weinberg and D. Gould, *Foundations of Sport and Exercise Psychology Web Study Guide,* 6th ed. (Champaign, IL: Human Kinetics, 2015).

To enhance your riding and gain a competitive advantage, getting into the zone and holding it is a highly desirable state. You'll peak your efficiency and your safety and will gain much more enjoyment and satisfaction from your rides. This transcendence of consciousness can be achieved by anyone with the right state of mind. And once you've got it, you'll have found your Zen.

CHAPTER ELEVEN

On the Move

EVERYTHING COVERED IN the previous two chapters is integral with the activities described in this chapter. Body positioning, braking, pedaling, shifting, vision, breathing, balance, and your state of mind are all necessary components that must work together for successful trail riding. By applying these techniques to the following subjects, you'll become a more proficient rider who can take on and conquer just about any challenge.

Obstacles

Obstacles are anything that obstructs or hinders your progress. They could be rocks, roots, water-bars, or some kind of tree debris. They could be fist sized, boulder sized, or anything in between. They could be sharp and jagged or round and smooth. Sometimes a trail can have a mixture of all these descriptions. Every situation will be unique and must be dealt with accordingly.

The first step is to identify the possible line options on these random landscapes. It's common to have more than one to choose from, resulting in the need for rapid decision making. And the best line may not always be the smoothest one; it could actually be the one that takes you over an object instead of around it. This situation could arise if the smooth path takes you toward some other, less manageable objects or dangerously angles away toward the side of the trail. Look up the path for the easiest and flowiest line, such as rocks that form a "V" channel that you can pass through. Choose a line that allows you to glide through with the least amount of trouble without sending you into a dangerous situation.

In addition to acute vision skills, you'll need to be balanced, steady, and ready. Unless you're climbing, this means getting into the attack position, loose and limber, and ready to respond to the trail. You should be prepared to move up, down, forward, aft, left, right . . . .whatever is required. Rough trails will beat you up, rattle your bones, and tense up your muscles until you're completely worn down. The attack position will allow your arms and knees to flex and absorb a good degree of the impacts and shaking, easing the beating on your body while allowing you to be more relaxed.

If the bumps and rocks are small enough, you can ride right over them at just about any speed. But as the sizes get larger, a higher speed may be needed to help your tires ride on the tops of the bumps. Riding controllably fast without brakes on bumpy terrain has the effect of making the trail feel smoother and the big bumps feel smaller, effectively keeping things under control. Just beware of rocks that are on top of a base of smaller rocks and sand. This tends to create a mushy surface that can seriously impede your forward progress and could even cause your front tire to plow if you were to turn or brake suddenly.

Going fast over the rough stuff can occasionally be a little unnerving and may even feel as though you're on the verge of losing control. If this happens, try not to tense up; this will only break your confidence and reduce your responsiveness. Do your best to stay confident and relaxed. As your bike shakes and bounces below you, maintain the attack position while keeping your weight centered on your pedals, adjust your speed, and most importantly, look far ahead.

When the path you're traveling on is a minefield of objects, like a garden of baby-head sized rocks, you'll need to dodge and parry your way down the trail using quick reflexes to avoid hitting them. It's a dance of carefully orchestrated balance, control, and vision. Pedal strikes can be common in these situations, so to avoid this, put the pedal in question to the topmost position as it passes over the object. Sometimes there are objects on both sides, and you'll be forced to ratchet your cranks (pedaling with quick quarter-turn backpedals) to keep both pedals high.

If you're squeezing your way through two rocks, be mindful of where your rear tire is tracking because it needs to make it through that gap as well. When swerving around rocks, it's possible that your rear tire will hit them even though your front tire has cleared them. Although this is controllable, bigger rocks will need a wider berth to ensure that both your pedals and your rear tire go around them. You'll also need to be careful not to allow your rear derailleur to hit any rocks, as this could cause serious damage to it.

While squirming around objects can work a lot of the time, sometimes the trail will dictate that you have to go over them. If it's medium sized, maybe up to five inches, you may be able to simply run into it and ride over (something that 29ers excel at). But for bigger or sharp-edged obstacles, step-shaped rocks, small logs or big roots, the following maneuvers will help to get you up and over:

The Manual: This is a maneuver that lifts the front wheel up a ledge or an object so that you can continue on without stopping. Lifting the front end needs to be an instinctive action, and to consistently lift long enough and high enough under various circumstances, it should be practiced regularly. If you're new at this and worried about falling, practice on grass to help soften the landing, although the best control will be on asphalt and pavement.

1. Start on flat ground by rolling along at a jogging pace. A lowered seat will help to complete this maneuver. Get into a low gear with your crank arms level and your body in the attack position. Just before the lift, push your weight down with your chest, bending at the elbows and knees while compressing the forks as much as you can. This is called preloading, and it's kind of like pushing down a diving springboard.

2. As your forks rebound, lean your weight back while simultaneously straightening your arms until they're locked out, pushing down with your heels and extending your legs. All of this is done in one fluid motion and should result in the front tire rising upward.

3. Normally, your center of balance is on the bottom bracket, but to aid the handlebar pull and remain balanced long enough to ride forward, your center of gravity should momentarily be shifted rearward, balanced on the tire.

4. Cover your rear brake in case you overlift. The rear brake can be skillfully used to control the lift, although this is better accomplished by balance and speed. The rear brake can also move the g-force forward and kill the lift, if needed.

5. Initially, practice this lifting maneuver on something easy, such as a roadside curb. You'll find that you only need to unweight the front tire enough to pull it up and over. If you lift too high, you'll lose your flow; too low, and you'll bash into it. Timing is also critical, so practice until you can flow over it using only your peripheral vision.

6. Performing a manual while riding uphill will require some strategy to prevent a loss of momentum. As you approach the ledge or object, there's a probability that you'll be seated in a climbing position. To maintain your momentum, you'll need to stand just before the lift and give a strong pedal stroke. You'll find that the front end will rise easier on an incline and that pedaling through this maneuver keeps your hill climb right on track.

7. Whenever you've lifted your front tire onto an object or ledge, the rear tire will hit a split second later. At this point, you'll need to shift your weight forward to unweight the rear. How much to shift depends on the height of the object. For smaller lifts, simply returning your weight to neutral and allowing the rear to follow like a trailer will suffice. On higher lifts, you'll need to heave your weight forward and upward by the hips to unweight the rear end, bending your knees as the rear end comes up. Keep your weight forward until both tires are up, using pedal strokes until the maneuver is completed.

The bunny hop

The Bunny Hop: There may come a time when you find yourself rolling along at a pretty good pace with nothing in the way, and then suddenly a log appears, crossing over the path right in front of you. In this situation, jumping both tires up and over the log with only a minimal loss of momentum is the way to go. This fantastic maneuver is called a "bunny hop," and it is not hard to learn if you're already proficient at manuals. Practice using these steps:

Set up a small object to jump over, such as a stick.

1. Like the manual, get into the attack position with your seat lowered and proceed toward the object at a fast jogging pace. As you approach the object, keep your pedals level and your rear foot slightly toes-down.

2. Like the manual, preload the shocks by bringing your chest further down and forward, close to the handlebars in one hard motion, and then lift the front end just as you would for a manual.

3. With your front end up, arms extended, knees slightly bent, and your body more or less upright, abruptly spring your feet upward by moving your hips back while bending the knees. It should feel like you're scooping the bike forward. At this point, your rear tire should come off the ground. This takes good timing and needs to be done in one fluid motion. If you're using clip-in pedals, they can be used to cheat the rear up, but the basic premise should be to use the ground like a springboard.

4. Your timing is dependent on the speed you're traveling, so practice using a variety of speeds.

5. Once you get the timing right, try hopping over larger objects. One of the best places to practice is over parking lot speed bumps.

6. When you feel proficient at it, practice your new skill on the trails whenever the opportunity arises.

The following are some additional things to consider when you're hitting technical terrain:

- **Regulate your speed:** When you're tackling obstacles out on the trails, the first thing to consider is your speed. Too much speed could cause you to become scared and tense, leading to a loss of control and possibly a crash; too slow of a speed may not allow you to clear the objects without coming to a stop. Regulating your speed is critical, and every situation is different and needs to be evaluated on its own merits.

- **Stay relaxed:** Stay relaxed and allow your arms and legs to absorb the impacts to ensure that you can control your balance. Let the bike move below you while your head and torso stay relatively level. Tensing up can be your biggest obstacle. You'll end up clutching the bike tightly and being jolted around by every bump. This will make it much harder to absorb impacts and stay in control.

- **Don't stare:** Keep your head up and always concentrate on keeping your central vision moving further up the trail. Pick the best lines through and over the obstacles ahead of time, and follow through using your peripheral vision when the object is close. It's important, as it always is, not to stare at the object you're going over, even if it caught you off guard because you didn't see it.

- **Slippery when wet:** With recent rain, it's best to assume that every root and rock is slippery. They have the potential to catch you off guard and cause your tire to slide out from under you. To help prevent a wash-out, do your braking before you get to the wet objects, not on top of them. Don't pedal on top of them either, as this could cause your rear tire to slip. Instead, let off the power and carefully coast over it. If you can lift your front tire completely up and over the object, that's even better. If it's a root and contact is inevitable, crossing at a 90-degree angle will help to prevent a sideways slide.

Managing Momentum

"Managing" momentum can be defined as: 1) using it to carry you forward as much as possible without pedaling, 2) avoiding unnecessary braking, and 3) preventing excessive momentum from creating a dangerous situation.

It takes power to build momentum, but it takes skill and experience to maintain it. While pedaling is the usual source of power, it's something purely derived from energy that the body produces. Because there's an upper limit to this energy, it's important to use strategies that extend your energy reserves. This includes taking advantage of any opportunity to gain momentum from other sources. Downhill riding is one good way, but it isn't the only option: varying terrain can offer ample opportunities to build and maintain free momentum.

When the terrain rises up and dips down, energy can be gained from the small bits of downhill, but simply rolling down them will not be enough. To take full advantage of these trail contours and extract maximum energy from them, the bike needs to be pulled up or pushed down in response to these small elevation changes. Pushing the bike downward on the down-slopes has the effect of adding weight for increased momentum, and pulling it up on the up-slopes subtracts weight to help preserve momentum. These body motions, commonly known as "pumping," will add more energy to your forward motion.

Let's say there's a small mound on the trail, perhaps a two-foot rise that you'll be rolling over. You may be tempted to catch some air on this, which can be fun, but try instead to take advantage of it by using the following steps in a smooth, fluid, and quick succession. This will maximize your pump and create as much momentum as possible:

1. Lower your seat if you have a dropper-post. This will give your body a greater range of motion to maximize the influence of your weight.

2. Get into a high attack position.

3. If the incline is steep, you can lean forward and down to preload your front end just prior to hitting it, much the same way you would for a manual.

4. When you begin to roll up the mound, pull the bike up by bending your elbows and knees in unison with the rise in elevation. If you did a preload, you'll need to spring your weight back enough to get it off your front tire.

5. As you cross over the top, center your weight over the pedals.

6. As you begin to roll down the other side, push the bike downward by extending your arms and legs while simultaneously pushing forward into the handlebars. Use the power of your legs to really drive it down.

7. At the base of the down-slope, return your weight to center.

8. You'll be extending your arms and legs in the low parts and bending them on the high parts. Throughout this maneuver, you should get the feeling that your torso is more or less level while the bike is moving up and down beneath you. Your limbs will seem to be flexing equal to the height of the rises in the terrain.

A dip in the trail will have the same concept as the mound, except in reverse. When you hit the dip, drive it downward, and when you rise out of it, pull the bike upward. These body motions should be performed throughout your ride whenever the trail has any changes or irregularities and is not limited to just the general ups and downs of the trail. You can pump many objects such as big rocks and roots, which will not only help with momentum by taking advantage of their back sides but also keep you light on the front sides so that you're not bashing into everything. Berms and corners are another great place to pump.

One way to learn how to be proficient at pumping is at a pump track. This is a specially designed course with a series of rollers and berms set up in a continuous loop. Once you get moving and it's done correctly, you should be able to pump these rollers and berms without pedaling and still maintain momentum around the track. These tracks are becoming more and more common, so if there's one in your area, you may want to practice on it to increase your proficiency.

Lifting up and pushing down. It's all a part of keeping the bike connected with the trail while staying in better control, no matter what the trail situation is. Use your eyes to study the path ahead and where you can take advantage of momentum-gaining opportunities. If you're always on the lookout and responding to everything you see, you should be quite busy with your elbows and knees. While faster speeds and more aggressive terrain will require faster pumps, it should still feel like you're smoothly passing over the terrain while your bike bucks and rolls beneath you. If you can pull this off, you'll be flowing with the trail . . . and you'll get faster.

Practice pumping on every ride, but don't be overly concerned with it because it's something that needs to develop naturally. Start by trying it in slow motion in places that can be obviously and easily pumped. Just remember to keep your muscles relaxed and always have fun with it.

Cornering

If riding faster is your goal, perfecting cornering techniques is the best way to speed up and bring flow to your ride. Confidently whipping through the turns will make your rides fast, fun, and satisfying. You'll be far less likely to crash, and you'll be able to take on increasingly difficult challenges.

As a new mountain biker, skilled cornering is one of the harder things to learn. It involves a variety of different techniques used over various types of terrain. The corners could be long and wide, short and sharp, bermed, flat, off-camber, uphill, downhill, rocky, gravelly, sandy, muddy, tacky, loamy, hard-packed, or any combination of these. The conditions will need to be assessed before you enter the turn while simultaneously deciding what actions need to be made, both consciously and subconsciously. The following sections break down and analyze the tasks and techniques to use. The goal is to put them together into one seamless operation to make your cornering smooth, fast, and precise.

Use good vision and select the best line: To sweep through corners, you have to see ahead to make an assessment and choose the best line. You need to know the surface conditions and evaluate your entry point and your angle of attack well ahead of time. Your evaluation will also determine speed, pedal position, the degree of lean, and how to brake.

As you approach a corner, study it from as far ahead as possible. There could be a variety of conditions that need to be considered in a second's time. Making your pre-assessment early is the best way to give yourself enough time to properly set yourself up for the corner at the right speed and on the right line.

Most often, you'll want to line up on the outside and start the turn wide, and then cut toward the apex on the inner side of the turn, followed by exit on the outside edge. This is an aggressive method that cuts down the sharpness of the corner, flows better, and nicely sets up your trajectory for the next turn, making it an overall faster way to go. There are, however, many circumstances that can change this strategy. For example:

- The normal route is so worn and grooved from other riders that avoiding these lines is safer and faster.

- Braking bumps before the turn force you to ride on a smoother part.

- The turn has obstacles that must be avoided.

- If it's half solid surface and half loose gravel, it's often best to stay on the hard pack.

- If it's bermed or has a small lip on the outside edge, ride on it for the fastest speed.

- If the turn is off-camber (the inner edge is the high side), it would be better to stay on the high side at a slower speed due to reduced traction. As you come around the corner, drop to the lower side for the exit.

These are just a few examples; each corner will need to be quickly evaluated and followed through with decisive action. Avoiding certain things may put you on a line that weaves, but it will still be faster than bashing into something or sliding out. Keep your chin up and look far ahead. Much will come from experience, so practice taking corners slowly, and then speed up as your comfort level rises.

Correctly place your pedals: In most cases, corners are best executed with the outside pedal at the bottom (six o'clock) position. As you begin your turn, drop that outside pedal and bury your weight onto it while keeping your knee slightly bent. This will center your weight onto the bottom bracket and drive it squarely into the ground, giving a significant increase in traction that allows you to rail the corners at faster speeds. As you're exiting the corner and ready to resume pedaling, your upper foot will then be in position to apply power.

Putting the outside pedal down may not come instinctively, especially if you're not used to it. And when you're taking successive lefts and rights, it's easy to get mixed up. Practice foot placement on pavement and on every trail until you get it right. (Think about pedal placement until you no longer have to think about it.)

There are circumstances where level pedals are advantageous. Large rocks may require various balancing moves and pedal movements to make sure that they clear the objects. While keeping both knees bent and ready to soak up the bumps, you can quickly move the pedals up or down as necessary to avoid strikes.

In other places, the ground may be firm or loamy and traction is less of an issue. This kind of corner can be flowed through and pumped for momentum using level pedals. Keep your inside foot forward, as this makes it easier to face into the corners while putting a little extra weight on the outside pedal. When leading with your non-favored foot, it may feel unnatural, but this awkward feeling can be overcome with practice.

Lean the bike and position your body: There are two ways to turn, by leaning the bike or by turning the handlebar. Leaning the bike is the most efficient way to turn, providing better traction and increased speed. When you lean the bike, it turns by self-directing the handlebar in the direction it wants to go. All you have to do is control the amount of lean and lightly hold the bar to set its direction.

Although leaning the bike will be the primary method of cornering under most circumstances, there are some situations (such as a sharp turn) where a leaning turn will need to be assisted by turning the handlebar. Be careful not to forcefully turn the bar too much because over-steering can cause your front tire to wash out. If you're going so slow that you can't lean, then just turn the handlebar.

For the most efficient cornering, it's important to nail it with the proper degree of lean, which is determined by your speed, the sharpness of the corner, and the angle of the ground. If you're leaning correctly and you ride a lot of tight single-track, you should notice tire wear on your side knobbies, not just in the center.

Body positioning is an integral part of leaning the bike in corners. The idea is to stay as upright as possible while the bike is leaning over. Slow and/or soft corners can probably be taken in the seated position, but the majority of corners will be off the saddle. Picture yourself doing the following and then give it a try:

1. If you have a dropper post, lower it for a greater range of movement.

2. Get into the low attack position.

3. Initiate the turn by leaning the bike. Your hips and torso will remain more upright in relation to the bike.

4. As the saddle moves down along the inside of your leg, put the outside pedal to the bottom position for the best tire traction and stability. On softer or slower turns where grip is less of a factor, level pedals are fine.

5. Your inside arm will be straightening while your outside arm will be bending.

6. Continue leaning the bike until you obtain the required amount of turning. The furthest lean will be at the middle point of the corner (the apex).

7. Make sure you find a fore/aft balance point that puts equal weight on both tires. If it's a downhill turn, you could easily be aft of the saddle. Be prepared to quickly increase pressure on either tire if there's a break in traction.

8. Your hips and knees should be swiveled to face the direction of the turn. Your head should also be turned to see down the trail.

Learning to lean the bike in the turns is a critical mountain biking skill that many riders get wrong. Experience will help you find the right balance and body positioning, and once you get the feel of instinctively leaning the bike, you'll be ripping through the corners.

Know when to brake and set your speed: Going too fast and braking in the turns is risky. The reason for this is simple: When you're steaming through a corner, linear momentum pushes you toward the outside radius. At the same time, your tires will be leaning and riding on the edge of their tread, giving them a reduced contact area with the ground. If you use your front brake in the middle of all this, your tire is susceptible to locking up and washing out from under you. For safe but fast cornering, setting up the correct speed beforehand allows the wheels to move freely through the arc of the turn. Get to the desired speed by completing the braking just prior to initiating the turn but no later than just before the apex of the turn. There should be no braking after that. Mastering the timing of this will take practice. It's something that needs to become instinctive. Once you have it nailed, you'll be cornering faster and more safely, and you'll be able to focus your attention on perfecting other cornering techniques.

Try out your timing on pavement to both the left and the right, increasing your speed as you get better. While you're braking, your weight should be slightly shifted back and then returned forward as you're positioning for the turn. This subtle weight shift will help to put pressure on the front tire to reduce the chances of it sliding out. Work on these techniques with the goal of making it instinctive. If you think you have it figured out, practice on some easier trails before advancing to the more challenging ones.

Deciding on the best speed for any particular corner will come from experience. On a basic level, turns that are wide, have a grippy surface, or have a usable berm can all be taken faster. Turns that are sharp, have loose surfaces, or are flat or off-cambered need to be taken slower. If you're on a snaking downhill trail, you'll be repeatedly grabbing your brakes before the turns. If you're travelling down a gravelly trail or fire road at a fast speed, brake early and get your speed way down before the turn.

During the action, a circumstance may develop where you haven't slowed down enough prior to a turn and you find yourself coming in hot with no time to slow down. It may be a situation where you're traveling downhill at a high rate of speed but failed to look far enough ahead to anticipate the trail veering off to the side. If you get into this type of situation, you'll inevitably have to do some hard braking while you're in the turn. What you don't want to do is lock up the front tire and wash it out. If possible, lightly use the rear brake throughout the turn without skidding. If this is not possible, a controlled rear tire skid can be used to pivot the bike. This great save is known as wheel drift. Proper execution of this maneuver will take some skill development using the following steps:

1. Find a location where skidding won't cause any harm or negative impact, such as a fire road. Start with a turn that's only about 45 degrees and has a somewhat wide arc. While riding at a relatively slow or moderate speed without braking, begin the turn with your outside pedal down. Lean forward a bit to put more weight on the front, and hit the rear brake with enough pressure to briefly lock the tire into a skid. You can momentarily put your inside foot on the ground, if needed (this is where flat pedals rule). During this brief skid, you should feel the rear end pivot to the outside of the turn, at which point you'll let off the brake to regain traction.

2. Try again on a 90-degree turn, this time holding the skid a little longer while lightly counter-steering by slightly and briefly turning your handlebars toward the outside of the turn. This will straighten out the bike and keep it on course as you pedal your way out.

3. Try it in both directions and incrementally increase your speed.

You've just learned a technique that can potentially save your skin, although skidding shouldn't be made into a regular practice if it can be helped. It causes ruts and braking bumps that are formed by tires scraping away the dirt. Other riders will then avoid these parts of the turn by going around the damage. This ends up widening the trail. Add a little rain to the mix, and the trail will erode even further. And if the trail doesn't have good drainage and riders are on the trail while it's wet and muddy, it ends up a total mess with long-lasting damage. Skidding is completely avoidable and doesn't have to happen. It's bad trail etiquette, bad bike handling, and should be avoided if at all possible. To prevent it, always practice good vision to anticipate your braking requirements. This will help to keep the trails smooth and everyone happy.

See through and beyond the turn: The most important aspect of cornering is seeing through and beyond the turn. You should be looking for the exit right from the beginning. Using good vision in this manner will allow you to properly execute the entire corner and the trail beyond it, and then set up for the next corner. This can't be understated; work on making it second nature. Never get into the habit of looking only a few feet in front of you because this will be your big downfall.

Resume pedaling: As you pass the apex of a corner and begin to rise from the lean, you'll need to resume pedaling (if it's not downhill). You should come into the corner prepared by anticipating the correct gear for the speed coming out of the corner. This is a judgment call that comes with experience. It will allow you to generate full power without delay when you need it the most and is a good way to speed up your ride, even if you have to soon brake for the next corner.

Don't tense up: Remain loose and flexible, ready for changing conditions.

Switchbacks

A switchback is a sharp turn in the trail that can take you as much as 180 degrees from the direction that you came from. The reason these exist is usually that the trail is on the side of a steep hill and a zig-zag path is required to effectively get up or down. This type of corner can be tricky and requires a different approach than regular corners.

Before you attempt a switchback, you should be well-adept at clipping and unclipping from your pedals. Switchbacks are tricky maneuvers that can be easily botched. If this happens, you need to be ready to drop the foot that's on the opposite side of the cliff so that you can lean away from the edge.

Downhill Switchbacks: You can get ten different pieces of advice from ten different people on how to ride switchbacks. This is due in part to the fact that not all switchbacks are alike. Each one needs to be assessed and executed in a manner that works best for the individual corner. Here are a few possible varieties.

- Smooth, rounded, bermed, not steep
- Smooth, angular, steep
- Rocky, rounded, not steep
- Rocky, angular, narrow, steep

From those examples, there's distinct variation in how these switchbacks could be handled. Smooth, rounded, and bermed means that you can take it faster, possibly remain seated, and possibly drop your outside pedal. Rocky and angular means that you'll have to slow way down, get into the attack position, possibly use level pedals, and possibly go so slow that you end up doing a track stand. Steep means that you'll have to shift your weight way back. In spite of the variations, there are some techniques that can be consistently applied to all switchbacks:

1. The number-one technique to remember is to look through, around, and beyond the switchback. This will allow you to pick the best line through any obstacles, help to set the best trajectory, and keep your gaze away from the edge of the cliff. Because switchbacks are sharply angled in another direction, you'll have to turn your head a little further to get a good visual.

2. Switchbacks are a sudden change in direction that will require steering input instead of bike lean. Twist the handlebar to get the degree of turning that the corner requires.

3. If the switchback is new to you, approach it at a slower speed than your skill can handle. Brake until you get to the apex of the corner. You can take it faster after it becomes familiar.

4. As you approach the corner, line up on the outside of the edge. What you do from there depends on the switchback.

That's where the similarities end. Other techniques have options that are dependent on the nature of the switchback and your personal preferences and skill level. Consider the following sets of choices:

A. Follow the switchback all the way around the outside edge to reduce the amount of steering input. This may also help to reduce the angle of decline.

B. Many switchbacks are better taken by cutting across to the inner edge at the apex and then back out to the outer edge for the exit. This is a faster way to take the corner; just make sure that you don't cut across too early or you'll make the turn too sharp. If the trail is on the wider side, it'll give you more space to perform this maneuver.

A. Level pedals will give you better fore/aft balance and greater control of the weight that's applied to each tire. If it's a rapid series of switchbacks going down the hill, it's easier to deal with pedal placement when they're kept level.

B. Outside pedal down can keep you ready to put the inside foot down if the corner becomes too difficult. If this happens, use the inside foot to scoot yourself along a few steps until your bike is better aligned with the trail.

A. In most cases, the rider and the bike will remain in-line with no leaning.

B. Some riders like to lean their bodies toward the inside edge while keeping the bike upright. This allows the tires to remain firmly connected to the ground while keeping their weight safely away from the cliff's edge.

A. Steep declines are best handled by lowering the seat post and keeping your weight way back behind the seat. This will help to keep things under control.

B. A decline that's "not so steep" may be best handled with the seat post up so that intense pedaling can resume directly after the switchback.

Uphill Switchbacks: As you're approaching an uphill switchback, move over to the side of the trail that puts you on the outside of the turn. Look through and beyond the switchback to evaluate your best line and for any obstacles in the path. When you reach the switchback, remain along its outer radius if possible. This will reduce the sharpness of the turn while making it less steep and more manageable. During a sharp turn, your rear tire will not follow the same line as your front and will actually cut across the switchback. When the turn is executed properly, there should be enough real estate that the rear tire doesn't run into the inside edge. Always be mindful of any obstacles that your rear tire could hit and cause you to stall or become imbalanced.

You will not be leaning the bike on an uphill switchback. As with any uphill climb, you will need to position your body more forward over the handlebar. As you're rounding the switchback, turn your head and shoulders so that your eyes can stay peeled in the direction you want to go. Your hips can pivot a bit in this direction as well.

You won't have the luxury of switching gears in the middle of a switchback, so you'll need to make sure that you're already in an appropriate gear. How much power you need to put into it all depends on the steepness of the climb. This can change while you're in the middle of it, so be prepared to apply more power as needed to maintain momentum.

> *"Life is like riding a bicycle – in order to keep your balance, you must keep moving."*
>
> -- Albert Einstein

CHAPTER TWELVE

Ups and Downs

EVERY MOUNTAIN BIKE ride will most likely involve climbing and descending, at least to some degree. How much elevation change you experience is all dependent on where you live and ride. If you're fortunate, you'll have a variety of degrees of difficulty to choose from. Sometimes, you may want the challenge of a tall mountain, and other times, a rolling hillside may be more to your liking. In any case, there are techniques that will help to make all of them easier. Read on to find out how to improve both your climbing and your descending.

Climbing

Riding uphill, otherwise known as climbing, is an integral part of mountain biking. Softly rolling hills with small inclines can be handled by most riders. But if they're long and steep, they can take every fiber of your being to achieve. With your lungs searing, your heart pounding wildly, your legs burning with pain, and nausea setting in, they can sometimes be absolutely brutal. It sure would be nice if you could just climb without effort or even avoid these kinds of hills, but that's not the way it works. It's going to take effort, and you can't have the thrill of ripping down a descent without climbing a hill (except with a ski-lift). This inevitability makes successful climbing a top priority.

The differences between various climbs lie in the steepness and distance of the inclines, the technicality of the trail, and the total ascension over the course of the ride. Multi-mile fire roads that seemingly go uphill endlessly will test your endurance. The short, steep, and irregular climbs will test your leg power and your cardio performance. Your leg muscles, your heart, your lungs, and your mental toughness will all be pushed to extremes. Your performance will be compared against other riders and your abilities and shortcomings will be exposed.

Mountain biking is a fun sport, but let's face it - it's also work and exercise. There's no way around it. You could be really good at shredding technically challenging terrain and skillfully making your way down steep descents, but if you can't perform on the climbs, you'll fall behind other riders.

As a new rider, the hills will be especially difficult. Without any conditioning, even small climbs will hurt. If you've put little or no time into climbing, you'll need to begin your conditioning on small and easy hills while improving your techniques. If you find yourself on a hill that you're not yet capable of climbing, you'll probably have to walk your bike up. It's not that you're "not a good climber"; you just need to build yourself up. This situation can be frustrating: we would all like to be able to successfully climb every hill, every time, to get where we want to go.

Nothing can make climbing become easier than good old-fashioned cardiovascular conditioning. Clearly, if you train hard and ride often, you'll improve your physical strength and stamina and become a much better climber in a shorter period of time. However, there are ways to create immediate improvements to your power output and achievable distance. The following 30 tips and techniques will help you gain every possible advantage. Many of these topics have been previously covered in this book, but this is where they can be effectively combined for a single purpose . . . getting up the hills.

1) Assess the climbs: You need to know if the trails you'll be riding are close to your abilities. If they seem like too much, you may need to improvise your route. For new and unfamiliar locations, check with friends, consult a topographical map, and read online trail reviews to get an idea of the difficulty level. The total ascension, the incline percentages, and the technicality of the trails all need to be factored in.

The following descriptions will help with this assessment. Keep in mind that these do not factor in the trail surface. Loose sand, gravel, rocks, and roots will require more power and can significantly increase the difficulty.

1-3%: Slight uphill. Not significantly challenging.

4-6%: Manageable, but can cause fatigue over long distances.

7-9%: Becomes uncomfortable. This may be a significant challenge for new climbers.

10% - 15%: A difficult, strenuous incline, especially over longer distances.

16% +: A challenging and painful climb for all riders, even for short distances.

2) Prepare yourself: Strength and endurance training are always the best way to improve your climbing, but to take full advantage of your current capability, there are a number of additional things you can do:

a.   Make sure that you're well rested by getting enough sleep. You should also be in a good frame of mind, eager and ready to go.

b.   Be well hydrated. If your ride starts out with climbing, you'll need to drink water no less than 20 minutes before you begin to give it a chance to get into your system. Don't wait until you get thirsty to drink again; doing so means you've become dehydrated and your performance has been affected. Instead, take frequent sips of water and/or a quality sport drink.

c.   Have the right amount of fuel (refer to the nutrition chapter). Do not eat a meal less than three hours before your ride. Eat a small amount of food, such as an energy bar or an apple, about an hour before your ride. A gel-shot can be taken 20 to 30 minutes before the climb.

d.   Make sure that your shoes are cinched down tight. If your feet are flopping around in your shoes, it will subtract a small amount of pedaling efficiency.

3) Prepare your bike: For you to be at your best, your bike needs to be at its best. Aside from being lubricated and mechanically sound, here are a few things to pay attention to:

a.   Always check your tire pressure before you begin your ride. Your tires should be properly inflated to provide the best traction. If the climbs are on smooth hard-pack, a higher tire pressure would be best. If the trails are technical or have a loose, gravelly surface, a lower tire pressure will serve you better.

b.   Make sure that your handlebar and seat are properly adjusted to ensure maximum leverage on the pedals. If you have a dropper seat post, make sure it's all the way up. If you find yourself doing a lot of climbing, you may prefer to have the seat adjusted a little more forward to help with weight distribution.

c.   Make sure that your rear shock's sag is set properly. If the setting is too soft, pedal bob will make your bike feel mushy and will detract from your forward motion.

d.   If the terrain is relatively smooth and your suspension is equipped with a lock-out feature, set it to lock before you hit the hill. This will make your suspension more rigid for reduced bobbing and better power transfer.

Your bike may even have a switch that can be set to "climb" for locking both front and rear at the same time. Locking out the rear suspension will have the biggest impact, while locking out the fork is less significant but still worth doing. Always be aware of whether you're locked or unlocked because if you ride into something technical, you may not be able to switch fast enough. Whenever a particular climb has been completed, remember to unlock your suspension . . . something that's easy to forget when you're feeling completely spent.

4) Get onto the right chainring: This does not pertain to bikes with a single ring. As you're approaching the incline, put the chain on the ring you want, which will probably be the small chainring if it's extremely steep. If you try to switch rings while riding up an incline, the high chain tension from heavy pedal pressure could result in a derailment or even a broken chain. If you do need to switch rings while ascending, letting off some pedal pressure as you shift will help, even if it robs some of your momentum.

5) Attack the hill: Build up speed prior to hitting the incline, usually as fast as you can go given the distance you have to work with. As you enter the climb and your speed begins to slow, down-shift one gear at a time at a rate that keeps your cadence steady and brisk. The rate of downshifting is largely dependent on the angle of the incline, the traction between your tire and the terrain, and your leg strength. Shift surely and rapidly by swiftly pushing the lever completely through its entire range of motion. This will prevent getting hung up between gears.

6) Maintain the right cadence: On hard-pack or on relatively firm gravel, a cadence in the range of 80-100 rpm would be appropriate. By keeping your cadence a little higher and the resistance lighter, you'll have the ability to deliver bursts of power when it's necessary. If you find yourself spinning with no resistance, switch to a higher gear for better power efficiency and a reduced chance of rear-tire slippage.

If the climb is super steep, technical, sandy, muddy, etc., you'll need a slower cadence. Try not to let your RPMs drop below 60 for more than a couple of minutes, or much greater muscle fatigue could set in. If you let it drop below 50, you'll run the risk of stalling out, especially if you hit something technical.

7) Pace yourself: Whether the hill is extremely steep or long and consistent, pacing yourself and maintaining a steady intensity is critical for making your energy last for the duration of the climb. Be careful not to go too fast, even if you're trying to keep up with someone, because if you "hit the wall" and come to a stop, you'll end up much further behind. Try to judge the average speed that will get you to the top. On long climbs, start out light and easy. If you're feeling pretty good at the halfway point, push yourself harder. This method will ensure that you make it all the way up.

8) Pedal-in-circles: During a tough climb is when pedaling-in-circles really pays off. Not only will this spread the effort over more of your leg muscles, but it also prevents pulses of power that can cause the rear tire to slip and stall your momentum. For increased power and smooth pedaling with little to no tire slip, pedal in circles as often as possible. If you have a single chainring, you may want to consider changing it to an oval ring, which is claimed to help smooth out the power stroke and lessen the chance of tire slip.

9) Change seat position: Optimizing your position on the seat will increase your climbing efficiency and performance and is the first climbing positioning adjustment you'll make. Your power into the pedals, your traction, and your balance are all affected.

Your saddle setback was adjusted for optimal pedaling efficiency while on level ground. But when riding uphill, your front tire will be elevated higher than the rear, which causes your center of gravity to move aft. This will reduce your leverage on the pedals. Sliding forward on the saddle will move your center of gravity forward and put you in a better position over the pedals. Your exact position will vary depending on the incline of the hill. When the angle of the terrain changes often, you'll be making frequent adjustments to stay centered. On the steepest hills, you may be sitting on the very tip of the saddle as you climb. If this is too uncomfortable, try tilting your seat down a little bit. If this doesn't help, you may need to try switching to a more comfortable saddle, perhaps a model with more padding in the nose for climbing.

Moving fore and aft will require you to change the position of your feet on the pedals. If you're using flat pedals, you can capitalize on this by moving your feet slightly forward on the pedals while slightly moving your toes down on the down strokes. You'll then be pushing deeper through the power stroke. If you're using clip-in pedals, the best you can do is point your toes down slightly while pushing further into the stroke.

10) Lean forward: The height of your chest, meaning how far you lean forward, affects your fore and aft balance, which is an important factor in keeping your weight evenly distributed between the front and rear tires. If you're too upright, your front tire will be un-weighted and could easily wander around or come off the ground. If you're too low, your rear tire will be un-weighted, allowing it to break traction and spin. How you position depends on the angle of the hill, the traction that you're experiencing, and the characteristics of your bike (i.e., head tube angle, wheelbase, tire size and type, etc.). Sometimes, the steepest hills require considerable lean. Whatever the case, you need to find a good balance point between front-steering traction and rear-power traction, which can often be a fine line. If your rear tire does slip, raise up a little and keep pedaling - you may be able to save it.

Remember, the first step is always scooting forward on the saddle; don't make leaning forward the default adjustment. Lean forward only enough to keep even pressure between the tires. Leaning way forward tends to restrict the diaphragm from performing full, deep breaths, so you should only be leaning as much as is necessary. Never allow your head to drop too much in relation to your torso because a slumped-over, head-down position could partially restrict breathing.

When the terrain varies, your positioning will need to be adjusted frequently. One benefit of changing positions is that it redistributes the workload between different muscles. Sitting upright will use more of your thigh muscles, and moving your chest down will use more of your buttock muscles. This change-up can play a small role in delaying burn-out of individual muscle groups.

11) Elbows out: On rough climbs, keep your elbows relaxed and pointed outward. This will give you the best leverage and flexibility for moving up and down to deal with the trail irregularities. Elbows out also allows your chest to expand more easily during heavy breathing. When it's steep and your chest is down low, your elbows will be pointed more down and back.

12) Relax: It's quite easy for your hands, wrists, and shoulders to become tensed up during a hard climb. But when these muscles tense up, they use more of the oxygen that should instead be going to the muscles that are doing the work. Just as scuba divers must keep their full body relaxed to conserve oxygen, mountain bikers must keep their non-working muscles relaxed so that more oxygen can go to the legs.

Tense muscles will also cause your motions to be jerky at a time when you need to finesse your front wheel with soft, micro-steering adjustments. If you catch yourself tensed up, simply remind yourself to relax. Start by keeping your hands light on the grips. One method that may help is laying your thumbs on top of the grips instead of hooking them under. From there, make sure that your arms, shoulders, neck, and jaw are also relaxed.

13) Breathe: Remember to use the previously covered breathing techniques. As the climb gets tougher and your body is under a lot of tension, maintaining steady breathing will become increasingly difficult. Don't allow yourself to start panting. It's especially important to focus on using deep, controlled, rhythmic inhales and exhales to provide maximum oxygen. This practice works to delay going anaerobic and helps to keep you relaxed and focused.

14) Look ahead and pick the right lines: Nothing can throw you off more than running into something or falling into a rut while you're on a difficult climb. That's why seeing what's ahead and choosing where you're going to go is so important. How far ahead you can look is commensurate with the angle of the climb. Normal climbs will have you looking ten or twelve feet ahead. Super steep climbs may only allow you to comfortably bend your neck enough to see three or four feet ahead. In spite of this, you'll need to occasionally glance up to see what's coming up on the trail.

The photo below depicts the optimal line to take on a steep trail. This hill has a water rut crisscrossing the path, along with loose and embedded rocks that make picking the right line critical to making it all the way up.

If you're faced with multiple choices of possible lines to take, it's often best to opt for the one that provides the straightest path with the best traction, even if means riding over obstacles. You'll want to avoid weaving so much that you run into more difficult objects that can cause you to lose all momentum and stall out. Sometimes, it pays to ride over one object to avoid the next one, but every situation is unique and will need to be evaluated independently. Whenever you're riding around an object, pay attention to what line your rear tire takes. You may need to make a wide berth around it so that the rear tire clears.

The rougher the surface, the more tense you'll be and the more energy you'll expend. Negotiating rocks and roots will tire you out much more quickly than a smooth hill with the same degree of incline, so it's important to slow your pace down and find a line that's smoother and doesn't cause too much weaving. The smooth part will typically be the most traveled part, which works well for providing the best traction on dry surfaces. However, if the surface is wet, it could be slick and slippery, which may force you to ride on the rougher part for the best traction.

15) Kick in your mental toughness: Climbing is where mental toughness will really pay off. When you approach a tall and steep hill, you need to hit it in the right frame of mind by using a strong can-do attitude. Don't pollute your mind by trying to justify why you won't make it all the way up. If you're trying to use some sophisticated reason such as your age, your weight, your bike, or the amount of sleep you got last night, you'll be setting yourself up for failure.

As you're climbing, you may reach a point where it seems like the pain is overwhelming and you can't go any further. Every fiber of your being wants to stop, and you're having thoughts such as "I hate this," "This is too hard," or "I'm never doing this again." You need to clear your mind of these debilitating thoughts. Instead of dwelling on how bad it hurts, just acknowledge the pain while detaching yourself from it: something that's there but not really a part of you. Convince yourself that the pain is nothing and that you're getting to the top of the hill no matter what. Your determination and self-talk may be the only things that keep you going[21].

When you're on the steepest of hills, it's important not to dwell on how insanely steep it is. Here's one solution that can help: when your torso is down low, you'll be looking just ahead of your tire, which will keep you from seeing the angle of the hill. In fact, it may optically appear that you're on flat ground. Go with this if it helps you psychologically.

Here's what it comes down to: when you think that you can't make it is when you set yourself up for failure. Failure will become a reality. It's that simple. Don't let your mind be your weakest link. This mind-control method doesn't come by itself; it's something that needs to be practiced and refined.

16) Repeat your mantra: Psychologically, using a mantra (a chant that you keep repeating in your head) can help to deflect thoughts of the discomfort you're feeling. It could be anything: "C'mon legs!" or "It doesn't hurt!" or "I know I can." It doesn't matter what it is or if it's true or not. Say it until you make it.

17) Play your music: If you like to listen to music while you ride, use the genre and songs that give you strength and endurance on the climbs. Some find that soft music puts them in a more trance-like state and helps to get their mind off the pain. For some, hard, edgy music gets them energized; and for others, something with more of a beat sets their climbing rhythm. Whatever works best for you is what you should listen to. As the pain sets in, you'll probably ignore it on the conscious level, but it can still provide a good distraction. For trail safety reasons, use a single earbud and keep the volume low.

18) Create mini goals: Some riders focus on the top of the hill and then hammer their way toward it. This method may be daunting for some. As you're laboring up the hill, it may seem like it's going on forever . . . and you're not even halfway! This can be discouraging. Instead of looking at the big picture, set smaller goals. Pick a rock, a tree, a leaf, or whatever . . . something that's a little way up the trail. When you reach that goal, identify your next target. Keep doing this, and before you know it you'll be at the top. It's a mind game that can keep you going. You can either pick targets that are far enough away to make it a challenging distance, or you can repeatedly pick short distance targets to keep your mind occupied until you make it all the way up.

19) Section it out: A ride up a mountainside will often consist of a series of inclines with sections in between that are level or not as steep. Look at these rises as individual goals that must be conquered. When you make it up one, pedal as light and slow as you can to let your heart rate come down. There may not be enough time and distance to make it come down as much as you'd like, but it'll make a difference. Just getting through that big gush of blood will put you in better condition for the next challenging incline. This is especially important if your heart rate is through the roof. Sectioning out the mountain this way has the additional benefit of giving you a psychological boost that can keep you going.

20) Pump the obstacles: If it's a technical climb, lift up and unweight the bike on the front side of the objects. If there's an opportunity to pump downward on the back sides, by all means do it.

21) Avoid the swervies: If your tire is swerving from side to side, you're wasting precious energy. You're probably moving too slowly and are tense. You may not have enough weight on the front tire, or you may not be on a good line. To remedy this, make sure you're in the best gear to keep a faster moving cadence, get your speed up, stay relaxed, adjust your weight forward, and if available, pick a line with a firmer surface.

22) Your first climb is a warm up: Your first serious climb (or the beginning of your climb) will be the hardest part because your muscles have not yet been activated, you haven't significantly increased your blood flow, and you may not be in the right state of mind. Subsequent climbs will be easier than the first one. It's important that you don't come to the premature conclusion that you're having a bad day. Doing so could make it a foregone conclusion.

23) Stand and climb: Standing on your pedals is sometimes just what's needed to get up and over the crest of a hill. Some strong riders stand and climb extremely well; it's their preferred method. But it's not always the most efficient way to go because part of your energy is used to support your weight. And the heavier you are, the more difficult this is, even though your weight partially adds power to the down strokes. Standing pedaling is difficult and exhausting over longer distances, but for those who can use it effectively, it can be a great method of powering up the steep pitches.

When standing, it's important to use the right technique because you'll have less control over minute weight adjustments. Corrections tend to be exaggerated, which can easily lead to a loss of wheel traction. To minimize this possibility, use the following methodology:

a.   While on an incline in the seated position, find your balance point and the best body positioning.

b.   Slowly raise your butt off the seat while keeping a bend at the waist. You'll only need to be two to three inches above the seat. This raises your center of gravity in relation to your crank arms, so you'll need to make a slight forward shift in your weight to prevent your front tire from becoming unweighted. Be careful not to move too far forward or your rear tire will break traction.

c.   As you rise, change to the next higher gear so that you don't over-torque and spin the rear tire from the power strokes. If necessary, move up another gear, but be aware that if you're about to stall out, it will be hard to downshift while standing because the pressure on the pedals will be putting a heavy tension on the chain.

d.   As the angle of the terrain changes, make small fore and aft weight shifts to keep centered between your wheels. This will require a higher degree of mental interaction than a seated climb.

e.   Pedal in circles as best as you can to maintain even pedal strokes.

f.   Hold the handgrips a bit tighter because the down strokes will tend to push your body upward.

g.   If you plan on sitting back down while still in the climb, be mindful that this will result in a net loss of power. To prevent from bogging down, shift to a lower gear as you sit.

24) Follow someone better: Following a stronger climber will inevitably cause you to push harder. It has a way of removing the tendency to go slower, stop and rest, or skip the climb altogether. The drawback of following is that you might not pace yourself correctly and end up "hitting the wall." But in the end, the strategy of following a superior climber will help you to become better.

25) Last ditch effort: You're almost there, but you feel that you can't make it. Before you quit, commit yourself to a few more revolutions of your cranks, say five or ten. When you complete those, do it again. Before you know it, you'll be at the top of the hill.

26) Heat Management: Riding uphill will make you hot. Depending on the temperature, you could become extremely hot, which will negatively affect your performance. Try these tips to manage your heat:

a. Do your climbing during the cooler part of the day.

b. Wear moisture-wicking fabric, such as polyester or Lycra.

c. Drink cold liquid. We're talking ice cold. Prior to riding on a hot day, fill your bottle and/or hydration pack with ice combined with water and/or an energy drink. The cold liquid will help to lower your core temperature, thus raising your effective performance.

d. Trees will often cast shadows onto half of the trail. Take advantage of this at every possible opportunity. The more you can stay out of the direct sunlight, the better off you'll be.

27) Stop and rest: Sometimes, you just can't make it all the way up. That's it. You've bonked. This is OK; you may fall further behind someone, but you'll be recharging your batteries and will have opportunities to catch up. Grab some water, take a shot of gel, and wait a little bit for your heart rate to come down. You'll find that after a short rest, the hill will suddenly become much easier. You can then continue onward with enough renewed energy to make it to the top. That being said, if you can instead stay on your bike and just spin slowly to catch your breath, you'll be mentally stronger and your ride will be much more gratifying. This will keep you in the game while providing better physical training.

28) Walk it up: Our goal is to ride all the way up the hills. But sometimes the hill is so steep that it's truly beyond our abilities, or it may be so rocky and full of ruts that it's unrideable by anyone. In these circumstances, walking the bike is the only option and shouldn't get in the way of your pride.

29) Take advantage of rolling hills: So you've made it up the hill and now you're spent. It's time to relax and coast down the other side so you can pedal hard up the next hill, right? Wrong. This method will actually use more energy and wear you out more quickly. The best way to take advantage of this type of terrain is to pedal downhill, then let the bike coast up the next hill as far as it will go. Besides being the most efficient way to distribute your energies, a fast and light spin also keeps the blood flowing in your muscles, helping to clear out the built-up lactic acid and alleviate any nausea you may feel.

30) Progress: If you're easily spinning up the worst part of the hill in your granny gear, it's time to use bigger gears. By continuously challenging yourself this way, you'll progress and become a stronger and faster climber.

Climbing can be one of the toughest things you do as a mountain biker, but it can also be one of the most rewarding. As you reach the top, a sense of pride and happiness will quickly replace the pain. You'll have done something incredibly good for yourself, and you'll know it. Cleaning a tough climb builds character and will make you a better person overall: able to take on life's challenges and persevere.

Over time, climbing will get easier. Don't ever be discouraged by your performance because you're getting stronger with every climb and you're doing great. Just keep hitting those hills and pushing your limits. You'll improve with every ride, and before you know it, you'll be looking back at hills you couldn't climb before and realize just how much better you've become.

Starting on an Incline

There may be times when you're tired or have become off balance and need to stop during the middle of a climb. Getting back on the bike and resuming pedaling will take some strategy, especially when the hill is steep. Hopefully you can just walk the bike past a difficult section to a spot that's not as steep or technical and then just get back on and ride. But if this isn't possible, there are techniques you can use for resuming your upward journey.

If you're not already in a low gear, you'll need to get into one. Click the shifter and lift the bike by the saddle using one hand while spinning the crank with the other hand. Another method is to squeeze the front brake lever and push the handlebar to get the rear wheel off the ground, and then use a foot to do the spinning. Whichever method works best for you is okay.

The height of the seat combined with the angle of the hill can make getting back onto the bike a challenge. Here are a few techniques to make this task easier:

1. If there happens to be a medium-sized rock next to you, use it as a step stool to get back on and steady yourself for the first down stroke.

2. If the trail is off-camber, use the higher, hill-side of the bike to get back on. This side has less distance for your leg to reach the ground and will also prevent you from tipping over toward the downhill side as you try to climb on.

3. If you have a dropper seat post, lower the seat. This will allow you to easily slide back onto the seat to make the first down stroke. Although it's best to be accustomed to starting with the seat in the normal position, lowering it is acceptable if it helps.

4. Once you decide the best way to get mounted, hold the brake levers and clip in your leading foot. Put this pedal near the top of the stroke where the leverage is maximized.

5. As you get ready to take off, you should have a general idea of the fore/aft balance point of the bike based on the angle of the hill. Bend your elbows and relax your muscles from hands to neck. Look up at the trail to strategize the best line to take.

6. When you're ready to begin the pedal stroke, release the brakes and give a little push off, if possible. On solid terrain, you can mash down hard on the pedal. If the terrain is loose, pedal softly until your tire grabs, then gradually push harder, being careful not to spin the tire. This is a slow-speed operation, which means that you need to stay loose and relaxed to remain balanced.

7. As you start to roll, carefully bring the other foot onto its pedal and clip in. By the time you complete your second down stroke, pop your seat post back up to obtain the proper leverage on the pedals. Doing these multiple tasks simultaneously will take coordination.

8. Ideally, it would be best to get clipped in right away, but in the heat of the moment this doesn't always happen. Don't be overly concerned about it because if you continue to wrestle with it, you could totally choke your launch. Just keep pushing down the pedals as you work on gaining momentum up the hill. Once the pedals are rotating, you'll be better balanced and your foot pressure on the pedals will lessen, making the task of clipping in much easier.

Descending

Successfully cleaning a descent, whether it's technical or smooth, can be one of the most fun aspects of mountain biking. As your speed increases down a hill, your adrenaline will be pumping and all of your skills will be fully engaged. It's a thrilling experience that always provides a triumphant feeling. But if you're not in control, it can be downright scary, which is why good technique is critical for staying safe.

The grade of the hill and the trail conditions, such as gravel, rocks, and gnarled roots, will determine how fast you can go, when to brake, and the positioning of your body. Doing it wrong could lead to a disaster that involves a lot of pain. It's important to know what the trail is going to do next and to have a plan of attack so that you're not tensed up and simply hanging on to the bars with a death-grip. Scan far ahead to anticipate any problems and pick the best and safest lines. If you get off your intended line, a quick decision will need to be made for an alternate. It's all about maintaining control of your situation while staying confident.

How your bike is designed has an impact on how stable it feels on descents. Bikes with a greater head angle (slacker) will put the tire further out in front, giving them a longer wheel base (distance between the wheels), which tends to make the bike feel safer on steep descents. It allows the rider to keep their body position further forward while staying centered and balanced on the pedals. Suspension also plays a role; longer suspension strokes, although heavier, help to keep the tires connected to the ground for better traction and allow bigger impacts without bottoming out.

No matter what kind of bike you have, descents will generally require you to be off the saddle and in the attack position. The question is: How far back do you position your body weight? This is dependent on how slack or steep the head angle is and the steepness of the descent. Use these positioning tips to get the best balance point:

- Lowering your seat post should be a routine on all descents. This allows you to easily respond to the changing terrain by getting your body low and shifting your weight with hip movements. If you don't have a dropper post, you can lower it manually prior to the descent, and then raise it back up when you get to the bottom. Putting a mark on the seat post where you normally keep it will give you an easy reference for a quick return to normal height.

- The fulcrum (center balance point) of your bike is at the pedals. For the best control, a balanced position on the pedals must be maintained, no matter what the angle of the decline is. Position yourself in a way that keeps you heavy on the feet and light on the hands. Dropping your heels slightly will help drive your weight into the pedals.

- Pedal placement is another consideration. When you're not pedaling, hold them level at the 3 o'clock and 9 o'clock positions to help avoid hitting rocks and to prevent them from scraping the ground in a turn. Which foot you lead with doesn't matter; many riders have a favored foot that they always put forward. However, switching them once in a while to get used to leading with either foot is a skill that can come in handy, especially in the turns.

- Keep your chest low for a lower center of gravity. This will greatly improve your ability to stay balanced when the trail gets sketchy.

- As you move your weight back for the downhill, don't allow yourself to pull on the handlebars; this means you're too far back. Your hands should lie on the bars naturally, a practice that is essential for optimal steering and braking. Squeezing the bars tightly will also cause your hands and forearms to get pumped up, achy, and less responsive.

- If a super-steep hill has you putting your butt well behind the seat with your body stretched out over the bike, you must still maintain some degree of bend at the elbows to allow them to extend if you hit any dips in the trail. With no elbow bend, the bike could harshly yank you downward. Another thing to remember is to keep your arms lower than your shoulders. This will give you the flexibility to raise your arms when the front end rises, thereby soaking up the bumps instead of being launched into the air.

- Sometimes, a trail will have a sudden, short, and steep decline. Before you get to the edge, rise off the saddle with your weight centered on your pedals. As you go over, smoothly shift your butt behind the seat to keep your weight driven into the pedals while extending your arms and lowering your heels. If it's rough, let your elbows and knees absorb the bumps. At the bottom, smoothly return to the normal position.

Some riders will automatically put themselves behind the seat even when riding down mildly pitched hills. Maybe this is done out of fear of going over the handlebars - an attempt to retreat from the danger. But this should never be a default position. This situation will make your front tire too light, allowing it to easily pop up from a bump, lock up and slide on anything loose, or simply make it more difficult to brake and steer - any of which could set you up for a crash. Although a far less common mistake, too far forward actually *could* send you over the handlebars if you ram into an obstacle. The bottom line is: when your weight is balanced on the pedals, it'll be properly distributed over both tires and your descent will be safer.

To get the feel of lowering your body and centering your weight on the pedals, it's best to first try out your descending skills on hills that are not too steep or technical. As you get better and more confident, you can gradually challenge yourself to more difficult hills. As with anything you're learning to do on your mountain bike, starting out easy and working your way up is the best way to build your skill base and to set yourself up with good habits that bring great safety and success on the trails.

Braking on Descents

As you're making your way downhill, you'll be faced with a variety of challenges that require both thought-out and instinctive use of the brakes. Your momentum plus your weight means that extra distance will be required to scrub off speed, so you'll need good braking strategy to allow enough time to choose the best line and avoid dangerous situations.

Being properly balanced is also critical for getting the best performance from your brakes. Centering your weight on the pedals will keep pressure distributed firmly and equally to both tires for maximum traction. If you squeeze the brake levers and your front tire easily locks up, you're probably too far rearward. This scary situation will make it impossible to control your steering and could easily result in a wipe-out. Leaning forward to add weight to the front tire will help keep it rotating during braking.

If the rear tire locks up or does a lot of bouncing, you're probably too far forward. A skidding rear tire is more controllable than the front, but it's a good indication that you're at risk of being pitched over the bars by the next trail irregularity. Shift your weight back to center it on the pedals. This should allow your rear tire to grab and stay better connected to the terrain while your front tire rolls smoothly over the bumps.

During hard braking, the force will want to push your body forward. You must not let this happen. This is the moment that you need to shift your weight back to resist this forward inertia. At the same time, dip your heels to push against the pedal axles and use the palms of your hands to push against the handgrips. It's important to time this correctly: shift your weight when hard braking actually begins.

Remember to modulate as required to help keep traction, and don't squeeze the brakes too abruptly. Constant adjustments in braking and balance are going to take a high degree of technique and skill. This doesn't happen overnight; you don't just instantly learn this. It comes with experience. It's a highly dynamic interaction between rider and bike. A seemingly tiny mistake on steep descents could lead to serious problems if you don't respond with instant corrections. Here are a few more helpful pointers to consider for various situations you may encounter:

- Don't be afraid to use your front brake. In fact, the front will provide the vast majority of your stopping power and should be used with emphasis.

- During downhill braking, you may feel your tires begin to skid, especially when the surface of the terrain changes below your tires. Some mini skids (chirping) of the rear tire is OK; just ease off the levers a little to keep both brakes working in sync.

- Try not to drag your brakes all the way down the hill. This will reduce control of the bike and can overheat your brakes to the point where they become less effective. Whenever possible, stay off the brakes completely and then brake hard when firm, smooth terrain is available. If you can sufficiently lower your speed using this method, you'll have much better traction and control during your descents.

- When the surface is soft and loose, feather your brakes to keep the tires from locking up.

- If the trail is sloped off to one side (off-camber), your tires will be connected to the ground by their edge. This creates a reduced tire footprint that could lead to a tire slipping toward the downside, especially during braking. In this situation, it's better to brake lightly or to simply reduce your speed before the trail changes to off-camber.

- If you have a suspension lock-out feature, make sure it's set to the descend mode. Utilizing the full travel of your suspension allows the tires to move up and down and stay in contact with the terrain. By having the tires better connected to the ground, you'll have improved traction, stability, and braking.

Drop-offs

Drop-offs (drops) are trail features that drop down in a way that makes them impossible to roll down. They're often unavoidable, and going over the edge will most assuredly result in a launch into open air. It can be one of the greatest thrills of mountain biking, but it can also be dangerous and cause serious injury if it's not well executed. The flight must be expertly controlled from pre-launch to post-landing and is not something that should be attempted until adequate core skills are in place and some experience is gained on smaller and easier drops.

First of all, you need to have complete control of the bike before you launch, which means that your vision, speed, and balance need to be spot-on. You must have good visual interpretation of what's on the trail beyond the drop so that you know where you're going to land and what you're going to do after you land. This may even take getting off the bike beforehand to check out the landing site. Your speed and body positioning will determine how far you'll travel through the air and what your bike's orientation will be (pitched down, pitched up, or level). With a mastery of these elements, there's no reason you can't enjoy successful drops.

As you can imagine, how and where you land is critical to pulling this off safely. The idea is to touch down as softly and smoothly as possible while staying in control as you continue down the trail. Using good technique to soften the landing, you'll have maximum control of your bike in the follow-through, and you'll greatly increase the size of the drop that your shocks can handle. The best orientation for your bike as you touch down will depend on whether the landing spot is level or down-sloped. Landing on flat ground reflects more of the landing force back into the bike, while landing on a downslope tends to be a fast-paced, high-energy landing. Here's a comparison of landing pitches on flat ground:

A. **Pitched down, front wheel landing first:** Landing on flat ground with your front tire first is not very controllable and has a tendency to pitch the rider forward. This can be made worse if you land on any sort of trail irregularity. A front-down landing is caused by the front tire dropping downward as you go over the edge of the drop-off. If this happens, it's also possible that the rear tire or even the chainring will strike the edge, which could result in the rider being thrown over the bars.

B. **Level, both wheels simultaneously:** This is a solid and controllable way of landing, but on the bigger drops, it has the possibility of bottoming out your suspension. For this reason, landing this way reduces the possible height you can drop.

C. **Pitched up, rear wheel landing first:** Landing with the rear tire slightly first allows you to split the impact in half, your rear tire and knees taking the first part and then your front tire and elbows soaking up the rest. This is an easy way to transition your weight and soften the landing. Just be sure not to lift the front end too high or you'll be landing hard into the handlebars. Think of it like an aircraft landing gently onto a runway.

Landing on a downslope projects your kinetic energy forward and downward. This changes the dynamics of the landing and how you should set your tires down:

A. **Front wheel first:** If your front tire lands slightly first, this is okay. It can be transitioned smoothly as your rear tire sets down. But if your front end is pitched too far downward when you land, you could get thrown forward or your front tire could swerve and wash out.

B. **Both wheels:** This is the best scenario. The impact will be soft as your forward motion smooths out your landing. When you can successfully land in this manner, you'll be set up to handle the trail challenges in the follow through.

C. **Rear wheel first:** Landing on your rear tire could cause you to heave forward as your front tire comes down. The resulting force will try to throw you over the bars. This is a less-controllable way of landing that could end up with a terrible outcome.

As you can see, landing on flat ground is best accomplished with the rear wheel slightly first, and landing on down-sloped ground is best accomplished with both wheels at the same time. Getting the bike to land the way you want requires launching at the right speed with the right weight distribution. If you're going fast enough and keep your weight back, your front end will, for the most part, remain elevated. If you're going slower, the front end will drop down. To overcome this, you'll need to do a manual just before going over the edge. Just make sure that you're not pulling the handlebars with your arms because this will throw your balance too far forward. It's a whole-body weight redistribution, just like any manual.

Once your rear tire clears the edge, you can return your weight to center. If you're landing on a downslope, shift your weight slightly forward while airborne to get the angle of the bike ready for touchdown. Always use your elbows and knees to help absorb the impacts, and never use your brakes before you touch down because this could lock up the tire.

Estimating the right speed and weight distribution as you hit the drop-off is something that comes from an escalation of experience on smaller drops. Practice by first dropping off something easy, such as a curb. Ride toward the edge at a moderate speed in a balanced attack position and with level pedals. Just as you reach the edge, perform a manual to get the front end up a little. The rear tire should land slightly first. Experiment with different speeds to change the timing. The next step is to find some easy drops on the trails, and when you're comfortable with those, progress to a bigger drop-off and apply the same techniques. You should be able to pick this up fairly quickly. Keep it safe and use extra protective gear if you're set on attempting something beyond your comfort level.

CHAPTER THIRTEEN

Crashing

A CRASH IS BY far the most negative experience you'll have on a mountain bike. The pain and disappointment can really damage the psyche. And if you become seriously injured, it will not only ruin your whole ride, but it could also wreck your confidence and potentially turn you off from the sport. What makes matters worse is that every rider will have an incident at some point in time. The good news is that, by taking all of the necessary precautions and using the right techniques, the risks can be mitigated and the chances of it happening can be significantly reduced. It's also possible to completely avoid serious injuries such as broken bones, lacerations, and concussions. Protective gear, how to ride, where to ride, how to avoid crashes, and how to fall are all factors that need to be examined to understand the best ways to save your skin and bones.

Wear Protective Equipment

For safer riding, protective equipment must be used every time you go out. Its sole function is to mitigate damage to the body in the event of a crash. It's not an injury end-all, but it can make a big difference. Wearing a helmet is, without question, an absolute must. Your eyesight is invaluable and needs to be protected with impact-resistant eyewear. Full-fingered gloves will protect your vulnerable hands. Elbow pads and knee pads will not only protect your skin, but also protect against possible joint injuries. In addition to the knee pads, shin guards can be used to protect your lower legs, which is one of the most common places to break skin.

Full body armor is highly recommended in the downhill, freeride, and enduro disciplines of the sport. This is where much bigger risks are taken and serious injuries can occur. It would be wise to use a full-face helmet and goggles; upper body armor to protect the chest, ribs, and spine; and a neck protector to further guard the critical spinal cord. Also helpful are padded mountain bike shorts with padding along the sides to protect your hips, quads, and tailbone.

Protective equipment can sometimes provide a boost in confidence that can keep you from tensing up and riding more stiffly. Just don't let this sense of security cause you to ride dangerously beyond your skill level.

Where to Ride and Staying within Your Skill Limit

It's true that riding on difficult terrain will improve your skill level, but not if the learning curve includes crashing because it was too much for your current abilities. There's also a good chance of getting badly hurt from a crash on rocks and such. Even if you do make it through a scary section out of sheer luck, this is no way to learn. Going beyond your abilities is when mistakes will be made. Try focusing on trails that provide a challenge but can still be handled with confidence. If it's too steep, too narrow, too rocky, too loose, etc., you're better off walking the bike through it. Take incremental steps when it comes to increasing the difficulty level.

Speed is another big factor. Try riding about 25 percent slower than the point at which you lose confidence and control. Three-quarter speed will greatly reduce your risk of crashing while allowing you to perfect your techniques. This is the best and safest way to improve. Before you know it, your three-quarter speed will be the equivalent of your previous maximum speed.

Are you tired? Fatigue can rob you of your ability to stay focused, balanced, and muscularly responsive. If you've been doing some serious climbing, chances are you're feeling drained and fatigued. It's important to recognize this and to make appropriate adjustments such as slowing down or even walking through something difficult. Don't put yourself at risk when you're more likely to bite it.

If you're riding with other people who are better riders than you or if they're familiar with trails that are new to you, following them is a safer way to get through it, as long as they're willing to slow their pace. You'll be able to see what the leader is doing and how they handled a tough section, then all you have to do is copy the moves. Just be careful because if they make a mistake that puts them off balance and you subsequently imitate that same mistake . . . you could get sent to the ground. A solution is to keep your distance - close enough to see them but far enough that you can change strategy if necessary. Never over-focus on the rider in front of you; make sure you're also looking at the whole trail before, around, and after them.

Trails that you're familiar with are always easier because you know all of the upcoming features and what to expect around every corner. You'll be prepared with the correct response, making you a much more confident and safer rider. Just be careful not to get too comfortable and thereby less attentive . . . getting too cocky will get you hurt. (This is a common mistake.)

When you're exploring new trails and riding on unfamiliar terrain, it can be interesting and fun, but you'll be at a higher risk of tensing up because you'll keep getting surprised by things. The answer here is to slow down and keenly use your vision techniques to anticipate what's coming.

Sometimes, you'll have no way of knowing what's coming up around a bend. There may be a surprise waiting for you, such as a hidden drop-off. If it's something dangerous, you'll want to know about it before you become committed to riding it out. Imagine yourself on a slope that puts you nose down at a steep angle with a spider web of rocks and deep ruts. As you wind your way down, you're trying to cope with it by deftly maneuvering with a dance of balance and braking. You come around a bend and suddenly reach a series of rock ledges with drops in the range of two to six feet, forcing you to decide quickly what to do. There should be no loss of pride by stopping, getting off the bike, and walking down to discover what's coming up and figure out the best way to get through it. Even the most experienced riders will do this.

Ride with Confidence

Worrying about how things might go wrong as you stare at the technical features of the trail and frantically dodge one danger after another is no way to ride. Always on the defense, fear and apprehension will cause you to tense up, resulting in reduced flexibility, compromised coordination, and poor trail vision. This is when things *will* go wrong. Don't let this happen to you! Instead, approach the trails with confidence.

This goes back to the lesson on mental state of mind. When you're riding confidently, your mind is sharp, you're looking far ahead at the whole trail to determine the best line, and you're not focusing on any one thing. You're relaxed, and your arms and legs are soaking up the bumps. You're balanced. Your speed is neither too fast nor too slow. You're riding the bike and not letting the bike ride you. You're flowing with the trail. This sounds good in theory, but it's not always automatic; it sometimes takes a conscious effort.

On the flip side, it's sometimes possible to relax and defocus too much. Maybe it's because the trail just got easier and you're feeling tired. If this is the case, you should stop and have some gel or a power bar, or even call it quits for the day, because crashes often happen when we're either wiped out or our guard is down and we're going slower. This is when off-balance mishaps are common. This sport always requires diligence and full attention. Don't let the trail give you a sucker punch.

Types of Crashes and How to Avoid Them

There seems to be a limitless combination of circumstances that lead to a crash, but there are some basic, common themes. Crashes will typically fall under one of the following examples:

The Slow-Speed Tip Over: One of the most common ways to crash is tipping over at a slow speed. This can be caused by a number of things, such as a lack of attention, a lack of balance, improper planning and line choice, or simply running into something without performing a lift. It could happen while picking your way through a rock garden, going around a switchback, climbing up a steep and slippery hill, or any other such place that has you going slow.

Regardless of whether the problem is your skill or your location, you need to pay full attention to what's going on and be ready to put a foot down if you get in trouble. There is very little forward kinetic energy with these types of crashes, so knowing how to do a track stand can be helpful, but ultimately, putting a foot or both feet on the ground when needed will ensure that you're not going down.

Flipping Over the Bars: This type of crash, otherwise known as an "endo" (short for end over end), can be one of the most injurious ways to crash and should be avoided like the plague. It typically happens whenever the front tire runs into some kind of object or hole. An unprepared rider will not have their body weight shifted back and will not lift their front tire. As the bike impacts, it will stop abruptly, and the rear tire will rise up. The rider's forward inertia will then cause them to lurch over the handlebars.

This kind of unexpected impact could also happen when riding through some overgrowth that's hiding the trail and any rocks and roots below. Because you'll be completely unprepared for the impact, you could be sent right over the bars. Proceed with caution in this situation. Another endo scenario can happen when the rider turns the bars too sharply while heading downhill. The downward pitch and the forward inertia could then throw the rider over the front.

Endos are avoidable. The best thing to do as you go down the hill is to shift your weight back as necessary to keep it centered on the pedals while feathering the brakes to keep your speed reasonable. Equally important is to continuously scan the path ahead of you for any upcoming danger. This is especially important if you're on an unfamiliar trail and you don't know what to expect. If you do suddenly have an object directly in front of you, shift your weight back and get the front tire up the face of it. Last but not least, if an upcoming tough section has you unsure if you can handle it, don't let your pride get in the way of stopping, getting off, and walking through it.

Sliding Out in a Turn: You have to respect the loose stuff. If the terrain is gravel over hard pack, your tires will handle it just fine when you're going in a straight line. But in the turns, whether it's a sweeping downhill fire road or a tightly turning single-track, you must be aware of the dynamics. Your tires will handle it to a certain extent if the bike is properly leaned over, but excessive speed or inappropriate braking could have you picking gravel out of your elbows and knees.

The best way to avoid a slide out is by judging how fast you should be going through the turn and doing all of your braking before you get to it. Sound familiar? It seems simple enough, but when you're trying to make good time on Strava, you're in a race, or you're just trying to catch up to some friends, there's a tendency to come into the turns too hot. When it comes to speed, you need to use good judgment.

If you do find yourself sliding in a turn, you'll need to save yourself by putting one foot down while leaning forward into the handlebar. This will put weight on the front tire so that it has traction. When the rear tire finishes its slide, you can then resume riding normally. This is a great way to pull off a save.

Stuck in a Rut: Rain often washes grooves, called ruts, into hillside trails. Whether you're going uphill or downhill, the threat of your tires falling into a rut is ever present. They will often crisscross the path, which can make avoiding them difficult. If you end up inside a rut, you may not easily get out because you can't turn sharply enough to ride up and out without throwing your balance off so much that a crash becomes inevitable.

Pick your lines carefully, even if it means riding the edge of the trail to avoid the ruts. If you find yourself stuck in a rut, try riding it out. An opportunity to get out should present itself shortly, especially if the rut takes a sharp turn and you can attack its edge at a more or less right angle. Sometimes, the rut can deepen or become too rough to maneuver through. In this situation, bring the bike to a stop and manually pick it up and out, then continue on your way.

Bucked by Obstacles: You've just run into a rock garden; you've misjudged their size and complexity and you're going too fast. The bucking you receive shocks and scares you, so you respond by tensing up and over-correcting. The next thing you know, you're tumbling over the rocks. Where did you go wrong? This comes down to experience and technical abilities. Either it's too technical for your skill level, or you've made some serious errors in judgment.

You need to keep your eyes peeled far ahead to anticipate what's coming, attack it at the right speed, pick the best lines, stay loose and limber to soak up the impacts, let off the brakes as you traverse the rocks or roots, and be in a good attack position with your weight centered squarely into the pedals. If this section of trail is more difficult than anything you've successfully ridden in the past, you may want to rethink attempting it. Consider an easier path or getting off the bike and walking through it.

Hitting Sand: Deep sand pits can frequently cause a crash when riders attempt to cross them. On crowded trails or during a race, there's a good chance that other riders will run into the downed riders and/or their bikes. If you see someone who has crashed in a sand pit, wait until they're completely out of the way rather than trying to get around them.

Riding through sand can be tricky and takes practice. Try to stay seated while moving your weight further back on the saddle to minimize front-tire plowing. When you hit it, you don't want to push your pedals downward as you normally would. This would make your tires sink in and bog down. Instead, scoot back on the saddle and push forward on the pedals with a power stroke that goes from about the 11 o'clock position to the 3 o'clock position. This will help to propel the bike forward without mashing deeper into the sand.

How to Fall

How you fall and how you land make a huge difference on how much you get hurt. Under most circumstances, a well-executed fall will prevent broken bones and may even prevent broken skin. The goal is to control the fall and absorb the impact without any sudden bone-crunching stops or skin-abrading slides. This is not something that's thought out as it's happening, it's a sub-conscious skill that must be developed to occur naturally and instinctively.

The pedals and chainrings are notorious for causing cuts and lacerations during a crash. Completely disengaging from the bike by jumping off the pedals and pushing the bars away and down is the best way to avoid them. This action is easier with flat pedals but can also be done with clip-in pedals; it's just a little more challenging until you're used to rapid unclipping. Proficiently and thoughtlessly unclipping using only muscle memory is the goal. If you're not there yet, practice sharp and rapid outward heel swivels to unclip whenever you come to a stop. Note: if you're using adjustable tension pedals such as the Shimano SPDs, you should set the tension low until you become accustomed, then up the tension to something a little more secure.

Once unclipping is second nature, practice the following steps for rapid unclipping during a controlled dismount. Find a soft, grassy area and use the utmost caution because there's always a potential for injury here.

1. While riding at a slow speed, unclip the pedal when it's at the top position and put that foot down on the ground. At the same time, lay the bike over to the ground while releasing your hand from the bar. When your foot is solidly on the ground, release your other foot from the pedal and swing it clear over the bike and onto the ground. If you're going down to the right, the sequence is: right foot, right hand, left foot, left hand.

2. Next, switch feet and do the same thing on the opposite side. This will likely be your more awkward side, so practice until you're accustomed to laying the bike over and jumping clear. The sequence is: left foot, left hand, right foot, right hand.

3. Now practice these exercises at a slightly faster speed. Your reaction time will have to be quicker, but if you can manage this, you've come a long way in preventing injury.

A solid impact with the ground has the potential to cause broken bones. You need to be aware that there's a natural instinct to stop your fall by extending an arm straight out, but trying to save yourself in this manner can cause serious injury. Your speed plus your weight will create a considerable amount of force, and strong-arming your fall will transmit this force from your palm on through to your skeletal system, commonly resulting in a break at one of the two weak points, the wrist or the collarbone. You'll need to short-circuit this bad instinct and retrain yourself to fall in a way that minimizes the chances of a catastrophic injury.

If you find yourself heading to the ground, the safest and most effective way to dissipate the kinetic energy of your body in motion is to separate from the bike and do a shoulder roll, pulling your arms in and against your body while bending the knees until you come to a stop. This technique is called a tuck and roll. It's something that can be done whether your crash is a flip over the side, a slide out, or even a headfirst flight over the handlebars.

Crashing is not something you can or want to practice on the trails, or anywhere else for that matter, but there are certain skills that can be mastered that can increase the likelihood of a well-executed tuck and roll. Practice the following steps to learn the basics of this injury-reducing technique until it comes to you naturally, athletically, and instinctively.

1. Practicing a tuck and roll may take a little getting used to. It's best done on a gymnastics mat or on soft grass. To make it more realistic, try these steps with your cycling gear on, including your helmet.

2. Get into a three-point stance (like a lineman in American football) with one hand on the ground and two staggered feet, shoulder-width apart, while bending at the knees and waist until your thighs and back are nearly parallel to the ground.

3. Slowly lunge forward, leading with the shoulder of your free arm while holding this arm slightly bent and tucked in, ready to collapse. Don't stare at where you're going to land; instead, tuck your chin down and away.

4. As soon as your arm touches down, roll onto your shoulder and allow your arm to fully collapse to your chest while protecting your face. As you start your roll, bend your knees and pull your legs in.

5. Allow your body to roll until it stops.

6. If you can roll back onto your feet, more power to you, but this is not too common in a real crash situation.

7. Try this again on your opposite shoulder until you're accustomed to doing it on both sides.

8. Practice from a slightly squatted down, two-point stance. This will get you accustomed to falling down from a higher position.

Sometimes, a slow-speed crash will have you falling over to one side with not enough time to put a foot down and not enough momentum to separate from the bike. Once again, do not use an outstretched arm to brace for impact. Instead, keep your hands on the handlebar while releasing your falling-side foot from the pedal. You'll start absorbing the fall by moving your foot outward until it touches the ground with its side, followed by your lower leg and knee, rolling up to your hip, and then onto your shoulder. Just before your shoulder touches down, you can release the hand on the down side and pull it in closer to your body. The key here is to remain loose and relaxed and to allow the side of your body to roll onto the ground from bottom to top to absorb the fall.

Another situation that may prevent you from separating from the bike is a slide out that happens so fast that you don't have time to react. Hopefully, you don't make the kind of serious misjudgment that leads to this type of crash because you could end up with some serious abrasions. In this situation, it would be best to remain connected to the pedals and to hold onto the bars while you ride out the slide. If you attempt and fail to separate from the bike, you could get entangled and sustain worse injuries.

Recovering from a Crash

If you had a crash that wasn't too bad and you came out of it unhurt, you can simply pick up the bike and continue riding. But sometimes its bad enough that you need to check your wounds and the condition of the bike. Before you do anything, get off the trail as a courtesy to other riders. This will also eliminate the possibility of being run into. Next, you'll want to assess your injuries. If you're certain that it's not serious, but you find yourself bleeding, you should tend to your wounds by cleaning, disinfecting, and covering them. Lastly, check your bike for any damage. Besides disappointedly staring at the new scratches, check that:

1. The chain is in place and the derailleur operates properly.

2. The handlebars are straight and the levers are properly positioned.

3. Your rims are straight and your tires remained properly inflated.

4. The frame is not cracked.

Do not attempt to ride the bike if it's in an unsafe condition!

After you've assessed the damage, gather up your water bottle and any other personal items that may have come loose. At this point, you'll be trying to figure out exactly what happened and where you went wrong. Ask yourself: "What should I have done differently that could have prevented this?" Maybe you could have taken a better line, or maybe you were pushing too hard on rough terrain and simply couldn't handle it. Whatever it is, run through your mind how you would change your approach. When it comes to crashing, there's a learning process that ends up making you a more experienced rider. It's your chance to increase your knowledge base and improve your riding skills. As in anything in life, we learn from our mistakes. With mountain biking, knowing where you went wrong and doing it correctly in the future will make you a much better rider.

When you get back on the bike, try to put the crash behind you because fear can control your actions. Remaining tensed up, afraid, frustrated, and angry could cause you to death-grip the handlebar, which in turn could lead to another crash . . . the last thing that you need. Do your best to clear it from your mind while focusing on the task at hand.

Fully recovering from a crash often entails facing down your fear by returning to the site and giving that spot another go-at-it. This can sometimes be intimidating. Fear is something that all riders will experience at some point in time no matter what their skill level is. As you learn from your crash experiences, you'll find that you have much more confidence and control.

When you put together and follow all of the riding advice we've covered in this book, you'll become a much better rider and will be far less likely to crash. Things such as making good use of the ready position, relaxing, looking far ahead, braking at the right moments, and properly leaning the bike in the turns are all factors in riding skillfully, confidently, and safely.

> *"Leave all the afternoon for exercise and recreation, which are as necessary as reading. I rather say more necessary because health is worth more than learning."*
>
> -- Thomas Jefferson

PART FOUR

Fitness Training

MOUNTAIN BIKING IS a very physical sport that can sometimes put a high demand on the body. The better physical shape one is in, the better these high demands can be handled. Indeed, it will not only determine how well you can handle technical terrain, but also how well you can climb hills and how long you can ride without bonking. It should be every mountain biker's strong desire to improve their physical fitness along with their bike-handling skills. There are several components that make up physical fitness, each of which is important for mountain biking and each requiring personal dedication to bring continuous improvement:

1. **Cardiovascular Endurance:** This is a measure of your cardiovascular system's ability to sustain pedaling effort over a period of time. It's gauged by how long and intensely you can ride until you reach VO_2 max.

2. **Muscular Endurance:** This is a measure of your leg muscles' ability to sustain pedaling against resistance over a period of time. The point at which you hit your lactate threshold and the subsequent "hitting the wall" is a good way to measure muscular endurance.

3. **Strength:** This is a measure of your muscles' ability to move against resistance. The steeper the hill, the more leg strength that will be required to rotate the cranks.

4. **Flexibility:** Flexibility is your muscles' and tendons' ability to stretch without injury. With mountain biking, flexible muscles throughout the body are important for reducing injuries and for remaining loose and limber for technical riding.

Everybody is different. We all have differences in our metabolisms and how we process energy. We also have differences in our musculoskeletal genetic makeup, which means our natural ability to improve endurance, strength, and flexibility will vary from person to person. But one thing that's consistent is our ability to improve. All it takes is the right mental can-do attitude.

Another hindrance to performance in this sport is excessive body weight because unnecessary body fat has to be carried by your legs up the hills, which further taxes your endurance. Again, this is something that can definitely be improved. Everybody needs body fat to survive, but too much of it is the concern. As we age, the percentage of fat to body weight goes up, but it's the body's shape and appearance that reveal if there's room for improvement. Look at the charts below[22]. Clearly, the images to the right are more preferable, and the images to the left are less preferable. For men in this sport, the 12-15 percent body fat range is ideal, and for women, the 20-25 percent range is ideal.

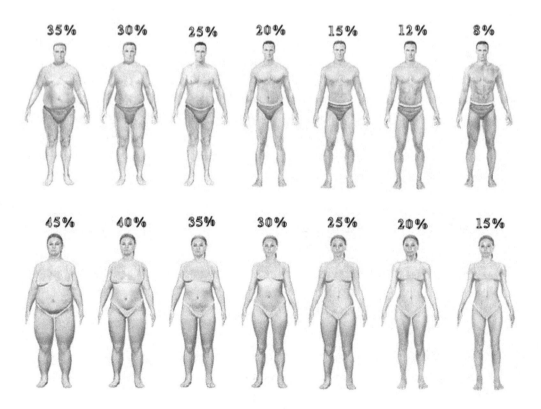

When you're active in this sport, you're an athlete, even if you consider yourself a recreational rider. As such, athletes strive to improve themselves so that they can better perform their activities. When you train to improve, you're working to increase your endurance, strength, and flexibility. You're also conscientious of your eating habits and your nutritional intake. When you do these things, you get the bonus benefit of a reduction in body fat. It's a win-win situation, but it's up to you to have the perseverance to follow through. The following chapters will outline what it takes to make improvements in these areas. Follow closely for success.

> *"Physical fitness is not only one of the most important keys to a healthy body, it is the basis of dynamic and creative intellectual activity"*
>
> *-- John F. Kennedv*

CHAPTER FOURTEEN

Endurance

CROSS-COUNTRY AND AGGRESSIVE trail riding are the best disciplines to increase your mountain biking endurance. Nothing else can match the combination of steep climbs and terrain challenges. The combined requirements of good technique, balance, visual prowess, strength, and cardio are unlike any other sport.

Extended riding and climbing will push the limits of cardiovascular intensity and endurance, as well as muscular endurance. This continuous, extended muscle tension and strain will cause your body to react and adapt; you'll have an inevitable increase in your performance. While this is desirable and achievable, it's something that can only be improved slowly; a quick transformation is not possible. It takes hard work and serious motivation. You need to be dedicated and mentally ready to give everything you have each time you exercise because how much you push to be ever-better and to achieve your goals will determine your fitness destiny.

Note: Whenever you start a new exercise program or you're planning to begin riding at higher intensities, it should be cleared by your doctor first, especially if you have any pre-existing medical conditions. To get an idea of what your starting intensity should be, you'll need a realistic evaluation of your current fitness level. If you've been relatively sedentary and are now ready to make changes for the better, you'll be starting out with low-level exercise. If you already get some form of exercise but need to increase your endurance, you'll still be taking gradual steps, but you can begin at a somewhat higher intensity.

All muscle tissue is made up of fibers, but not all of these fibers are alike. There are two generalized types: slow twitch fibers that use more oxygen than glucose (aerobic) and fast twitch fibers that use more glucose than oxygen (anaerobic). Different people have different ratios of slow and fast twitch. Someone with a higher percentage of slow twitch fibers may be better at sustaining exercise over a longer period of time, such as a long-distance runner. Someone with a higher percentage of fast twitch fibers may have more explosive power, such as a sprinter. With mountain biking, both kinds of fibers are important and should be trained to work better.

Cardio Endurance (Increasing Your VO₂ max)

As you begin your physical fitness journey, adopting cardio endurance training is a good way to establish a fitness base that you can grow upon. This involves prolonged moderate intensity exercise from significant time on the saddle, primarily working the slow twitch fibers of your muscles. This kind of fitness training will form the basis of everything else you do and will pay big dividends with all aspects of riding by improving your cardiorespiratory system's ability to deliver oxygen.

If it's your first time on a mountain bike ride, start with something short, say a couple of miles/kilometers. Skip the big hill climbs and stick to rolling terrain for now, but keep adding distance every time you go for a ride, preferably a few times a week. When you reach about ten miles/kilometers, you'll be ready to pick up the pace and start climbing some moderate hills. You should be pushing your heart rate significantly faster, your breathing should be harder, and your legs should be feeling constant tension. As you're doing this, the tiny capillaries in your leg muscles will be developing[23]. This will improve blood delivery and bring oxygen where it's needed, thus helping you get through your rides without becoming overly fatigued.

Building a fitness base and increasing your VO₂ max is best accomplished with rides that last at least two hours. As your muscles adapt and produce more energy, keep adding distance to your rides. There's no shortcut, but with a little hard work and strategy, you'll be able to achieve long distances and fast times.

Muscular Endurance (Increasing Your Lactate Threshold)

Once you have a good base of aerobic training, you'll be ready to work on delaying the onset of lactate burn. Raising your lactate threshold will reward you with big climbing ability - the power to make it up longer and steeper hills without hitting the wall. Of course, you want this, but it'll take hard work and dedication.

One training technique to enhance your progress involves climbing hills at an intensity that's either right at your lactate threshold or just below it. When you start to feel a light burn, you'll know you've hit it. This is an intensity that you should be able to hold for up to an hour. By continuously pushing this boundary, it can be moved steadily higher. If you feel the burning getting too intense, you may have to ease off a little or choose a less challenging hill because walking the bike up will defeat the purpose. To make it all the way, longer hills that are not too steep are the best option. If you can get in some serious saddle time at this level of intensity, you'll make some great progress and notice that the hill climbs are getting easier. You can then challenge yourself with the steeper hills.

Another good way to raise your threshold is with a technique called "interval training." This is done using short bursts of power to push your system well beyond your lactate threshold. You'll be intentionally allowing your legs to burn heavily as the lactate builds up in your muscles. This is followed by a recovery period, which should be double the time of the power burst. Recovery involves using slow and easy pedaling to clear out the lactate. If your power burst is 30 seconds long, your recovery period will be one minute; if your burst is one minute long, recovery will be two minutes, etc. Repeat this overload and recovery several times. As you get better, you'll be able to shorten your recovery time.

High intensity training will force your system to become better at clearing lactate, thereby raising your lactate threshold. Keep in mind that intensity training will also increase your endurance, but endurance training will not increase your intensity. Basically, intensity training will make you a much stronger rider, which should make "pushing until it hurts" a high priority.

Using a Heart Rate Monitor

The rate that your heart beats is directly related to the amount of exertion your body is going through. As such, your beats-per-minute number is an accurate reflection of your exercise intensity at any given moment. A heart rate monitor is a device that provides you with this number so that you can adjust your intensity as needed. You'll be able to tailor your exercise for maximum cardiovascular fitness gains or to keep yourself in a certain zone to prevent over-exertion.

The best monitors for biking use a strap around your chest to measure the electrical pulses of your heart. These wirelessly connect to either a cycling app that provides audible announcements or to a cycling computer that mounts to your handlebar. Although a cycling computer can provide a visual heart rate number at all times, this can be distracting and difficult to look at when there's a lot of trail action. These are better suited for non-technical rides and for road cyclists. If you use a cycling app, further details of your various heart rates throughout the ride can be obtained by analyzing the stored data when you're done riding.

If you're working on building cardio fitness while staying below your lactate threshold, you'll want to push your heart rate as high as possible without feeling the burn. Once you know this heart rate number, you can hold it just below your threshold level and sustain the exertion over longer periods of time. As your fitness increases, you'll find that you can hold higher heart rates without burning out your legs.

Road Biking

Road biking can be a great way to build your cycling endurance, especially if you're not close to readily accessible trails or ones that can serve as a good fitness training ground. Trying to get in some serious fitness building miles/kilometers on varied off-road terrain can sometimes be difficult. If your local trail system inhibits you from long distance riding with an uninterrupted and sustained effort, road cycling can provide the opportunities to significantly improve your fitness and may be your best alternative. Even though it's not the preferred cycling experience of mountain bikers, it's definitely something that should be considered when you're trying to make improvements to your cardiovascular performance.

The roads will allow you to accurately adjust your power output and speed to keep you right on the edge. Hill climbing on the road is usually a long and predictable incline, which will allow you to accurately stay just below your lactate threshold. If you're doing intervals, road riding will give you complete control of your power surges and recovery periods.

Another advantage that road cycling offers is the opportunity to practice your pedaling stroke technique. The problem with trying to perfect your circular strokes while mountain biking is that it ends up being the last thing you're thinking about when you're negotiating rough terrain. Instinctively pedaling in circles is definitely advantageous, but it takes practice to make it second nature. Focusing on this while on the roads is easier because, as it pertains to the tasks at hand, there's often not a lot to think about.

The dangers of road cycling are distinctly different. With mountain biking, a crash is almost always some kind of mistake that could have been prevented by doing something differently. On the road, the drivers of motorized vehicles pose a different kind of risk. When they make a mistake and hit a cyclist, there's often nothing the cyclist could have done to prevent it. The risks can certainly be reduced by sticking to bike lanes, never riding alone, obeying the laws, vigilantly using a rearview mirror, using front and rear flashing lights, and remaining continuously attentive to drivers' actions. When considering road cycling, keep the ever-present danger of vehicles in mind.

Group Indoor Cycling Classes

Indoor cycling classes don't provide the outdoor experience that mountain bikers enjoy so greatly, but they can be extremely effective at increasing cardiovascular fitness and should be given due consideration. For many people, packing up the bike and travelling to the trails on work or school days is just not feasible, especially when daylight gets shorter. Difficult winter weather can also make outdoor riding problematic.

If you're riding too seldomly to make significant gains or to maintain your fitness, group indoor cycling classes can be the next best option. Of course, you won't be practicing trail skills, but these classes do offer a way to improve your leg strength and cardiovascular fitness.

With the lights down low, the music thrumming in your ears, the instructor commanding your intensity, and motivated people all around you, it can be highly stimulating. The instructor will tell you to pedal faster or slower, to increase or decrease the resistance, to sit down or stand up, and may run you through various exercise programs that are designed to push your limits.

Sometimes the instructions are extremely intensive, and sometimes they're of average intensity to allow most of the participants to keep up. If you feel you're more advanced than the others, by all means push harder than what's being called out. Be a leader. This takes mental discipline, but it's how you'll make the most gains. Remember, you've got mountains to climb!

If you're lucky, the bike you're using will have a digital display that shows information like RPMs, gear number, wattage, and cycling time. The most important number to pay attention to is average wattage, which is usually displayed at the end of your session. This is the number you need to best yourself on every time you're on the machine.

Another useful feature is Bluetooth connectivity for heart rate monitors. With this information, you can figure out your lactate threshold heart rate, your heart rate at maximum effort, and the amount of time it takes to get your heart rate down to recovery level. This is good information to know when you're trying to understand your perceived exertion.

There's no better opportunity to practice spinning in circles than on an indoor bike. With a stable machine, you can really get a feel for applying circular power. You can even test your smoothness by doing one-legged pedaling since there is little chance of tipping over. Just don't try it during class time, and be careful not to hit yourself with the loose pedal.

Indoor cycling classes have a reputation that is often tarnished by substandard instructors. If he or she doesn't understand what's required for a serious cyclist to raise their VO_2 max and lactate threshold, doesn't understand the importance of pushing big gears to simulate hill climbing, doesn't have a commanding presence, and/or uses a lot of "fluff" such as rocking, gyrating, or taking your hands off the bars for any reason, it's probably not a class worth attending. But if you can find a class in your locality with a quality instructor who understands outdoor cycling and has like-minded, enthusiastic students, then you've scored. The rest will be up to you psychologically.

As an alternative to these classes, you could try a stationary bike at home, or you could use a trainer that your bike mounts to, but these take some seriously consistent motivation that may or may not occur when you're by yourself. Classes can be the answer because all you have to do is show up and the motivation will come.

While indoor cycling is not as good as the real thing, consistently doing a one-hour class at least three times a week will accelerate your fitness and make those big hills feel smaller. At the least, you'll be able to maintain your fitness when you can't get outdoors. Don't knock it until you try it.

Cross Training

If the winter months are putting a damper on your cycling and indoor exercise just doesn't cut it for you, there are still many sports that can be used to enhance your mountain biking abilities and fitness level. Don't just waste away in the off months. Try something physical and fun. There are several activities that can be done year round that will definitely benefit not only your fitness and coordination, but the way your mind interacts with your body. Try working one or more of these activities into your life:

Jogging/Running: Although this isn't going to have a significant impact on your coordination, it will have a direct impact on your endurance. It's something that can be done just about anywhere and is fairly easy to work into a busy schedule.

Basketball: This is a great sport for improving your cardiovascular system while greatly enhancing your eye-hand coordination and your balance.

Swimming: This is a serious cardio workout that will build and tone a vast array of muscles while regulating and deepening your breathing. It's an all-around great workout that will have a positive impact on your fitness and performance.

Snow Skiing and Snowboarding: These sports are excellent for developing your vision techniques, response time to various situations, and your overall athleticism. All of this will translate very nicely to your mountain biking skillset.

These are just a few good examples of cross-training activities that can maintain or even improve your mountain biking endurance and skills. There are many more activities that can be beneficial in various ways. It's just a matter of working them into your life and doing it consistently and in a competitive-minded way.

CHAPTER FIFTEEN

Strength Training

MOUNTAIN BIKING REQUIRES strength. Not just the strength to turn the cranks during steep climbs, but also the strength to withstand the rigors of the trails. Repeatedly pushing, pulling, lifting, turning, etc., to negotiate with the terrain puts a big strain on the human body. After a while, it can become extremely tiresome. And when fatigue takes over, crashes become much more likely. Strong and durable upper body muscles will fare much better in this sport.

You may have concerns that increasing your muscle mass will increase your weight on the bike, but you can rest assured that the benefits of extra muscle exceed the drawback of increased weight. Besides, cardio alone may not burn off the excess body fat that you may be trying to lose. Having more muscles means that your internal fire is burning more calories, and hence fat, all hours of the day. An exercise program that includes both cardio and weightlifting is the best way to trim down and tone up.

If you *are* interested in seriously beefing up and looking more athletic, this can also have distinct advantages with mountain biking. We're not talking about emulating the bodybuilders on the covers of weightlifting magazines, just adding some musculature if you have a thin frame. You'll not only feel better about yourself, but you'll have more athletic prowess.

Another important factor to contemplate is the extra padding and protection muscles provide in a crash. This consideration should not be taken lightly, as everyone will crash at some point, and muscle thickness really does make a big difference on how serious the injuries will be. Bear in mind that broken bones are the most common serious injury in a crash. Muscles will not only pad the bones but also help to hold everything together. Strong, thick, and flexible muscles are truly your best internal protection.

As far as leg exercises, there's some debate on the efficacy of weight training on cycling performance. The most current studies show that, while it does not provide an endurance advantage, it can have a positive effect on explosive type power, such as what is needed to get up a sudden, steep incline[24]. Making this kind of strength gain is a matter of doing the appropriate leg muscle workout with the optimal number of repetitions for a cycling application.

Dangers & Precautions

Note: It's recommended that you check with your doctor before you begin any exercise program. Use of a certified personal trainer will greatly reduce the chance of injuries. Whenever you start any exercise program, you have to ease into it to prevent injuring previously underused muscles, tendons, and ligaments. Resistance exercise stresses the muscles, making them stronger and more resilient. But in the process, it's entirely possible to cause small tears to tendons and ligaments, the tissues that connect muscles to bones. One way to help prevent injury is by slowly easing into it until your muscles are more conditioned and able to take on the stresses. Tight, weak, and unconditioned muscles are more likely to allow damage, while strong and flexible muscles are less likely to allow damage.

It's relatively easy to become injured if you've never done strength training before or if you're just resuming your training after taking some time off. It's imperative to start out with much lighter weights than you're capable of lifting because too much too soon is a major cause of injury. Your body simply needs time to adapt before you can push harder. Another big cause of injuries is poor lifting technique. Any motion under a load that's done the wrong way can easily pull or tear tissues. If you're inexperienced, you may want to consider the guidance of a personal trainer.

Age is another factor that affects rates of injury. Youths under supervision and adults in their 20s have a fairly low risk of injury[25]. Strength and flexibility will begin declining after about age 30 to 35; after about 50, many people will start to develop some kind of joint problem regardless of their activity level; and after about 55 to 60, muscular strength will quickly diminish. A lot of these maladies can be reversed, prevented, or slowed down with a proper exercise program. The question is: what is your age when you decide to start? Clearly, starting at an older age will require more caution.

Repetitions and Sets

A repetition is the full motion of one exercise - all the way up and all the way down. A set is a group of repetitions, regardless of how many are accomplished. The number of repetitions, the amount of weight, and the degree of effort during the last couple of repetitions in the set will determine the intensity level. If you're an experienced lifter looking to make the most gains, you'll want to take it to full intensity by pushing the weight until you hit the point of failure. In fact, you can even go beyond this with a spotter (another person who helps by lightly assisting you to complete the repetition or repetitions.)

The following categories represent the various intensities that can be used for weight training. Which one you choose depends on the particular exercise and your goals. Mixing it up every couple of weeks is a common way of getting the best results. If you're new to weightlifting, you'll want to keep it light to prevent injuries until you become more conditioned. If you're experienced with weightlifting, use the highest weight possible that still allows you to complete your chosen number of repetitions.

Heavy: Three sets of eight to ten repetitions, resting two to three minutes between sets. This will give you the fastest muscle and strength gains.

Moderate: Three sets of ten to fifteen repetitions, resting one to two minutes between sets. This is a good range for developing muscle tone.

Light: Two sets of fifteen to twenty repetitions, resting less than one minute between sets. This is good for developing muscular endurance and a tolerance for lactic acid build-up.

Mountain Biking Muscles

There are nearly 700 named muscles in the human body, many of which work in groups to perform certain motions. Different types of sports, including mountain biking, will activate specific groups of muscles that are primary to the sports' unique actions. Resistance exercises can be tailored to work out these specific muscles for maximum effectiveness and performance.

Entire books have been written on resistance exercises/weight training/body building. The variety of exercises that can be performed at the gym and at home is quite expansive. Additionally, the methods for performing correct motions and the techniques for maximizing muscle gains can be detailed. For serious bodybuilders, there's a lot to learn. The details of the exercises are beyond the scope of this book and are not defined here, so further research will be required. The intent of this chapter is simply to raise awareness of the positive effects that resistance training has on mountain biking, and to point out some of the specific exercises that target "mountain biking muscles."

Everyone's workout routine will be different; much depends on individual level of experience. Which exercises to perform and in what sequence, how many times per week, how much weight to use, and how many sets and reps are all in play. The combinations that make up a routine are countless. Since mountain biking is fluid and uses "groups" of muscles, it can be beneficial to do exercises that rely on groups to keep the muscles working fluidly together, while muscle isolation is the best way to build raw strength. A routine that combines both of these approaches will bring the best results.

Calves: There are several muscles on the front, sides, and back of the calves that connect in a variety of ways to the knees and the feet. These muscles will assist the quads with power and pedaling. Well-conditioned calves will also help to reduce the fatigue that happens while continuously holding the pedals in position during off-the-saddle riding.

There are a number of calf-strengthening exercises that can be done on gym equipment including: <u>Standing Calf Raises</u>, <u>Seated Calf Raises</u>, and <u>Calf Presses</u>. A combination of various exercises will usually give the best results.

Quadriceps (quads): This is a group of four muscles that run from the knees up to the hips on the front and sides of the thighs. These powerful muscles extend the legs at the knee and are the main driving force of your pedaling. Working out these muscles will give you more power when it's needed. Another consideration is that cycling doesn't fully contract and

extend the quads and tends to concentrate the work to the outer sides of the legs. This has the potential to put uneven strain on the kneecaps and the adjoining tendons, which could then lead to injuries. Resistance exercises to fully develop the quad muscles can compensate for this[26].

The granddaddy of all quad exercises is the <u>Barbell Full Squat</u>. It's the single most effective exercise for strength and muscle gains and is the best weight-lifting exercise to complement your mountain bike training. It will hit multiple other muscle groups including calves, hamstrings, glutes, and lower back. A word of caution: This exercise can be dangerous if proper form is not used, so make sure to get good instructions and don't overload the weight. <u>Machine Leg Presses</u> and <u>Machine Leg Extensions</u> can also aid in a more even development of the quad muscles. A couple of other great quad exercises are <u>Lunges</u> and <u>Step-ups</u>. Both of these can be done with either a barbell or with dumbbells and will also hit the calves, hamstrings, and glutes.

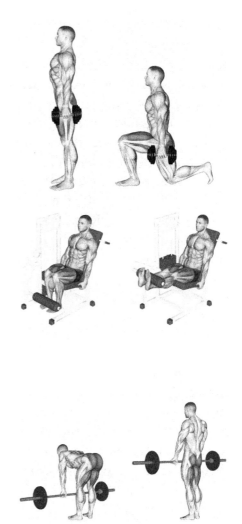

Gluteus Maximus (glutes): These large muscles constitute the majority of your buttocks. They help to raise you off the saddle when you need to get up, and they straighten the legs at the hip when standing pedaling. They connect to and work in tandem with your quads to complete full motions. Strengthening this muscle is beneficial for many mountain biking situations.

<u>Squats</u>, <u>Lunges</u>, <u>Step-ups</u>, and the <u>Deadlift</u> are highly effective exercises for the glutes. The Deadlift can be done with either a barbell or with dumbbells and will also hit the lower back and the forearms.

Core: The core refers to the body's midsection and includes both the abdominal muscles (abs) and the muscles of the lower back. Your core is the muscular connection between your upper body and your lower body and is critical for mountain biking. These muscles

move your upper body in all directions. They will also hold your upper body still by resisting motions such as twisting and bending. After riding for a while on rough terrain, this area of the body can easily become exhausted. Once that happens, pedaling performance will be negatively affected due to the legs' and the core's common connection with the hips. Enough can't be said about the importance of strengthening this area of your body.

Multi-muscle exercises such as Squats and Deadlifts will also use the muscles of the lower back. A great exercise that isolates the lower back is Back Extensions. For the abdominals, there's a wide variety of exercises including Crunches, Sit-ups, and Leg Lifts. No fancy equipment is needed, but they can be assisted with a mat, a BOSU-ball,

or a stability ball. These should be done several times a week for the quickest gains.

Back: The back has several major muscles that in total perform a wide variety of functions including pushing, pulling, and lifting. They directly support the muscles of the shoulders and the upper arms. This makes strong back muscles a must for mountain biking.

There are many great exercises for the muscles in the middle and upper back. One such exercise is Bent-over Rows, which can be done on a machine or by using barbells, dumbbells, or kettlebells. Seated Cable Rows and Lat Pulldowns are a couple additional back exercises that can be quite effective.

Shoulders: No matter how the bike is moved . . . up, down, back, forth, turning . . . the shoulders are involved. Each shoulder has three deltoid muscles (front, middle, and rear) that can provide both the strength to deal with the rigors of mountain biking and the dexterity for body positioning and weight shifting. Making these muscles stronger will also help to prevent common injuries such as a torn tendon at the rotator cuff.

The shoulders need to be worked out using a combination of exercises. The <u>Shoulder Press (a.k.a. Military Press)</u> can be done on a machine or by using barbells, dumbbells or kettlebells. This exercise will also work out the triceps. <u>Lateral Raises</u> isolate the shoulders and are done with a machine or with dumbbells. The trapezius muscle (traps) connects the shoulders to the neck. <u>Shrugs</u> will isolate the traps and can be done with a cable machine, a barbell, or dumbbells. <u>Upright Rows</u> will work out both the shoulders and the traps and are done with a barbell or a curl bar.

Another exercise that should be tried is the <u>Russian Kettlebell Swing</u>. Kettlebell exercises typically hit multiple muscles, which can be very useful for fluid motions. This particular one is the most popular of them all. While it has the biggest impact on the shoulders, it will also hit the back, hips, glutes, and quads. It's recommended to get personalized instructions for safe and proper technique.

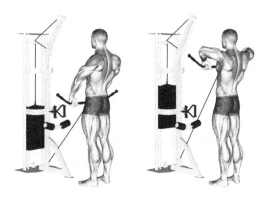

Triceps: These are the three muscles at the back of the upper arm. They extend the arms at the elbow, giving the ability to push. This works with turning, making your way around obstacles, maintaining the ready/attack position, and providing support when the ground is bouncing the bike around. They can also help to pull up on the handlebars when necessary. They get a lot of use, so it's important to have strong triceps.

There are a number of excellent exercises that concentrate on the triceps. One of the most effective is the <u>Arms Overhead Extension</u>. Because this arm position stretches out the triceps, it has the biggest impact. It can be done through a variety of methods including cables, machines, dumbbells, and kettlebells. <u>Lying Extensions</u> are also extremely effective and can be done with a machine or with a straight bar, a curl bar, or a triceps bar. <u>Dips</u> will hit the triceps at a different angle and should also be tried. A <u>Close Grip Bench Press</u>, while also hitting your chest, is another good option for the triceps.

Forearms: The group of muscles in the forearms will get a lot of use during mountain biking, especially on rough terrain. They work with the hands to maintain a grip while simultaneously flexing and extending as your body and your wrist position changes. Well-conditioned forearm muscles will help delay the fatigue and soreness that can sometimes lead to mishaps and crashes. The forearms will typically get a workout when any type of upper body exercise is performed, but sometimes it may be necessary to specifically target this area. <u>Wrist Curls</u>, <u>Reverse Wrist Curls</u>, and <u>Wrist Rollers</u> are all great options.

Training all of these muscle groups will definitely pay off on the bike. You may have noticed that a few of the major muscle groups didn't make it to this list. It's not because you won't use them; it's because they have a lower impact on the sport. Most notable are the biceps, the chest, and the hamstring muscles. Because biceps are primarily used for underhanded pulling, they don't play a major role in mountain biking. Chest muscles' main use is to move the arms across the body. Other than helping with some steering input, this is not an action that requires a lot of strength. However, if you're a man trying to develop a muscular look, the biceps can definitely be a standout feature, and nothing will make you look stronger than a well-developed chest. Try <u>Barbell Curls</u>, <u>Preacher Curls</u>, or <u>Dumbbell Curls</u> for your biceps, and <u>Bench Press</u> combined with the <u>Dumbbell Fly</u> or the <u>Machine Fly</u> for your chest. The hamstrings are the muscles on the back side of the thighs. These can play a minor role in standing up and with stabilization. Because they don't get heavy use, it's common to see cyclists with large quads but underdeveloped hamstrings. To attain a balanced look, you may want to consider performing resistance exercises that will beef them up, such as <u>Leg Curls</u>.

Find out all that you can about these exercises and any others that you may want to add to your routine. Look them up online, buy a book, or hire a personal trainer. Wherever you get the information, carefully follow the directions and find a routine that you can commit to. Learn to do them with the strictest form for maximum effectiveness and a reduced risk of injury. Performed correctly and on a consistent basis, these exercises can bring awesome results.

> *"Notice that the stiffest tree is most easily cracked, while the bamboo or willow survives by bending with the wind"*
>
> -- Bruce Lee
>
> Martial Artist and Actor

CHAPTER SIXTEEN

Flexibility Training

A GREAT NUMBER OF people have a tendency to neglect their muscle flexibility, especially non-athletes. But for the athlete, stretching is a critical component of conditioning the body for performance. Virtually all world-class athletes stretch as part of their fitness routines . . . and with good reason. The gains far outweigh the time penalty of performing these exercises. Consider the following benefits of stretching as you're deciding whether or not to commit to a routine:

Increased flexibility: This extra flexibility means that your muscles and joints will have a greater range of motion. This will make you more nimble on the bike and able to push your body to perform maneuvers with greater ease.

Increased coordination: Flexible muscles tend to have better coordination and, therefore, better technique.

Increased balancing ability: The increased range of motion of muscles and joints will help with the coordination and balance required to remain upright.

Increased fluidity and speed: The vigorous movements on the bike will benefit from the faster motions that flexible muscles and joints can provide.

Increased blood flow: Your blood circulation will increase as a result of the increased flexibility. This benefits your cardiovascular system.

Reduced rate of injury and recovery time: Stiff and inflexible muscles have a much higher risk of injury, including leg muscle strain . . . a common sports-related injury. Flexible muscles and joints are less susceptible to strains and pulls. If one does occur, it will be less severe and the recovery time will be shorter.

Reduced post-ride soreness: Without good flexibility, your muscles will become more stiff and sore, especially the day after the ride.

Stretching is an important factor when it comes to increasing the body's ability to perform and is a crucial activity for every mountain biker. But how stretching is performed is also important. If it's done incorrectly, the benefits will not be realized because bad technique can actually cause injuries. Basically, if you force the stretch to the point that it's painful, you're overstretching and causing too much tissue damage; and if you're bouncing, you can pull a tendon. At the least, you'll be causing excessive micro-tears to your muscle tissues that end up leaving you overly sore and discouraged.

The way to gain flexibility is with repetitive, gentle stretching. This is best accomplished by pulling just enough to feel tension and slight discomfort. Do this often, and the muscles will respond by elongating. You may not notice any difference from stretch to stretch, but over time, you'll be rewarded. Shoot for performing each stretch for anywhere between 20 and 60 seconds, repeating the stretch two or three times and doing it two or three times per week. This may sound like a lot, but in reality, it doesn't take that much time.

There are two basic methods of stretching: static stretches, which entail holding a stretching pose for a period of time; and dynamic stretches, which are done using motion. In each category, there are countless different stretches that can be used, but a good basic stretch for each body area will be enough. New poses and movements can be tried as you progress. There are so many variations that it would be well beyond the scope of this book to list them all, but an internet search will provide you with plenty of good options. One more important note: Always remember to keep breathing while stretching.

Static Stretches

Static stretching can be a highly effective and beneficial activity but can reduce the muscle's ability to provide power for a certain period of time[27]. Serious stretching with cold muscles can also lead to injury. For this reason, the best advice is to stretch within ten minutes of completing exercise. This will ensure that your tissues are "warmed up" and more receptive to elongation. The following are just a few examples of basic static stretches:

Quadriceps Stretch: While standing and supporting yourself with one hand, pull your foot with the other hand and bring your heel toward your buttocks until a stretch is felt in front of the thigh. Keep your leg close to and parallel with your other leg. Your knee should be pointing to the floor. Switch legs and repeat.

Hamstring Stretch: This can be done either seated or standing. If seated, you'll be on the ground with one leg straight out in front of you and a slight bend at the knee. The other leg is bent with your foot facing inward for balance. Lean forward until you feel the appropriate amount of stretch. Switch legs and repeat. If standing, you'll need something to prop your foot on, such as a chair, and something to hold on to for balance. Prop your foot up with your leg straight out or with a slight bend at the knee, and then lean forward for the appropriate amount of stretch. Switch legs and repeat.

Calf Stretch: Put your hands against a wall straight out in front of you, and then leave one foot in place while taking a big step back. Make sure your feet are facing forward and are flat on the ground. Next, slowly lean in toward the wall by bending your elbows and forward leg until you feel the appropriate amount of stretch on your rear leg's calf. Switch legs and repeat. Another way to stretch your calf is to prop the ball of your foot up on something, such as a 2x4 piece of wood, and then lean forward.

You can also sit on the ground with one leg straight out as you grab your toes and pull back.

Hip and Glute Stretch: Sit on the ground with one leg straight out in front of you and the other leg crossed over the top. Support yourself with the arm that's on the same side as the top leg. Put your other arm against the outer side of the top leg and twist your body. You should feel the stretch on the side of your hip. Switch sides and repeat.

Neck Stretches: This can be done seated or standing. With your hands hanging loosely at your sides, slowly tilt your head to the side until you feel the appropriate amount of stretch. Hold and repeat on the other side.

Shoulder Stretch: This can be done seated or standing. With the back of your hand, pull your opposite elbow to bring your arm across and into your chest. Pull enough to feel the stretch and then hold it in this position. Switch arms and repeat.

Triceps Stretch: This can be done seated or standing. Raise an arm over your head and completely bend your elbow to point it straight upward. This will position your hand behind your head. Use your other hand to pull and hold the elbow while leaning your body to the opposite side. Switch arms and repeat.

Biceps and Chest Stretch: This can be done seated or standing. Reach both arms behind your back and interlock your fingers. With your arms straight, raise them up and away from your body, keeping your shoulders back and your chin up.

Dynamic Stretches

Some riders like to warm up before they hit the trails so that they feel more loose and limber, especially during cold weather. That's where dynamic stretching comes in. These exercises use motions to activate and warm up the muscles, thus preparing them for the upcoming activity. This does not elongate tissues the way static stretching does; it simply brings them to their maximum range of motion.

The following is a sampling of exercises that are compatible with the motions and muscles used during mountain biking. They can be an effective warm-up routine if you don't mind doing them at or near the trailhead. None of these will require you to get on the ground.

Lunges: These are great for warming up your quads and glutes. Start in the standing position with your feet together and your hands on your hips. Take a big step forward while keeping the other leg straight and in place. Don't step so far forward that your knee extends past your toes. Lower onto your forward foot until your thigh is parallel to the ground. Spring back to the starting position and then repeat with the other leg. Try doing six to eight repetitions per leg.

Note: A variation to this adds a torso-twist. Instead of putting your hands on your hips, clasp them in front of you. As you're lowering down, twist your torso to the opposite side of your forward leg, then return to center as you're coming back up. This stretches your lower back while activating your core muscles.

Alternate Toe Touches: Stand with your feet spread far apart. Bend over at the waist and reach a hand toward the opposite foot. Do not stretch more than what is comfortable. Switch and reach with the other hand to its opposite foot. Continuously alternate for six to ten reaches per side.

Jumping Jacks: This is old school but a great warm up that stretches the arms, legs, and torso. Stand straight with your chin up and your toes pointing forward. With a jumping motion, extend your legs out to the sides with a slight bend at the knees. At the same time, swing your arms out to the sides and all the way over your head. Return to the starting position and repeat for 30 to 60 seconds.

Shoulder Rolls: Standing straight and relaxed, roll your shoulders in big, circular movements. Stay relaxed while keeping it smooth and fluid. Do this ten times in the forward direction, then ten times in the reverse direction.

Neck Rolls: Standing straight and relaxed, slowly drop your chin to your chest, and then slowly roll your head toward one shoulder. Stop at the point where your ear is closest to your shoulder, using care not to tilt your head back too far. Slowly roll your head forward and around to the other shoulder, pausing in the middle to look down. Do it five times to each shoulder.

Ankle Rotations: While seated, raise one of your legs off of the ground and support it with your hands. Rotate your ankle in a circle five to ten times in one direction and then the other direction. Repeat this procedure with the other leg.

CHAPTER SEVENTEEN

Nutrition & Hydration

YOU'VE ALREADY LEARNED that raising your VO_2 max and your lactate threshold takes hard work and proper nutrition, so it should go without saying that what you ingest is critical to the success of your athletic aspirations. Food, beverages, and supplements play a big role in how your body regulates and expends energy. Too often, fuel and nutrition are not what people think about when making food choices. For mountain bikers and athletes in general, this is something that must always be considered.

Excessive body fat can be a hindrance to mountain biking, especially when it comes to climbing hills. Conversely, this sport can play a big part in weight maintenance and weight loss. Good habits and choices of food and beverages are also important to enhancing your performance and reaching your goals. In this chapter, we'll cover the basics of good eating habits, nutrition as it applies to energy production, supplements, and the value and methodology of proper hydration. This advice is particularly important and should be more-or-less adhered to if you truly want to succeed in this sport. Once you have control of this, you'll feel a general sense of well-being that will positively affect many other aspects of your life.

Eating

Eating . . . one of the most basic things that we do. And the food and beverage industry does a good job of providing what we want and need. But a want is not always the same as a need, and it's the wants that often get us into trouble. Many food and beverage corporations are extremely keen on catering to what we want, and they know how to drive up our desires for the purpose of enhancing the sales of their products. Added sugars, salt, and fat are prime examples. All too often, the resulting effect is weight gain from overeating and eating the wrong things.

As an athlete, you're burning more calories and will therefore need to ingest more calories than non-athletes. You'll also require more protein and more complex carbohydrates than non-athletes. Don't take this as a ticket to eat whatever you want and however much you want, because you can't exercise your way out of a bad diet. Portion size, frequency of eating, and eating the right things all need to be considered to have the right equilibrium.

When it comes to portion sizes, you should never stuff yourself. Stop eating the moment the hunger is gone and you feel satisfied. You can use a smaller plate to limit your portions, or you can get into the habit of leaving some uneaten food on the plate. Try drinking a big glass of water before you eat to help curb your appetite. Also, don't wait until you're hungry before you eat because it'll cause you to seek out too much food. Instead of three big meals a day, try grazing on small amounts of food six to seven times a day. This will keep you satisfied while keeping your energy level steadier throughout the day. Go for seven to nine servings of fruit and vegetables per day, and try to get a little protein with every snack. Don't eat a big meal in the evening. Instead, make breakfast your biggest meal and lunch your second biggest. These are just a few of the widely recommended suggestions to manage food intake and prevent overeating.

Too much sugar in your diet is a problem. It leads to a host of problems including weight gain, sharp peaks and valleys of energy, cardiovascular disease, diabetes, and more. Sugars added to processed foods and beverages are the biggest culprit of excessive sugar in the diet. Often, it's hidden in the list of ingredients under a variety of names: evaporated cane juice, brown sugar, high fructose corn syrup, maple syrup, sucrose, dextrose, glucose, lactose, and galactose . . . to name just a few. No matter what the name, they're all a variety of simple sugar, put there to make things taste better and keep you coming back for more. Hopefully, you're ready to eliminate these added sugars from your diet. The problem is that it's hard to get away from because it's seemingly in everything. Supermarkets are a minefield of processed foods that contain added sugar. You have to be a savvy shopper to avoid them, but it can be done because there's always a big selection of real food to choose from. Consider "real food" as anything that hasn't been processed: food that's been picked, gathered, farmed, milked, hunted, or fished.

Fat intake is another thing to consider when making food choices. Too much of the wrong fats will lead to weight gain and clogged arteries. You should not eliminate all fat from your diet because fat is necessary for survival. What's important is limiting the wrong kinds of fat and getting enough of the right kinds of fat. This includes substituting saturated and trans-fats with non-hydrogenated, unsaturated fats, which are found in food sources such as nuts, peanut butter, almond butter, avocados, avocado oil, and olive oil. Saturated fat intake should be minimal and occasional, and only from real foods such as eggs, butter, and grass-fed red meat.

Nutrition and the Ride

Once you have control of your day-to-day eating habits, you can focus on tailoring your nutrition intake to meet your cycling goals and needs. As an athlete and a mountain biker, you have specific nutritional requirements to help you ride at an optimal level of performance. What you consume pre-ride, during your ride, and post-ride are all important considerations, each with their own unique requirements.

Pre-ride: To ensure that you have enough energy for your ride, you need to be fueled up. But this fuel needs to be absorbed into your system via digestion. Undigested food in your stomach hasn't been converted to energy yet. It will make you feel weighted down and could exacerbate nausea on the toughest climbs. As a general rule of thumb, a meal should be eaten two to three hours before the ride, although there are factors that change the rate of digestion, including the variances from person to person. When you're deciding what to eat before riding, consider the following:

- How much you eat is determinative of how long it takes to be digested. It's best to go for a moderate-sized meal with a moderate number of calories. If you're a smaller person, your portion size will be smaller, and if you're a larger person, your portion size will need to be a little larger.

- Different kinds of foods will digest at different speeds. Fats take the longest to digest and should be avoided in your pre-ride meal. This includes red meat and cheese, among other sources.

- Some lean protein should be consumed in a pre-ride meal. This will put amino acids into your bloodstream, which will promote muscle regeneration and help to prevent muscle breakdown. (Your muscles can actually degenerate after all other fuel sources have been exhausted.) Try eating foods such as turkey, chicken, eggs, and cottage cheese . . . they'll keep you going strong.

- Avoid sugary food. This will only spike and crash your energy before you even begin your ride.

- Carbohydrates are your best source of fuel. It should be a mix of complex and simple carbs. Foods such as vegetables, whole wheat bread, and oatmeal have complex carbs for longer-term energy; fruits will provide simple carbs for more immediate energy.

- About 30 to 45 minutes before your ride, you may want another boost of simple carbs. Try eating a small banana, a small apple, or a healthy energy bar. Within 20 minutes, you can take a shot of gel. This will provide fuel right when you need it.

During the ride: As you're hitting the hills and burning energy at a high rate, your body will be depleting its store of energy. To continue to ride strong, it's important to keep some fuel in the tank so that you don't hit the wall and bonk out. To do this, you'll need to take in some carbs on a regular basis, being careful not to consume too much and subsequently develop stomach issues. Use the following tips to guide your replenishing needs:

- Unless all you had was gel, your pre-ride meal and snack should be enough to get you through the first hour of your ride. If it's been all uphill, you may want to start sipping a quality sport drink after a little while. Otherwise, there's no need to replenish during this time period.

- During the second and third hours, frequently sip the sport drink. You should finish it by the end of the third hour. Take a shot of gel every 20 to 30 minutes or eat a healthy energy bar every 40 to 50 minutes. The gel will give you a quicker boost of energy and the bar will sustain you longer. Alternatively, you can combine the two, eating half a bar and half a gel shot every 30 to 40 minutes. The hardest part is remembering to keep fueling at the proper intervals.

- If your ride is going to be longer than three hours, you'll need a second bottle of a quality sport drink so that you can maintain proper electrolyte levels in your system. At this point, you may want to eat another banana. As you continue, you'll need to keep ingesting bars and gels as you did in the second and third hours.

- If you're on an all-day ride, you'll need to interrupt it with a small meal, such as a sandwich.

Post-ride: Every mountain biker hopes to improve their conditioning with each ride, but if you don't get the right post-ride nutrition quickly, your muscles won't be able to recover and build on their efforts. Basically, you'll need to eat as soon as possible after you're done . . . ideally within the first 30 minutes, preferably within one hour and never more than two hours. This is the time that your body most needs nutrients to repair, recover, and grow your muscles. Trying to make up for it later in the day just won't cut it.

Specifically, you'll need both carbohydrates and protein at a ratio of about three parts carbs to one part protein. Both will play an important role in your recovery. Carbs are needed to restore the glycogen reserves in your muscles so that it can be readily converted to glucose for energy on the next ride. Remember, your muscles will be hungry for these carbs right away, so rapid refueling is essential.

Protein will help repair muscle tissue that was broken down during a hard ride. The amino acids in the protein will help to grow the muscle tissue, a necessity if you want to be a stronger rider. Repairing muscle tissue as soon as possible will also reduce some of the soreness that typically hits hardest the following day. In any case, it's still beneficial to eat protein with every subsequent meal and/or snack in the day.

Bringing some food with you to the trailhead to snack on when you're finished is a great idea, and a healthy meal would be the best. There are a variety of healthy bring-along food items that can be combined to provide both carbs and protein. Items such as apples, bananas, grapes, 100% fruit juice, yogurt, cheese, sandwiches, nuts, and energy bars are all good options, as long as you have them readily available. It's entirely possible that you won't be hungry after your activity, so at the least, you should be drinking some kind of recovery drink made for this purpose. You can then have a post-ride meal later on. Nutrition is an essential aspect of mountain biking; get it nailed down, and you'll have much better success.

Supplements

An internet search on supplements will display a vast array of recommendations and sales pitches. It's a big business that makes big money. You certainly don't want to waste your money, but when you're trying to push the limits of your abilities, you may wonder if there's something safe and effective that you can take to help you perform better.

Clearly, if you have a good diet and eat nutritionally rich food, your requirement for supplementation goes down, but there still may be some room for improvement. This is not to say that there's a magic pill that will quickly transform you into a better athlete. Getting proper nutrition will ensure that you're taking every advantage of your hard work and that you're not deficient of any essential nutrient. It's about maintaining good overall health, which will help to keep you at your best. The following are some of the more important supplements that you may want to consider:

Carbohydrates: As a mountain biker, you should never let yourself become depleted of carbohydrates, both on and off the bike. As long as you're riding frequently or semi-frequently, you should maintain a certain amount in your system. Unless you're riding all-day or multi-day, gel shots and energy bars are the way to go. Even though they're food products, they can still be considered supplements because of their concentrated nature. Carbohydrate sport drinks and post-ride recovery drinks are supplemental beverages and are commonly available from supplement companies.

Protein: Post-ride is when your protein requirements are at their highest. This is when you need a big intake of protein, in the range of around 25 grams. If you can't eat a large volume of protein-rich foods, you may want to consider supplementing with some quality whey protein powder mix.

Omega-3 Fatty Acids: A study has shown that omega-3 fatty acids can increase neuromuscular function and performance in athletes[28]. What this means is that they can improve the nerve activation of muscles, effectively making muscles quicker to respond, which increases cycling performance. Another benefit is the ability to offset post workout inflammation. Decreasing inflammation in muscles will improve recovery. Omega-3 is usually sourced from marine life such as salmon, tuna, and sardines but can also come from plant-based sources such as flax or chia seeds. You probably can't get enough from your diet alone, so supplementing with fish oil pills containing DHA and EPA omega-3 fatty acids is the way to go.

Multivitamins & Minerals: Even the best diet may leave you short of certain vitamins and minerals. For example, vitamin D and magnesium are essential for certain bodily functions, but most people don't get enough. As an athlete, you especially need to be stocked up with all of the various micro-nutrients. A daily A-Z multivitamin and mineral pill will ensure that you're getting everything that you need. Look for one that provides 100 percent of the recommended daily allowances (RDAs). If it falls short on some nutrients, additional supplementation may be necessary. Consuming these nutrients has not been conclusively proven to give a performance edge, but deficiencies could lead to health problems, and hence, performance issues.

The supplements listed above are the basics, and taking them will ensure that your body is getting what it needs. Much of it is part of a healthy lifestyle, which will ultimately have a positive effect on performance. Substances such as caffeine[29], nitrates[30], creatine[31], and beta alanine[32] are said to enhance performance, but they are not essential for maintaining a well-functioning body, which is why they're not on this list of recommendations.

Hydration

Because dehydration will negatively affect performance, proper hydration is an essential component of mountain biking. Dehydration can reduce your endurance and strength and has the ability to cause heat cramps. In extreme cases, it can even cause heat stroke. "Proper hydration" does not translate to "the more you drink, the better you'll do." What it means is drinking enough to satisfy your requirements. Your digestive system can only process fluids back into your bloodstream at a certain rate. Exceeding this rate doesn't do any good. So this raises the question: How much should I drink? There are many variables that affect perspiration, so this answer will have to be in the form of a percentage of what you lose[33]. As a rough figure, you should try to replace roughly 75 percent of what you sweat to prevent any loss of performance. This should keep you from exceeding a two-percent loss in body weight[34].

Since most mountain bikers will not be weighing themselves before and after rides, it's hard to determine how much weight has been lost. Therefore, how much to drink will take some experimentation on the part of the rider. Variables such as the ambient temperature and humidity, personal sweat rate, body size, amount of exertion, and time will all affect the actual volume that needs to be consumed.

We've already covered the need for a quality sport drink while you ride, but plain water should be kept on hand as well. Keep the sport drink in a bottle and the water in either a second bottle or in a hydration pack. The following are examples of recommendations for a 170-pound rider using a combination of water and sport drink:

- A ride of less than one hour: a 16-ounce bottle of water
- A one to two-hour ride in cool weather: a bottle of sport drink and a bottle of water
- A one to two-hour ride in hot weather: a bottle of sport drink and 40 ounces of water in a hydration pack
- A ride of three hours in cool weather: two bottles of sport drink and 40 ounces of water in a hydration pack
- A ride of three hours in hot weather: two bottles of sport drink and 70 ounces of water in a hydration pack

This is just a rudimentary guideline. How much you bring will need to be customized and will be learned from experience. Remember, it's always best to err on the side of bringing a little too much water rather than not enough. If the ride is longer than three hours, it will require planning and strategy, such as a larger hydration pack and a way to get the containers refilled. In any case, always remember to gulp some water every so often to prevent dehydration.

Lastly, it's of the utmost importance to be properly hydrated before you begin your ride. This doesn't mean just drinking a bunch of water right before you take off. It's about maintaining your bodily hydration at all times. Get in the habit of drinking more water. Try to consume at least 68 ounces of water per day, more if you can. Look at the color of your urine; it should be light yellow.

If you're in a situation where you haven't hydrated and you have a ride coming up, you'll have to quickly try to normalize your hydration level. When it's about four hours before ride time, drink a bottle of water an hour, stopping one hour before your ride so that it can process through your system. This will ensure that your body's hydration level has balanced out. If you want, a drink just before you take off would be fine.

PART FIVE

Everything Else

WE'VE LEARNED ABOUT the bikes, the equipment, how to prepare both yourself and the bike, and how to ride. This section will cover everything else that can either benefit you or provide a deeper insight into the sport. Racing, caring for your bike, and trail issues are all important subjects that need to be covered and understood.

CHAPTER EIGHTEEN

Racing

Y OU'VE LEARNED SOME great bike-handling skills and you've gotten better on the trails. Maybe you're climbing hills that you could never climb before and you're feeling great. Maybe you're showing up all your buddies. Whatever the case may be, you've got some confidence instilled and now you're wondering how you would do in a race. This is how it all begins. If you're the competitive type, it's a natural progression.

On the flip side, there are many riders who don't want to progress to racing. It's just not their thing; they prefer to keep riding the way they always do . . . for fun, camaraderie, adventure, and exercise. With racing, you truly have to have a strong desire to compete against other riders, because it will be the hardest riding you'll ever do. You'll be pushed to ride faster than anything you're accustomed to.

If you're naturally competitive but you've never had the experience of racing, it should be something that you try at least once. Racing in itself has a way of making you a better rider. Once you're scheduled for a race and it's on the calendar, you have a set amount of time to further improve in the hope of doing better. It's safe to say that how much you push yourself is dependent on the strength of your desire to place better in the final standings. In any case, you're going to come out of the experience a better rider.

In spite of the pain that comes with pushing your body to the limits, racing can be a positive experience. You'll find that there's a lot of camaraderie with the other racers, they'll often help each other out, both on and off the course. These are your people . . . fellow mountain bikers. You may make some new friends or at least some acquaintances. From talking to those that have previously raced the course, you can find out what it's like and what to look out for . . . maybe you'll hear some interesting stories. And after everything is said and done, you'll feel great about yourself and what you've accomplished, no matter how you placed.

Types of Races

There are several types of mountain bike races to choose from, so if you've never raced, you should decide which one is best suited for your riding style and capabilities. No matter how good you think you are, you should always start out by registering in the beginner classification. You'll be surprised how many good riders are out there. It can be humbling. Besides, your first time going through the process will be an opportunity to figure out ways of doing things better in future races.

The following is a rundown of some of the more common race types, but there are other specialized types that are not mentioned here:

Cross-country: This type of race tends to be the most popular. Just about every big venue will have some kind of cross-country event. Racers will start in a big pack, and then after some distance the pack will spread out. Expect a variety of terrain including climbs, descents, and turns. Usually the course has some technical parts, but it's never overly technical. They will have some combination of single-track, double-track, fire roads, and maybe even some paved roads. They'll have different categories of races to accommodate the various experience levels; the difference being the distance or number of laps that must be accomplished. Racers will usually race by age group, but the range of ages in each group is dependent on the expected number of registered racers. Race distances can vary between venues, and timewise they can take one, two, or three hours . . . or it could even be an ultra-endurance event that lasts eight, twelve, or twenty-four hours.

Downhill: If you're considering downhill racing, your bike handling skills are already exceptional and your bike is only meant for downhill riding. This is a time trial event, meaning your rip down a hill is timed from start to finish, and is compared with the other racers. They will begin at the starting gate, one after another at designated intervals of time ranging from half a minute to every few minutes. The course will be steep and rocky, with berms, jumps, drop-offs, etc., all done at high speeds.

Dual Slalom: This is downhill event that has two racers competing with each other on parallel man-made tracks. These tracks are designed to be identical: the same jumps and berms at the same locations on the hill. The first one across the finish line is the winner, who then advances to the next round against another competitor. The loser gets knocked out of the races.

Enduro: Enduro is a racing format that falls in between downhill and cross-country. The beauty of it is that it doesn't have the extremes of either DH or XC. No travelling downhill over treacherous terrain at speeds that would scare the daylights out of most riders, and no gut-wrenching endurance tests typical of cross-country races. This is not to say that it's not challenging or physically demanding, it's just that it falls in between the two extremes. The bikes used for this event appropriately fall in between the DH and XC bikes, as described in chapter one. Only the downhill portions of this race are timed, but you still have to ride uphill to get to the top of the hills. The winner is the one with the lowest combined downhill times.

Preparing for a Race

You should be aware of the race you want to enter several months in advance to give yourself time to prepare. You can then tailor your training to match or exceed what you can expect at the upcoming venue. This will be every bit mental as it is physical. The idea is to be strongly confident as you reach a peak level of performance.

Training harder than the race is easier said than done. Take for instance cross-country racing: You're surrounded by other riders; you're trying to pass some of them at every opportunity, usually where the trail widens. At the same time, others are persistently trying to pass you. All of this creates an atmosphere of competition that will continuously push you to go faster, resulting in a high degree of pain and suffering. This doesn't happen under normal riding circumstances, so it's a challenge to train harder than this.

To overcome this training deficit, you'll need to develop rides that exceed the geographical parameters of the race course. The downhills should be longer, faster, and more technical. The distances, the total ascension, and the degree of the inclines should all be greater.

Frequency and time on the trails are also critical for making improvements. You should be riding often and putting in extra time and distance. This is your chance to refine your bike handling skills and push your endurance. If you're a cross-country rider, your leg strength, your heart strength, your lung power, and your endurance over time will all need to be pushed. Keep climbing and pushing your limits . . . make it hurt. Work on your downhill speed and technique, because that could be a way to outpace the other racers. Nail down your cornering technique, because corners can often be the spots where you overtake other racers. Make it a habit to consistently tell yourself to go faster, because finding the motivation to continuously ride at a strenuous race pace can be difficult. One method that can help is by trying to beat your previous times on Strava. Attempting to make personal records and a higher placing on the leaderboards will push you to go ever faster, whether it's on the downhills, uphills, or on the flats.

The months leading up to the race is the perfect time to lose that excess body weight you've been thinking about. You'll have time to make dietary changes to a low sugar, healthy fat, high protein diet. You should be regulating your portion sizes and keeping your alcohol consumption to a minimum. With a proper diet and frequent exercise, you won't believe how quickly the pounds fall off. Come race day, you'll be lean and mean.

The week leading up to the race is a critical time for mental and physical preparation. By this time, your fitness level is what it is. You're not going to make any gains in your last week. When you enter the race, you want your legs to be rested and with no soreness or "pumped up" feeling. At the same time, they should be crisp, strong, and ready for action. To get them into this state, when and how much you exercise needs to be strategized. Here is one example of how you can taper down before the big day:

7 days before the race: This is your last big hurrah. Do your biggest, most intensive ride.

6 days: Take a day of rest to allow your legs to recover from the previous days' effort.

5 days: Pre-ride the race course. Learn its contours and devise your race strategies . . . what lines to take, where you're going to push hard, where you can do some passing, and where you should conserve energy. If you're able to, make a Go Pro type video to study over the next few days so that you don't forget anything.

4 days: Do a ride that's half the distance of your normal ride, but keep the same intensity.

3 days: Take a day of rest to allow your legs to recover from the previous days' effort.

2 days: Do a ride that's half the distance and half the intensity of your normal ride.

1 day: Do one hour of easy riding just to keep your legs active.

If you plan on racing a downhill event, it's imperative that you become familiar with the course. You should know all the drop-offs, jumps, and turns. You must know exactly what to expect as you traverse down the hill. Do an initial walk down the course and give it a good evaluation, then take some practice runs. This should happen within the last few days leading up to the race. Don't shy away from doing some cross-country conditioning rides as well, because leg strength and endurance will help with your performance.

No matter what kind of race you're entering, you should be getting plenty of rest during the last week. A good pattern of sleep lasting seven to nine hours per night will help you perform better[35]. (This should be the norm whenever you're in training.) Your eating habits should remain unchanged, the same healthy diet you adopted during training. Just make sure that you're getting some carbohydrates after your training workouts to restore your glycogen level. There is no benefit to "carb-loading"[36], which entails eating massive amounts of carbs. This will only make you feel bloated. You just need to eat a moderate amount of things such as bread, pasta, cereal, bananas, etc., especially on the last day before the race. As far as hydration goes, drink plenty of water a day or two ahead of the race to ensure that your body has a balanced level of hydration.

Race Day

To start race day without any additional stress, it's important to get all of your things ready the night before. Have all of your equipment picked out, organized, and ready to go. You should know exactly when and what you're going to eat in the morning and you should have all of your energy foods packed and ready to go. You'll also need to figure out how much water / energy drink you'll need to bring. Remember, if it's a well-organized XC race, there are designated rest stations where you can get refilled. This will allow you to bring less, thereby lightening your load. Have the container(s) filled and chilled the night before.

Your bike should also be ready to roll. Any maintenance issues should have been previously accomplished. Your suspension adjustment should already be set. Your drivetrain should be clean and freshly lubed. Your tires should have plenty of tread and be in good condition. It's also important to know what tire pressures you want to use in the race. Some XC racers like to set it high for reduced rolling resistance. If you've seen the course and you know its level of technicality, you should have an idea of what pressures to use. Set them the night before, adding a little extra as needed to compensate for any known leakage.

Get to the race and to the start line fully ready to race no less than 15 minutes before start time. This means you've had your energy supplements, you've taken your last drink, you've relieved yourself, your gear is on, and you've done some warm-up riding to activate your legs. Use this extra time to run through the course in your mind. Think about how you're going to ride it.

Performing in a Race

You've trained for this. You've read this book and applied what you've learned. Now it's come down to this race and you're waiting at the start line. You feel physically ready, but where is your head? There's a good chance that your nerves are getting the best of you. Maybe you're worried about how you're going to do. No matter what kind of race it is, this can be a negative factor.

Having your head in the right place is important. Self-confidence is important. If you're confident on your training rides, there's no reason you shouldn't be confident at the race. Clear your mind of negative thoughts and focus on what you're good at. This is what's going to give you the edge in the race. Knowing that you're a performer and that the other racers are going to struggle against you is a mental boost that will make you faster.

If you're in a cross-country race, you'll be in a line up with your peers. As the time gets close, there will be a countdown and a "go" or a "pop". If you've properly tapered down your training the week before and you're freshly warmed up, you should be able to take a leading position. This is important because you don't want to fall too far behind before you hit the single-track, at which point it becomes harder to pass.

You're going to have a lot of distance to cover and you'll be riding faster than you're accustomed to. You will be uncomfortable. It will be a test of how much pain and discomfort you can maintain over a long distance without hitting your "red line". Keep in mind that it's important not to burn out too fast. You'll start out with fresh legs, which means your heart will be racing to keep up. As distance goes by, your legs will begin to tire and your heart rate will come down in response. To compensate, you'll need to pay attention to your heart. Establishing a pace that keeps your heart rate a little lower in the beginning will better allow your legs to stay fresher and push harder throughout the race.

When you're racing with a single-minded conviction, it's important to remember to occasionally sip from your water bottle and to replenish with gel. If you don't remember to do these things timely, you could disadvantage yourself. Also, you may forget to adjust your shocks' descend, trail, climb switch. If this is a problem, just leave it in trail mode. That should get you through most of it.

If you're coming up on another racer that you want to pass, call out and then do it without sacrificing momentum. Since you know the course, you'll know the best places to do this. If somebody wants to pass you, do your best to let them by . . . again without losing any of your momentum.

On downhills, do your best to leverage your skills. If you do well here, you can really make some good time. Some of your competitors may be roadies first and mountain bikers second. They may not do as well as you on downhills/ technical sections/ switchbacks/ turns. This is where you can shine. Just be sure not to go faster than your abilities can handle. Your practice runs should have already established your best speed; hopefully your natural ability and your learned skills propel you to greatness. There's an interesting study that shows what makes a downhill rider perform better[37]. It concludes that: "In order of importance, rider skill, handgrip endurance, self-confidence, and aerobic capacity were identified as variables influencing DH performance."

"The expectations of life depend upon diligence; the mechanic that would perfect his work must first sharpen his tools."

--Confucius

CHAPTER NINETEEN

Bike Care

YOUR BIKE IS an investment in what you love doing. But even if you've spent a ton of money on a model with high end components, these mechanical parts will still wear out and/or break. There's no getting away from eventually doing maintenance work or paying somebody to do it. Yes, this means spending more money. But if you stay on top of things and routinely give your bike some TLC, you can prevent premature wear and unnecessary breakage. This requires frequent inspection, proper lubrication, and some basic maintenance.

If your bike needs a more serious type of work accomplished and you would like to do it yourself, a specialized book that provides in-depth bike maintenance instructions can be extremely helpful. If you go this route, you should be mechanically inclined and ready to buy the proper tooling.

Keeping your bike in tip-top shape requires thorough inspections to ensure that nothing detrimental is missed. Checking the condition of every part of your bike and knowing where the trouble spots are will ensure that your machine remains in top working order. A few things to look for were presented in Chapter Four, Buying a Used Bike. These are good items to check for regularly, but a more thorough inspection should be accomplished for ongoing care. The following topics provide information on general bike care, what to inspect, and where trouble can arise.

Washing the Bike

It's generally not necessary to wash your bike after every ride, especially if it's just a little dusty or has a few spots of dirt, in which case wiping it down with a moist rag will do. But if it's caked with mud and other trail remnants, hosing it down becomes a necessity. Mud will not only make the bike heavier, but the grit will excessively abrade and wear out your drive train, get into all of the mechanisms, work through the shock and forks' dust seals, and get into the bushings and/or bearings of the suspension linkages.

Cleaning your bike has the additional benefit of providing an opportunity to take a close look at how it's holding together. As you're getting dirt out of the crevices and thoroughly drying every surface, you can't help but notice all the details of your wonderful piece of machinery. This is when you can look for loose fasteners, broken or bent parts, frame cracks, abraded cables, and other such issues. To give the bike a good cleaning, you're going to need a few things:

- A water hose with an adjustable nozzle
- A bucket
- Liquid dishwashing soap or bicycle cleaning soap
- Two cleaning brushes or a bicycle cleaning brush set
- A large sponge
- Some rags

Washing the bike should be accomplished with a soft or a medium spray so that water and dirt aren't forced into places they shouldn't be. Always avoid shooting pressurized water at the ends of the wheel hubs, the bottom bracket, the headset, the fork and shock seals, or any other place that has a bearing seal.

Putting your bike on a repair stand is the best way to hold it in place as you wash it. If you don't have one, other options include leaning it against a wall or turning it upside down on the ground. If you choose the latter, put something (such as a towel or a doormat) under the handlebar to protect the levers from scraping the ground.

To get the majority of the dirt off, start by carefully blasting the excess from the tires, rims, and frame with a medium strength spray. The next step is to fill the bucket with soapy water and repeatedly dip a long-bristled brush into it as you clean your drivetrain components, including the cassette, the rings, the chain, and the derailleur assemblies. Make sure you get in between each cog of the cassette and behind the rings and pulleys. Pedals will also need some attention because dirt tends to cling to them; a condition that could prevent them from spinning freely and/or make it harder to clip-in.

The best method to clean the chain is with a chain-cleaning tool that uses internal rotating bristle brushes along with a chamber for the degreasing fluid. The unit snaps onto the chain, and as the cranks are rotated, it goes to work, giving you a beautifully cleaned chain. There are several manufacturers that make this type of chain cleaning system. For lightly soiled chains, sometimes all you need is a can of cleaner to get the job done.

Next, use a rag and the soapy water to clean out the crevices of the suspension linkages, sliding the rag in and out to get all the dirt out. Carefully rinse the drivetrain and suspension linkages using a soft spray of water. From there, all that's needed is the sponge and more soapy water to do a cosmetic cleaning of the frame, rims, handlebar, seat and seat post. The tires are best cleaned with a stiff bristle brush. Follow up all of these washings with a light rinse off.

Thoroughly drying the bike will prevent standing water from causing corrosion. To get a good amount of the water off, pick the bike up about a foot and allow it to drop a couple of times to shake loose the excess water. Next, use clean, dry rags to wipe down all of the surfaces. To help to prolong the life of the fork and shock, give a special wipe to their stanchions and accompanying dust seals to ensure there is no remaining dirt or water stains. You can even use a q-tip soaked with isopropyl alcohol to thoroughly clean the seals. This will also provide a good opportunity to inspect their condition. Finally, let the bike sit (in the sun, if possible) for a while to ensure that the chain and drivetrain are completely dry prior to lubrication. A completely dry chain will allow the lubricant to fully penetrate the internal surfaces.

If you really want to make your bike shine, a nice wax job will do the trick. If possible, avoid spray on polishes as they run the risk of contaminating the brakes. If you must use this type, cover the brake and rotor with a rag or simply spray the polish into a rag and then wipe it onto the bike.

Chain and Drivetrain

One of the more important tasks in keeping your bike properly maintained is to regularly lubricate the chain. This will protect it against corrosion and reduce the amount of wear on the moving parts, including the valuable cassette and chainrings. A dirty chain can also make it harder to pedal and can affect shifting. Chain lube and cleaning products are relatively inexpensive and should be purchased right away when you buy a bike. If your bike and/or chain are brand new, the chain will have factory lube that's permeated into all of its internal surfaces. This lubrication works well and should last through the first couple of cleanings.

You'll need to have a lube picked out based on your trail conditions and your personal preferences. Which one is best is controversial, but basically a wet lube should be used in wet conditions because it's less likely to wash away, and dry lube should be used in dry conditions because it attracts less dirt. Just make sure that you select a lube that's specifically made for bike chains. Using anything else (e.g. motor oil) can cause problems. For a quick and easy clean and lube, there are two-in-one cleaner/lubricants available on the market. Although this is not optimal, they do well enough to keep you going.

To apply the lube, slowly rotate the cranks while dripping it onto each and every link. Make sure to also lube the moving parts on the derailleur. Some of the dry lubes on the market won't require wiping off the excess, but some of the wet lubes will splatter, so wiping may be necessary. If you're using lube that's dispensed from an aerosol can, take every precaution to protect the brake and rotor from contamination.

The chain is usually the first item in the drivetrain to wear out. As it wears, it "stretches", which then causes the other components of the drivetrain to wear out. The best way to dramatically increase the life of your drivetrain is by replacing the chain when it reaches a certain amount of stretching. Chain manufacturers recommend replacement when 0.5% to 0.75 % stretch is reached. The best way to check this is with a chain wear indicating tool, which is simply a go / no-go measuring device. To replace the chain yourself, you'll need a good chain tool to take apart a link.

After checking the chain and lubricating the drivetrain, take the bike for a quick spin. Shifting gears should be smooth and easy. If you're having problems such as skipping gears or if shifting feels off in some way, there's something else going on. Check the cassette and chainrings for worn teeth and make sure they have a good profile. If they look narrow or curved in the opposite direction of the chain travel, it's probably time for a replacement.

Poor shifting can also be attributed to a misaligned derailleur hanger, which is the piece that holds the derailleur mechanism to the frame. This is one of the most fragile parts of the bike and can sometimes become bent by a fall to the right. If you suspect that it's out of alignment, it will need to be trued up to the rim, which can be accomplished by any quality bike shop.

Another possible cause of poor shifting may be due to the derailleur being out of adjustment. There are various adjustments on the derailleur that affects how it shifts. Unless you know what you're doing, this would also be one of those things that are best done by the professionals at the bike shop.

Wheels and Tires

When you're jumping, dropping off ledges, and bouncing around rocks and roots, it can be quite common to bang the rim and develop a slight wobble. To check for this, raise your tire off the ground and give it a spin. Any rim wobble is undesirable and will need to be corrected. This can be done by increasing or decreasing the tension of certain spokes by turning the nipples with a  spoke wrench. Making this operation work requires a certain degree of experience, so if you're not sure about what you're doing, have it done at your local bike shop. If the rim is seriously dented or bent, you'll likely need to replace it.

The condition of the wheel bearings are another thing to pay attention to, even though they should last a long time without servicing. All that needs to be done to check this is to remove the wheels from the bike and spin them while holding the axle. They should spin freely and smoothly. If you feel and/or hear any roughness, there's something wrong with the bearings and it will need to be serviced.

The tires should be inspected regularly for damage such as punctures or tears. This is especially true if you've been riding in locations with sharp-edged rocks. If you have a gash on the sidewall, it could burst at an inopportune time and put your safety at risk. Patching the sidewall is never a good idea and is not recommended. If it's damaged, you'll unfortunately have to replace the tire . . . but look at it on the bright side: it's a perfect opportunity to try out a tire with different tread, width, and/ or sidewall thickness.

Check the tread for missing knobbies and excessive wear. Deciding when to replace the tire is a matter of the tires' performance. If it's not hooking up as good as it used to in the turns, or the rear is slipping more easily on the climbs, you might want to consider some fresh treads. Just don't wait until the knobbies are completely gone.

If you're rolling with tubeless tires, the sealant inside will need to be replaced roughly every two to four months because it dries up and becomes clumpy. At this point it'll no longer be able to perform its job of sealing small punctures and tears. Due to the frequency that this needs to be accomplished, it's a good task to learn how to do on your own. Even if you just need to replace an inner tube, removing one of the tire beads from the rim and then reinstalling it is something every biker should know how to do.

If your wheel(s) have been removed and reinstalled for any reason, it's always a good idea to double-check that the quick releases are tight and the wheels are secure before you start your ride.

Brakes

Flying down the side of a mountain is not the best time to find out that there's something wrong with the brakes. It's critical to your safety that the brakes are in good operating condition at all times. These are one of the most important parts of the bike and cannot be ignored. Regular inspection, adjustment, and repair will ensure their dependable operation.

A number of things can cause braking problems, but the most common is worn brake pads. They're designed to wear down to protect the rotor from wear, and as such, they'll need to be replaced when their minimum thickness is reached. How often this happens is all dependent on how often you ride and how much you're on the brakes. You may begin to notice some operational degradation as they wear down, but it's not necessary to check the pads after every ride; every so often will suffice.

To check them, remove the wheel so that you have an unobstructed view of the pads. Using a flashlight, visually check the thickness of the pads. The bare minimum that they should be allowed to get is 1mm thick (3mm if you include the metal backing). Once they reach that thickness, they'll need to be replaced or you'll risk wearing them down until the metal backing is scraping the rotor. If you're still not sure of their condition, you can remove the pads to get a better look. Not all pads are removed in the same manner, so check with the brake manufacturer for the exact method.

If the brakes are squealing, the pads could either be contaminated with oil or dust, or they could be glazed over. To try to remedy the contamination, remove the pads and clean them with isopropyl alcohol. Keep in mind that there's oil on your fingers so you need to be careful not to touch the pad surface. To remove glazing or more serious contamination, a little bit of pad material can be removed by laying them down onto fine grade sandpaper (280-320 grit) and gently rubbing them using a figure-8 pattern.

The rotors may also be part of the problem. If you suspect they're contaminated or they appear soiled, they can be cleaned with a paper towel that's wet with isopropyl alcohol. If you notice they're squealing on and off, the rotors may be warped.

Check for this by giving the tire a spin; if it wobbles enough to touch the pad, it'll need to be straightened. The best tool to bend it straight is a <u>rotor truing fork</u>. If the wobble is excessive, it may need to be replaced.

If you have hydraulic brakes, it's important to check all of the fittings and lines for signs of leakage. It may look oily or it may just show up as a clump of dirt. If you find something, chances are that air can get in through the same leak. A bubble of air in the line will diminish braking performance and give it a spongy feel. Too much air can cause a total loss of braking. This is a very serious condition that must be fixed right away. Take the bike to a shop if you think that the hydraulics needs servicing.

If you have mechanical brakes, the main issue will be cable stretch. As time goes by and the brakes have had a fair share of use, the cables will grow longer. This will change the reach of the levers, so they'll need occasional adjustments to keep it optimal, as discussed in chapter seven. Eventually (maybe every 2-4 years), you'll reach the max adjustment limit, at which point

you'll need to replace the cables. Also check both ends of the cable for frayed wires, which could impair the operation of the brakes. If they're in bad condition, it's another reason to replace the cables. Occasionally putting a little lubricant on the cable ends and the pivot points will help to keep them operating their best.

Torque Specifications

One issue that you need to be aware of is the proper torqueing (tightness) of the bike's bolts, screws, and nuts, especially before performing any maintenance. Factory installed parts should be at the proper torque and should not work loose. Whenever a part gets replaced, it's imperative that the correct torque is applied so that there is no unintended damage from over-tightening or premature loosening from under-tightening. Recheck the torque after a couple of rides. To be able to properly torque the full range of the bike's fasteners, you'll need to invest in a couple of <u>torque wrenches</u>; one with a range of 20 – 200 inch/pounds for the smaller fasteners, and a bigger wrench that goes up to 700 inch/pounds for things such as the bottom bracket, the cranks, and the wheel hubs. Torque wrenches that are preset to specific inch/pounds or newton/meters are also available and are convenient for use on the smaller fasteners. You will also need the necessary <u>sockets and bits</u> for the variety of fastener types on the bike. Always check with the manufacturer for the correct torque specifications. The following are some examples of the common areas where fasteners could possibly loosen:

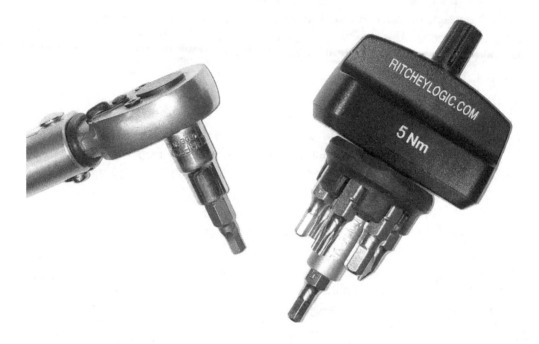

Stem to handlebar bolts: If the handle bar moves when you pull or push it, there's definitely a problem. If you have carbon fiber bars, it becomes especially important not to overtighten these.

Stem to steering tube clamp bolts: Check that your handlebar is perfectly perpendicular to the tire and that the fasteners are properly torqued.

Brake and shifter levers: If the levers easily move on the handlebar, put them at the optimal position and properly torque the fasteners.

Pedals to the cranks: Check the security of the pedals; clockwise to tighten the right pedal and counterclockwise to tighten the left pedal.

Rear suspension pivots: Check the bolts using the proper torque to prevent damage.

> *"Our mission is to create, enhance and preserve great trail experiences for mountain bikers worldwide"*
>
> -- The International Mountain Bicycling Association

CHAPTER TWENTY

Trail Love

WE THE MOUNTAIN biking community absolutely love riding trails in the great outdoors. It sets us free, thrills us, challenges us, cleanses our minds, and connects us with nature. Many of us have made it a huge part of our lives. In fact, it's in our very nature to want to expand our horizons by riding more often and exploring new lands. We certainly don't want this freedom to end or get disrupted. But the truth is . . . we are not alone out there.

We share the great outdoors with other riders, other types of recreational enthusiasts, and the plants and animals. But sometimes negative encounters occur; sometimes things don't quite work out. We should always strive to minimize or eliminate these negative situations so that we can be favorably viewed as responsible members of the outdoor community. It's in our best interest to have symbiosis with all trail users. When we're viewed with negative eyes, it works against us and makes it harder to gain respect.

It's also important to be safe, free from anything that could hurt us beyond the already-accepted risk that comes with mountain biking. Safety is compromised when something or someone is unexpectedly on the trail in front of us. How we respond and whether or not we were following the rules will in large part determine the outcome of this encounter.

Pay close attention to the following subjects; because your responsible involvement will not only help set the course for current mountain bikers, but also for the generations that come after us. Together, we can make a difference.

Trail Etiquette

Trail etiquette is the code for polite conduct while riding. The idea is to avoid offending, annoying, or risking the safety of other trail users, whether it's bikers, hikers, trail runners, or equestrians. We have to get along and have symbiosis. If our interactions are not civilized, some of those users could complain to the land owner, the authorities, or to local government entities. This in turn could jeopardize our access to the trails and/or prevent our ability to gain access to new ones. And that's not what we want to happen.

Don't ever assume that you're the only one on the trail. Use good speed judgement and acute vision skills to spot the other trail users well in advance. Always be aware of possible hidden danger around blind corners. Knowing what's ahead will give you the time to react and do what you need to do. Most often, this means yielding. What you should specifically do varies with the type of user you encounter, their numbers, their direction of travel, and the width of the trail. Here it is broken down by user type:

Mountain Bikers: Wherever you may be riding, there's always a high likelihood that you'll come across other bikers, especially on the weekends. Collisions on single-track can and do happen on occasion, but this danger can be mitigated if a few basic guidelines are followed. It's also a matter of giving respect and common courtesy to fellow riders.

Single-tracks can sometimes be narrow and tight with no room for riders to reasonably pass each other. Add in some blind corners and you have a recipe for disaster. Some parks will have one-direction trails, which simplifies things as long as everybody adheres to the rule. For multi-directional trails, it's a little more complicated, especially when it comes to uphill rider vs. downhill rider. Many will say that the uphill rider has the right of way, but there are other things to consider.

Some trails are just natural for bombing down at high rates of speed. Often, these trails are known to the local riders as the "downhill trails". If you're going to ride up a single-track, you should know what the situation is with that trail, because it's at best disappointing for someone on a good downhill rip to have to stop for you, and at worse, they may not be able to stop in time. If it's a trail that's commonly used for downhill runs, consider taking the long way around to get up the hill, possibly on some fire road. You can then try your hand at ripping down that same single-track.

That being said, if you're heading downhill and you see someone coming up, the right thing to do is to stop, pull over, and let them pass. The common thinking is that if the uphill rider were to stop to pull over for the downhill rider, they would require extra energy to get started again. Also consider that the uphill rider may be exhausted and delirious while on the steepest climbs. Their gaze may be just ahead of their tire and they may not be able to maneuver to the side quick enough. It may stink to have to stop on a good rip, but its common courtesy. If an uphill rider does pull over for you as you're heading down, that's great. Just be sure to slow down a bit and give a big "thank you".

Passing another rider coming toward you on level single-track is a different story. Both riders should try to make way. Stay on the same side of the trail that you would if you were driving (in that country). The features on your side of the trail may allow you to pull over further than the rider on other side. Take advantage of this and make way as best as you can. You should also tell them how many more from your group are behind you (if they're not within sight). Relaying this information applies in any passing situation; whether it's bikers, hikers, up, down, or level.

If you're trying to pass someone from behind, call out which side you're going to pass. If there isn't a good place to pass, call out and let the rider know that you would like to pass when there's a chance. More than likely that rider will make way for you at the first opportunity. Just don't ride aggressively behind their wheel. Give them some space and the time they need to move over. As you're passing, don't forget to thank them. Reverse the situation if someone wants to pass you.

Hikers: Unlike our fellow mountain bikers, many hikers don't understand us too well. When they see us coming at a fast rate of speed, they either freeze up with fear because they don't realize how well our brakes work, or a group of them will scatter to both sides of the trail, leaving you unsure of which way to pass. Some hikers will be friendly and courteously make way for you, while others will angrily block your way. While it's true that a hiker can more easily make way for a biker than the other way around, the simple fact of the matter is that unless it's a posted bike-only trail, hikers have the right of way. That doesn't mean that you can't pass, it just means that you need to adjust what you're doing and accommodate them.

Follow these simple steps to keep encounters with hikers civil and uneventful:

1. Slow down. If you're going fast, slow way down.

2. Greet them with a friendly salutation. If you have a bell, you can use that instead.

3. Move to one side of the trail and wait for them to move to the other side before you pass. Follow up with a "thank you".

4. If the trail is too narrow for you to ride by them, come to a complete stop and wait for them to pass.

5. If you're coming up from behind, announce your presence and politely ask if you can pass. Once they make way for you, follow up with a "thank you".

6. If you're coming up on a blind corner, call out in case someone is around the bend. This could prevent a catastrophe.

Horses / Equestrians: You may not agree with horses being allowed on the multi-use trails you ride on. After all, their hooves cause deep impressions on soft trails, and their riders never clean up the fecal matter that they leave behind. But the fact is that they have the right to be there, and they do have the right of way.

How you approach a horse will be significantly different than a hiker. Horses can get frightened, some more easily than others. Because they're big and powerful, a frightened horse can be a danger to you and its rider if it tries to abruptly turn around or it rears up on its hind legs. Since you don't know the disposition of the particular horse you're approaching, you have to always assume that it's on the skittish side. The following guidelines will ensure trouble free encounters:

1. When you first see them from the front, come to a stop. Horses are farsighted, so things up close are blurry. Stopping further away allows the horse to properly identify you as a human.

2. Talk to the rider. It could be about anything. This also lets the horse know that you're a human and not a predator. This applies whether you're approaching from the front or from behind.

3. If you notice that the horse is sidestepping and snorting, it's probably agitated by your presence. The rider may not be able to speak to you because he/she is trying to calm the horse down. If this is the situation, talk in a calm voice and slowly move away.

4. If all is well, ask the rider how you should pass. Follow the passing instructions, whether it's you staying still, dismounting and moving off the trail while they pass, or you passing slow and steady on one side or the other.

Trail Rules

Although our preference is to have care free riding experiences, there will always be rules, laws, and common courtesy issues that need to be followed. You may find them on posted signs, on the parks printed literature, or on the park website. Every rule has a reason or some kind of justification, even if it isn't spelled out. Some you may agree with and others you may not, but we still need to follow them to be good participants of the outdoor community.

Access: One of the big rules that you should be aware of is staying off the trails and areas where mountain bikes are forbidden. These are places that are typically restricted to hikers only, or hikers and equestrians. Staying off these trails and out of these areas will keep you out of trouble, even though it may be frustrating when there's some great single-track just out of reach. There's a variety of possible reasons for these restrictions. It could be that they're trying to protect a certain fragile ecosystem from damage, or maybe its private property, or maybe a conservationist group managed to convince the land manager to create a restriction. Whatever the case is, it must be followed.

Speed Limits: If there's a posted speed limit, there's always a possibility that there's a ranger with a radar gun waiting to catch and ticket speeding cyclists. This law is only in certain parks, so make sure you know what the situation is where you're riding. This can be disappointing, especially on flowy downhill trails, but it's put in place in an attempt to protect the safety of other trail users from the perceived danger of speeding cyclists. Forget trying to set a Strava record where speed limits are in place.

Littering: Littering is a rule / law that if not followed, will have undesirable consequences in the way that mountain bikers are viewed. You need to be especially conscientious about this one. Take your empty gel packs, energy bar wrappers, old inner tubes, etc. with you. There's a common saying for mountain bikers: Leave No Trace. This in part means whatever you went in with comes back out with you.

Trail Damage: Leave no trace also means avoiding trail damage. Do your best to avoid skidding and to stay off muddy trails that are easily damaged by your tires. Don't go around the puddles either because that will damage the natural vegetation and widen the trail. Never try to make a new trail or make a shortcut on an existing trail, because doing so damages nature and leaves more than just a trace.

Gates: Close the gate behind you, even if it was already open when you got to it. Gates are usually in place to control ranch livestock, such as cows, horses, and goats. Closing and latching the gate behind you is a simple common courtesy that prevents the animals from going places they shouldn't.

Respecting Wildlife

We share the areas we ride with a large variety of wildlife, which means we have a responsibility to treat these animals with respect, whether they be predator or prey. We must avoid conflict with them because many of these species are a critical part of a healthy ecosystem that should be protected and preserved.

Some of the animals near high use trails have grown accustomed to us and will generally stay away. Young animals and those near low use trails will not be accustomed to bikes and will get quite scared. For example, a deer or a rabbit may be on your trail, and when they see you they'll take off down the trail in the direction you're travelling. Their speed may not allow them to easily exit the trail, forcing them to just keep running scared in front of you. In this circumstance, the best thing to do is immediately stop and let it move on without putting it into a panic attack.

Predators can also become scared, but their reaction can be quite different. Since mountain bikes are quiet and fast, there's a high likelihood of surprising something. Startling a predator will turn their fear into a defensive mechanism. Depending on the species, this can result in various degrees of aggression. It's important to know what kind of predatory animals exist in the area you plan on riding and what you should do if you end up in close vicinity of something potentially dangerous. The following are brief behavior descriptions of a few common predators and what actions work best when you encounter them:

Bears: Bears don't like to push their way through the bushes; they prefer to use trails. So if you see a bear, it's likely to be on or near your trail. There are two species that a mountain biker could potentially have an encounter with, the black bear and the brown bear (also known as grizzlies in North America). Each has a different temperament and way of behaving, so it's important to know the characteristics of both and be able to identify which one is which. With either type, there are some basic rules that you should follow when riding in their territory:

- Never ride alone. There is no record of a bear attacking a large group of people.

- Talk or sing as you ride to let the bears know that you're there and that you're a human.

- Don't use your iPod. Your full sense of hearing needs to be intact.

- Always carry bear pepper spray and know how to use it. For quick deployment, you can have it in a personal holster or keep it in your water bottle cage, held in place with an adapter such as the one from this manufacturer: http://counterassault.com/store.htm

- Stop as soon as you see a bear. If it's still far away, go back the way you came. Find a detour if you still need to get to the destination. They care a lot about their personal space, which, depending on the bear, can vary between 10 and 50 feet.

Black bears in the wild will likely be scared of you, but they should still be treated with respect and caution. Black bear attacks on humans are extremely rare; in fact, the bear will probably leave quickly when it sees you. If it doesn't run away, it may be curious, which is indicated when it stands on its hind legs or walks a few steps toward you to get a better view. Although unlikely, it could become aggressive if it has cubs nearby or it's protecting a food source, such as the carcass of an animal. It'll display behaviors such as huffing and snorting, swaying its head, and stomping a foot. In this circumstance, do the following:

- Get your bear pepper spray out and have it ready to use. Remain calm.

- Make direct eye contact with it to show that you're not intimidated.

- Talk to it loud and clear so that it knows you're a human and that you're not intimidated.

- Slowly back away to give it the space it wants. Never run from a bear.

- If it seems to have lost its focus on you, consider riding back the way you came.

- If it charges toward you, go ahead and use the spray. Don't let it get closer than 25 feet before you use it. Remember, this is your most important defense. Aim just above its head so that the spray lands in its eyes. Continue spraying until it stops charging.

- An attack is highly unlikely, but if it happens, fight back using any means and weapons you have. Go for its eyes and nose.

A brown bear is a more dangerous species because they're more likely to be aggressive when they're surprised, so it's imperative that you know when you're riding in their territory. Although attacks are rare, an encounter with one of these is still very serious and every possible precaution must be taken to prevent an attack. In addition to the previous advice, apply the following:

- Ride slower. This will help you assess your surroundings. This is especially important at blind corners where there's a possibility of being surprised by something around the bend.

- Keep your eyes out for clues that a bear has been there. As they forage for food, they'll overturn rocks, break up decayed logs, and dig up plant roots. Look at the trees; bears scratch them with their claws and they leave clumps of fur when they rub up against them. Look for paw prints. If you see any of these signs, a bear is probably nearby. Turn your bike around and hightail it out of there!

- If you're being attacked by a brown (grizzly) bear and fighting back is not possible, drop onto your stomach and lock your fingers behind the back of your head and neck. Lie still and play dead because there's a good chance that the bear will stop its attack. If it's still messing with you, it may try to flip you over onto your back. You must prevent this by holding your elbows and toes outward. After the attack stops, continue to play dead until you're certain that the bear has left.

Mountain Lions / Cougars / Pumas / Panthers: These are all the same animal. They're found in many areas within North and South America. This predatory creature hunts large animals such as deer, as well as a wide variety of smaller mammals. They are very reclusive and under normal circumstances will shy away from humans. This makes attacks highly unlikely, but it's not unheard of. Because they don't see in sharp focus or in color, they can sometimes mistake a hunched-over, fast-moving biker for some other kind of prey. For this reason, if you're riding in an area known to have mountain lions, you need to have awareness and follow certain guidelines to stay safe.

- Don't ride at dusk and dawn. This is when mountain lions do most of their hunting.
- Riding alone increases the chances of an attack. Pair up with someone or ride in a group.
- Wear bright clothing with lots of contrast to make you look more human.
- If you see the carcass of an animal, there's a good chance a mountain lion will be returning to eat off it again. Leave the area immediately.

- Don't crouch down to fix your bike. This will make you look smaller and more like some kind of prey. On January 8th, 2004 in the Orange County foothills in California, a mountain biker was doing just this when a mountain lion attacked and killed him.

Following the above guidelines will help to keep you safe and will probably result in you never getting to see a mountain lion. But if you do have an encounter, there's a high likelihood that you can successfully scare it away with these actions:

- If you see a mountain lion, you can avoid setting off its instinct to chase by immediately coming to a stop while facing it and dismounting with the bike in front of you. You cannot outride this creature and turning your back to it gives it an opportunity to attack, since they always jump on their prey from behind to clamp down on the back of the neck.

- As it's looking at you, remain facing it while making eye contact, clapping, and talking loudly in a firm voice. Without bending over or crouching down, try throwing rocks, branches, or other objects (such as a full water bottle) directly at it. You could even try grabbing your bike by the stem and seat post and hold it upside down over your head (practice this) while you scream at it. This will make you look large and intimidating. Just don't advance toward it.

- Make sure the lion has a path to escape, never corner it in. If at all possible, you should not get between it and its dead prey or its cubs. In this scenario, it won't back down.

- Slowly back away without ever turning your back to it.

- In the unlikely event that you're attacked, remain upright and fight back using any means and weapons you have. You'll probably succeed in driving it away.

Wolves: This is another predator species that mountain bikers need to be aware of. They can be found in certain areas of North America, Europe, Asia, and Africa. Wolf attacks on humans are extremely rare and they will normally try their best to avoid us. However, because they're a wild species, running into an aggressive wolf is always a possibility. If you do have an encounter with one, scaring it off is quite easy using the same actions as listed above for the mountain lions.

Poison Oak / Poison Ivy

The memories of a great ride can be ruined when a case of poison oak or poison ivy develops in the ensuing days and weeks. Contact with these plants will cause a red rash with bumps that can turn into oozing blisters, resulting in a horrible and almost unbearable itching/burning sensation that never seems to end. Depending on how much contact is made with the plant, it can range from a small spot to a combination of major parts of the body. Poison oak / ivy is a serious trail hazard that mountain bikers must cope with, preferably by minimizing the risk of exposure or by avoiding it completely.

The oil from the poison oak and ivy plants contain a substance called urushiol. This substance will soak through the outer layers of the skin and into the epidermis layer where it causes an allergic reaction called contact dermatitis. About 85% of the population will have this kind of allergic reaction, while the other 15% is immune, although repeated exposures can create some sensitivity to it.

These plants only grow at elevations below 5000 feet (1500 meters), so there's no need to worry about it if you're riding at higher elevations. Poison oak can be found along both the Pacific and Atlantic Coasts of North America, and poison ivy can be found throughout most of North America except the Canadian province of Newfoundland and the U.S. states of California, Alaska, and Hawaii. Poison ivy can also be found in much of Asia including China, Japan, and Taiwan.

Identifying the Plants: The primary factor in avoiding poison oak and poison ivy is the ability to positively identify it. Issues that complicate this are the various ways that they grow as well as the different appearances they take through the seasons. It would be wise to learn as much as you can about these plants and look at as many pictures as needed to become familiar with their different appearances.

U.S. Western Poison Oak

Poison oak can grow as either a shrub or as a vine that usually stays low to the ground but can sometimes work its way up a tree. The leaves will typically come in groups of three and have somewhat of an oak leaf shape, although the size of the lobes on the edge will vary from plant to plant. The leaves are usually green at the beginning of the season and will start to turn red over the course of the summer, which is when the plant may also have greenish-yellow or tan berries on it. If the stems have thorns, or if the edges of the leaves are rippled or saw-toothed, then it's not poison oak.

Depending on the location, poison ivy will grow like a shrub (up to about four feet tall), as ground cover vines, or as a creeping vine that grows up trees. Like poison oak, it will also have leaves that come in three's, but they'll be pointed at the tip and will look closer to the shape of an almond. In the spring they'll start out bright green and shiny, glistening with the urushiol oil, and by the fall they'll turn bright red. The berries will be grayish white in color. This plant does not have thorns.

U.S. Eastern Poison Ivy

Preventing Contact: Once you know what to look for, avoidance will be your next line of defense. If you're riding in an area that's prone to having poison oak or ivy, certain precautions will need to be taken to keep both you and your bike from contacting the plants. Running over the plants, including the dead leaves, twigs, and branches, could transfer the oil to your skin from subsequent contact with the tires. For this reason, it's best to stay on the trails and keep away from the edges. As you're travelling, watch out for hanging vines and branches that could brush against you. And if you plan on going into the bushes or behind a tree to relieve yourself, be extra careful because this little walk into the woods has a risk of contaminating your hands and shoes. From there it could transfer to places you would least want a rash . . . your face or your private area.

Clothing can protect against direct skin contact. Long sleeves, tall socks, and pads for the knees, shins, and elbows can all help. If the weather is too warm and covering up is impracticable, there is another defense that can be used. A substance called bentonite has been proven to delay the absorption of urushiol[38]. Ivy Block® is a lotion that contains bentonite to create a protective barrier that will provide more time before the oil must be washed off. Take the bottle with you so that if you sweat it off, you can reapply it as necessary.

Once unprotected skin has been contaminated, you'll have about half an hour to wash it off. Maybe you'll have up to an hour, but why chance it? If you know it's gotten on you, you'll have to do something about it pretty quick before it penetrates the outer layers of your skin. Individually wrapped alcohol wipes can be helpful in neutralizing and wiping away the oils. Put a small handful of these in your hydration pack. Many people report that a liquid called Tecnu works well at neutralizing and washing away the oils. The big advantage of this product is that you can use it when there's no running water to properly wash up.

As soon as possible after your ride, thoroughly wash your skin in the shower with lathery soap and lukewarm water, even if you've previously used Tecnu. This will ensure that any trace amounts are washed away. Treat your clothing and gloves as if they're contaminated by putting them directly into the wash using a double rinse cycle. Your shoes, hydration pack, and your bike should also be washed off, as the oil can remain on surfaces for weeks and still come back to get you. By taking every possible precaution, it's possible to completely avoid getting contact dermatitis from poison oak or ivy.

Finding Relief: In the unfortunate event that you come down with a case of poison oak or ivy, you'll have to manage it as best as possible. Once the oil is washed off of you, your bike, and your possessions, it can no longer spread to other parts of your body. Fluid oozing from blisters is not contagious and will not spread the rash. Any subsequent outbreaks are simply due to secondary contact or trace amounts of oil that took longer to penetrate the skin.

Although there's no cure, some relief can be found with a treatment of hydrocortisone cream, calamine lotion, cool compresses, or a lukewarm bath in colloidal oatmeal preparation. Besides providing some relief from the itching, these treatments will also keep you from scratching the blisters and breaking them open, something that could lead to an infection and a longer healing process.

If you have a severe case that covers more than a few square inches of skin or if it's on your face or genitals, you should seek professional medical care. They will likely prescribe an oral steroidal medicine such as prednisone to help relieve the itching and swelling symptoms. A normal case of poison oak / ivy will usually last anywhere from one to three weeks. Hopefully you can avoid being contaminated by these plants and won't have to go through this malady as part of your mountain biking experiences.

Mountain Biking Advocacy

Without trails to ride on, it wouldn't be possible to mountain bike. We rely on networks of maintained trails to enjoy our sport. But all too often, there are forces that are working against our access to these trails, a condition that's more prevalent in some areas than others. When (for no apparent reason) bikes are denied access to trails that are perfectly suitable for riding, it can be disappointing, frustrating, and maddening. And the average rider will never get an explanation.

This is a serious issue. Whether you're riding on government land or private land, somebody in charge is managing that property and making decisions on whether you can ride there or not. These land managers use a variety of reasons to ban bikes from trails, commonly based on misconceptions of damage or dangers that mountain bikers purportedly create. Often times, influential outside groups such as The Sierra Club, The Wilderness Society, or The Backcountry Horsemen lobby to keep bikes off the trails, but their arguments typically don't match the facts.

Trail Damage: Opponents of mountain bike trail access like to say that we tear up the trails, that our tires cause excessive erosion that extends over long distances. But this notion doesn't hold water when it's been scientifically proven[39,40] that tire tracks do not cause more dirt displacement or trail erosion than footprints or hoof prints. This is the case even in wet conditions. Additionally, this argument based on trail usage is absurd because hikers still outnumber mountain bikers and probably always will, and their footprints are more noticeable because

Typical damage from footprints

they're typically concentrated closer to the trailheads. The only exception to all of this is when we skid . . . but as described earlier in this book, it's a habit that needs to be avoided, which most of us do.

When they say that mountain bikers damage the plants more than hikers, this has also been proven to be untrue. The vast majority of the trails we ride on are devoid of any vegetation, and it's the hikers that are more likely to trample the plants by straying where they shouldn't. When it comes to scaring animals, hikers are much more likely to walk toward them, which will cause a bigger disruption to their lives.

Trail Danger: Basically, this is an issue of perception. Hikers never seem to realize how well our brakes work and how good our directional control is. They also don't realize that we always see them long before they see us. As you know, mountain biking requires looking far ahead at all times, whereas hikers are most often looking down at the ground. By the time they see us, they may become confused as to which way to go and what to do . . . even when we slow way down and call out to them (which we should always do). A collision with a hiker is an absolute rarity and the danger that they perceive is greatly overstated.

The damage and danger that mountain bikers pose is there, but it's negligible. There are those that simply don't want to see us in their space. But this is how we recreate; we just want access to the trails that are suitable for riding and to amicably share them with other users. To our credit, it's common to find mountain bikers that describe themselves as environmentalists. We enjoy and care about these places just as much as any other trail user. We too want them kept clean and beautiful. Beyond that, the mountain biking community volunteers for more trail maintenance projects than any other group. This means that when mountain bikers are part of a multi-use trail system community, everyone benefits.

A Model for Trail Access: Where you live and ride determines how much access you'll have to trails; and one of the most trail accessible places in the world right now is Scotland. In 2003, Scotland passed The Land Reform Act[41], which was created to give everyone greater freedom to enjoy the outdoors, including mountain bikers. It also sets the guidelines that users, land managers, and those working in conservation must follow. A supplement to this document, The Scottish Outdoor Access Code[42], provides a reference point for responsible behavior in the outdoors.

The only caveat to having these access rights is that they are exercised responsibly. According to the Code, responsible access means not causing unreasonable interference with the rights of any other person. Here are some of the listed basic rules for responsible access:

- Think ahead about how to minimize your impact and be willing to modify your behavior.

- Respect people's privacy and peace.

- Take personal responsibility for your own actions.

- Respect the needs of other people enjoying the outdoors.

That doesn't sound too bad, does it? The preface of the Code states the following: *"Scotland has a long-standing tradition of tolerance and respect towards people's need to move freely through the outdoors, and this has been recognized by the courts. This freedom of access enables people to enjoy the outdoors for a wide range of recreational activities provided no damage or disturbance is caused."*

This level of access allows mountain bikers who ride responsibly to go just about anywhere. Scotland truly has one of the most progressive access rights in the world and should serve as an example to other countries on how to manage a symbiotic outdoor experience.

How to Advocate: The best method for advocating is by uniting together and speaking with a collective voice. When our community unites, we have much more power and a much better chance of achieving our goals. We also need to build partnerships and alliances with land managers so that we can come up with reasonable solutions and agreements for trail access issues. We need to coordinate with these land managers on the best ways to maintain the trails and occasionally volunteer to do a little trail clean-up and improvement work.

Luckily, we do have an organization that is doing just that. It's called the International Mountain Bicycling Association (IMBA)[43], which is the largest and most effective advocating group we have. If you're interested in participating with advocacy and trail maintenance on some level, this is the best organization to get involved with. Contact them and find out where there's a local chapter or an affiliated organization near you.

Wilderness Areas: In the United States, Congress passed the Wilderness Act of 1964 to protect vast areas of land from the incursion of commercial interests. These lands were labeled "Wilderness Areas" and became protected from the destructive forces of the expansion of civilization. They were secured as places of natural beauty that humans could visit and enjoy.

Although mountain biking did not exist at that time, bicycles were not specifically banned from wilderness areas. But as the boom of mountain biking began in the early 1980's, the Sierra Club and the Wilderness Society pressured the U.S. Forestry Service to reevaluate the intent of the Wilderness Act. Their goal was to have bicycles banned from wilderness areas. They were successful. In 1984 the Forestry Service reinterpreted the Act to include a ban on bicycling. Designated wilderness areas now stand at 109 million acres divided over 762 individual areas. Ouch.

This was a big blow to mountain bike trail access, but at the time our community was still in its infancy and didn't have an organized advocacy group. Times have changed and besides the IMBA, there's now an organization called the Sustainable Trails Coalition[44]. The STC is working to legislatively remove the blanket ban of mountain biking in wilderness areas. The idea is to put the decision making back to the land managers to determine which trails are appropriate to ride on and which ones aren't.

We're not talking about hordes of bikers invading these vast lands. Nor are we talking about bikers entering these areas to have races and build jumps and berms and make it a playground. We respect this land as much as any conservation-minded person. Some of us just want to visit these places of natural beauty the way we enjoy doing it . . . by quietly rolling through it.

As you can see, advocacy is important for continued and expanded opportunities to participate in our sport. When we band together, we can achieve great things. Mountain biking has the potential to motivate our youth to get away from their electronics and get out into nature. By passing on these ethics to every succeeding generation, the passion for the conservation and preservation of wild lands will continue well into the future. How great is that?

Endnotes

1. The Outdoor Foundation
   2017 Outdoor Recreation Participation Topline Report
   https://outdoorindustry.org/wp-content/uploads/2017/05/2017-Topline-Report_FINAL1.pdf

2. Industry Overview 2015: A Look at the Bicycle Industry's Vital Statistics
   National Bicycle Dealers Association
   http://nbda.com/articles/industry-overview-2015-pg34.htm

3. Incidence, risk factors and prevention of mild traumatic brain injury
   J. David Cassidy, Linda J. Carroll, Paul M. Peloso, Jörgen Borg, Hans von Holst,
   Lena Holm, Jess Kraus, Victor G. Coronado
   http://www.medicaljournals.se/jrm/content/?doi=10.1080/16501960410023732

4. HEATSTROKE Author: Robert S Helman, MD; Chief Editor: Joe Alcock, MD,
   MS
   http://emedicine.medscape.com/article/166320

5. Heat acclimation improves cutaneous vascular function and sweating in trained
   cyclists
   Journal of Applied Physiology Pub: 1 December 2010 Vol. 109 no. 6, 1736-1743
   DOI: 10.1152/japplphysiol.00725.2010
   Santiago Lorenzo, Christopher T. Minson
   http://jap.physiology.org/content/109/6/1736

6. National Oceanic and Atmospheric Administration (NOAA), National Weather
   Service
   Office of Climate, Water, and Weather Services
   http://www.nws.noaa.gov/os/heat/heatindex.shtml

7. National Oceanic and Atmospheric Administration (NOAA), National Weather
   Service
   Office of Climate, Water, and Weather Services
   http://www.nws.noaa.gov/om/windchill/

8. HYPOTHERMIA
    Jamie Alison Edelstein, MD; Chief Editor: Joe Alcock, MD, MS
    http://emedicine.medscape.com/article/770542

9. http://www.urbandictionary.com/

10. By Zyxwv99 - Own work, CC BY-SA 3.0, https://commons.wikimedia.org/w/
    index.php?curid=37052106

11. Gaze-Eccentricity Effects on Road Position and Steering
    Readinger, Chatziastros, Cunningham, Bülthoff. H., & Cutting (2002)
    http://people.psych.cornell.edu/~jec7/pubs/road_position.pdf

12. Balance Ability and Athletic Performance
    Con Hrysomallis
    http://link.springer.com/article/10.2165/11538560-000000000-00000#page-1

13. Muscle blood flow is reduced with dehydration during prolonged exercise in
    humans
    José González-Alonso, José A L Calbet and Bodil Nielsen
    The Journal of Physiology
    http://jp.physoc.org/content/513/3/895.long

14. Diaphragm structure and function in health and disease.
    Poole DC1, Sexton WL, Farkas GA, Powers SK, Reid MB.
    Medicine and science in sports and exercise, 1997 Jun;29(6):738-54
    http://www.ncbi.nlm.nih.gov/pubmed/9219201

15. Effects of respiratory muscle work on exercise performance
    Craig A. Harms, Thomas J. Wetter, Claudette M. St. Croix, David F. Pegelow,
    Jerome A. Dempsey
    Journal of Applied Physiology Published 1 July 2000 Vol. 89 no. 1, 131-138
    http://jap.physiology.org/content/89/1/131.short

16. The limit to exercise tolerance in humans: mind over muscle?
    Samuele Maria Marcora, Walter Staiano
    European Journal of Applied Physiology, July 2010, Volume 109, Issue 4, pp 763-
    770
    http://link.springer.com/article/10.1007/s00421-010-1418-6

17. It's All in the Mind: PETTLEP-Based Imagery and Sports Performance
    Dave Smith, Caroline Wright, Amy Allsop, Hayley Westhead
    Journal of Applied Sport Psychology, Volume 19, 2007 - Issue 1
    http://www.tandfonline.com/doi/full/10.1080/10413200600944132?scroll=
    top&needAccess=true

18. The development and maintenance of mental toughness in the World's best performers.
    Connaughton, D.; Hanton, S.; Jones, G.
    Sport Psychologist 2010 Vol. 24 No. 2 pp. 168-193
    http://www.cabdirect.org/abstracts/20103259744.html;jsessionid=3C0887A440 38EB09FA845BEDCE095336

19. Mental toughness, optimism, pessimism, and coping among athletes
    Adam R. Nichollsa, Remco C.J. Polmanb, Andrew R. Levyc, Susan H. Backhouse
    Personality and Individual Differences, Volume 44, Issue 5, April 2008, Pages 1182–1192
    http://www.sciencedirect.com/science/article/pii/S0191886907004175

20. The Zone: Evidence of a Universal Phenomenon for Athletes Across Sports
    Janet A Young and Michelle D Pain; Monash University, Melbourne, Australia
    Athletic Insight, The Online Journal of Sport Psychology
    http://www.athleticinsight.com/Vol1Iss3/ZonePDF.pdf

21. Effects of Motivational Self-Talk on Endurance and Cognitive Performance in the Heat
    Wallace PJ1, McKinlay BJ, Coletta NA, Vlaar JI, Taber MJ, Wilson PM, Cheung SS
    Medicine & Science in Sports & Exercise, 2017 Jan; 49(1):191-199
    https://www.ncbi.nlm.nih.gov/pubmed/27580154

22. Source: http://www.builtlean.com/2012/09/24/body-fat-percentage-men-women/

23. Capillary supply and mitochondrial content of different skeletal muscle fiber types in untrained and endurance-trained men. A histochemical and ultrastructural study
    F. Ingjer
    European Journal of Applied Physiology and Occupational Physiology, September 1979, Volume 40, Issue 3, pp 197-209
    http://link.springer.com/article/10.1007/BF00426942

24. Strength training improves 5-min all-out performance following 185 min of cycling.
    Rønnestad BR, Hansen EA, Raastad T.
    http://www.ncbi.nlm.nih.gov/pubmed/19903319

25. Resistance training among young athletes: safety, efficacy and injury prevention effect
    A D Faigenbaum, G D Myer
    http://www.ncbi.nlm.nih.gov/pmc/articles/PMC3483033/

26. Risk factors for patellofemoral pain syndrome: a systematic review
    J Orthop Sports Phys Ther. 2012 Feb;42(2):81-94. doi: 10.2519/jospt.2012.3803.
    Epub 2011 Oct 25.
    Lankhorst NE, Bierma-Zeinstra SM, van Middelkoop M.
    https://www.ncbi.nlm.nih.gov/pubmed/22031622

27. Acute effects of muscle stretching on physical performance, range of motion, and
    injury incidence in healthy active individuals: a systematic review
    David G. Behm, Anthony J. Blazevich, Anthony D. Kay, and Malachy McHugh
    Applied Physiology, Nutrition, and Metabolism, 2016, 41(1): 1-11, 10.1139/
    apnm-2015-0235
    http://www.nrcresearchpress.com/doi/full/10.1139/apnm-2015-0235#.VrP29
    vkrLIU

28. 21 days of mammalian omega-3 fatty acid supplementation improves aspects of
    neuromuscular function and performance in male athletes compared to olive oil
    placebo
    Evan J. H. Lewis, Peter W. Radonic, Thomas M. S. Wolever, and Greg D. Wells
    http://www.ncbi.nlm.nih.gov/pmc/articles/PMC4470064/

29. Caffeine and performance
    Erica R Goldstein, Tim Ziegenfuss, Doug Kalman, Richard Kreider, Bill Campbell,
    Colin Wilborn, Lem Taylor, Darryn Willoughby, Jeff Stout, B Sue Graves, Robert
    Wildman, John L Ivy, Marie Spano, Abbie E Smith and Jose Antonio
    Journal of the International Society of Sports Nutrition 20107:5 DOI: 10.1186/
    1550-2783-7-5
    http://jissn.biomedcentral.com/articles/10.1186/1550-2783-7-5

30. Dietary nitrate supplementation and exercise performance.
    Jones AM
    Sports Medicine 2014 May;44 Suppl 1:S35-45. doi: 10.1007/s40279-014-0149-y.
    http://www.ncbi.nlm.nih.gov/pubmed/24791915

31. Creatine supplementation with specific view to exercise/sports performance
    Robert CooperEmail author, Fernando Naclerio, Judith Allgrove and Alfonso
    Jimenez
    Journal of the International Society of Sports Nutrition20129:33 DOI:
    10.1186/1550-2783-9-33
    http://jissn.biomedcentral.com/articles/10.1186/1550-2783-9-33

32. Effects of β-alanine supplementation on exercise performance: a meta-analysis
R. M. Hobson, B. Saunders, G. Ball, R. C. Harris, and C. Sale
Amino Acids 2012 Jul; 43(1): 25–37. Published online 2012 Jan 24. doi: 10.1007/
s00726-011-1200-z
http://www.ncbi.nlm.nih.gov/pmc/articles/PMC3374095/

33. Exercise and fluid replacement
Sawka MN, Burke LM, Eichner ER, Maughan RJ, Montain SJ, Stachenfeld NS
American College of Sports Medicine
http://www.ncbi.nlm.nih.gov/pubmed/17277604

34. Rates of fluid ingestion alter pacing but not thermoregulatory responses during
prolonged exercise in hot and humid conditions with appropriate convective
cooling
Dugas JP, Oosthuizen U, Tucker R, Noakes TD
European Journal of Applied Physiology. 2009 Jan; 105(1):69-80. doi: 10.1007/
s00421-008-0876-6. Epub 2008 Oct 14
http://www.ncbi.nlm.nih.gov/pubmed/18853180

35. Sleep and athletic performance: the effects of sleep loss on exercise performance,
and physiological and cognitive responses to exercise
Fullagar HH, Skorski S, Duffield R, Hammes D, Coutts AJ, Meyer T
Sports Medicine 2015 Feb; 45(2):161-86. doi: 10.1007/s40279-014-0260-0
http://www.ncbi.nlm.nih.gov/pubmed/25315456

36. Dietary carbohydrate, muscle glycogen, and exercise performance during 7 d of
training
Sherman WM, Doyle JA, Lamb DR, Strauss RH
The American Journal of Clinical Nutrition 1993 Jan;57(1):27-31
http://www.ncbi.nlm.nih.gov/pubmed/8416661

37. Characteristics Explaining Performance in Downhill Mountain Biking
Joel B. Chidley, Alexandra L. MacGregor, Caoimhe Martin, Calum A. Arthur,
Jamie H. Macdonald
International Journal of Sports Physiology and Performance, Volume 10, Issue
2, March 2014
http://journals.humankinetics.com/ijspp-back-issues/ijspp-volume-10-issue-2-
march/characteristics-explaining-performance-in-downhill-mountain-biking

38. Prevention of Poison Ivy and Poison Oak Allergic Contact Dermatitis by
Quaternium-18 Bentonite
Marks, James G. Jr. MD; Fowler, Joseph F. Jr. MD; Sherertz, Elizabeth F. MD;
Rietschel, Robert L. MD

American Journal of Contact Dermatitis: Official Journal of The American Contact Dermatitis Society:

March 2001 - Volume 12 - Issue 1 - ppg 54 http://journals.lww.com/dermatitis/Citation/2001/03000/Prevention_of_Poison_Ivy_and_Poison_Oak_Allergic.20.aspx?sessionEnd=true

39. Erosional Impact of Hikers, Horses, Motorcycles, and Off-road Bicycles on Mountain Trails in Montana
John P. Wilson and Joseph P. Seney
Mountain Research and Development, VOL. 14, NO. 1, 1994, PP. 77-88
Published by: International Mountain Society
https://www.uvm.edu/~snrvtdc/trails/erosionalimpactofhikers.pdf

40. Managing Recreational Mountain Biking in Wellington Park, Tasmania, Australia
Luke Chiu and Lorne Kriwoken
University of Tasmania, Australia: Annals of Leisure Research Vol. 6, NO.4
http://eprints.utas.edu.au/2948/1/Managing_Recreational_Mountain_Bike.pdf

41. Part 1 Land Reform (Scotland) Act 2003: Guidance for Local Authorities and National Park Authorities
http://www.gov.scot/Publications/2005/02/20645/51837

42. The Scottish Outdoor Access Code
http://www.gov.scot/Resource/Doc/158552/0042992.pdf

43. https://www.imba.com/

44. http://www.sustainabletrailscoalition.org/#home

About The Author

Paul Molenberg lives in the San Francisco Bay Area. He has had a lifelong commitment to fitness and sport activities, including almost two decades of mountain biking a diverse range of trails throughout the United States and some of Canada. The coastal redwood trails of Northern California, Lake Tahoe's epic rim trail, the slopes of Maui's Mt. Haleakala, the downhill and cross-country trails in Park City, Utah, and the black diamond trails of North Carolina's Pisgah Forest are just a few of the challenges Paul has taken on and conquered. He has now leveraged his experience to create this comprehensive book on the sport of mountain biking.

CPSIA information can be obtained
at www.ICGtesting.com
Printed in the USA
LVHW060430300622
722398LV00005B/293